TWO BRITS IN ASIA

JOE TILSED

TWO BRITS IN ASIA

WAS IT ALL A DREAM?

Self Published

I wrote this book as a surprise 25th birthday gift to my lovely Sydney, who joined me on our travels in Asia.

POLICE AND AEROPLANES

BANGKOK | DAY 1

10th April 2022

https://twobritsinasia.com/police-and-aeroplanes/

We started the day trying to get our boarding passes online, however, the airline did not offer online check-in from London Gatwick, so we had to do it at the airport. Thankfully we didn't get charged a fee as we did with Ryanair, the week prior, on our trip to Mallorca.

I popped out to Argos to pick up a large bottle with a handle, which we could carry around with us while we go on our adventures. Syd stayed at home waiting for Toby, Toby's friend Isaac, Mum, Nan, and Syd's Dad, to arrive and give us a farewell.

Luckily, I arrived home before they did, Toby and Isaac were first, followed by Syd's Dad, then Mum and Nan. We sat and chatted for a bit, I did some final packing for us both and then loaded up Toby's car, as he was driving us to the airport. I said I'd drive there but he wanted to.

Syd's Dad left and we all went out for a roast dinner at Toby Carvery, we had invited him, but he was in a rush to get back for the horses, I think. Somehow Mum and Nan beat us to the carvery! This is a phenomenon as Mum makes it seem that she doesn't know that the car has more than 3 gears... We went in and enjoyed our meal, I was stuffed! After saying our goodbyes to Mum and Nan, we went quickly to Castlepoint the shopping centre, up the road, to pick up some new headphones for Syd as her other ones had broken, only letting sound out of the left ear. That would not do for the 14-hour flight ahead.

Once the new headphones were acquired and tested on her phone to check they worked and fit okay, we were off! Only stopping once in Fleet Services to relieve our bellies of the massive meal we had consumed about an hour earlier. Then back on the road and making good time to Gatwick.

Toby parked in the short-stay car park and walked us in, with Isaac too. Toby went to the loo again while Syd and I queued to check in and drop our bags off. It was taking quite some time, and those short-stay carparks are roughly £400 a minute, so I called Toby over and said no point waiting. We said our goodbyes and they went on their way back to Swansea. Thankfully we weren't charged for check-in this time!

We found a spot to charge up our phones and laptop more. Syd read some of her book, while I did some ETF trades. I'd recently bought a privacy screen for my laptop so anyone trying to look from the side wouldn't be able to see anything. I was just boosting off my phone's hot spot (which was using a VPN) instead of connecting to the airport Wi-Fi, I find it faster and much safer.

We were an hour late getting on the plane. Then it was delayed for a further two hours while we were sitting on it. Syd and I were in seats 31E and F, and behind us was a group of three clearly drunk and high male ne'er-do-wells. They were causing a right scene, throwing chocolate nuts all over the place, luckily neither of us has nut allergies.

Before sitting behind us they had tried to sit by the emergency exit, and for some unknown reason decided to break the housing that the oxygen masks sit in. An engineer entered the plane, but he was unable to fix it. Making these seats unusable, and the people who had actually paid for them had to be seated elsewhere.

Once these hooligans had been moved behind us, they were nothing but rude to the staff, demanding more alcohol, which they were denied as we had not taken off yet, but they opened their own supply instead. They each went to the toilets one by one, probably to take more drugs. One of them was even smoking an e-cigarette on the plane! The one directly behind Syd touched her head, which we found very disrespectful. They were also grabbing our chairs and rocking them about. I was in no place to turn around and say anything as quite frankly I was scared.

Police later boarded the aircraft and escorted them off the plane, which caused even more delays as one of them had hold luggage that needed to be found and removed.

COVID TESTING

BANGKOK | DAY 2

11th April 2022

https://twobritsinasia.com/covid-testing/

The earlier delays on the flight had caused a knock-on effect with our onward travel and subsequent Covid Testing arrangements, meaning we now had to isolate ourselves in our hotel room for longer than planned. How those three drunks were even allowed on the plane in the first place is beyond me. Right from check-in, through to boarding, they were a nuisance to all passengers.

As well as these three, there was an unrelated passenger on board, who during take-off, decided to start walking around the plane to find a better seat. All while cabin crew members were still in take-off positions. He had already asked them if he could move while the delay was going on, which they had rightfully told him, "not until we were in the sky". He was also clearly drunk, and he had bragged about downing a whole bottle of rum during the flight (once we landed). He kept a large portion of guests around him awake on this night flight, including us as he was only two rows ahead.

We had tried ordering food via the ScootHub QR code, and directly via their webpage. This is where we are supposed to order food and drink on this long-haul flight, however, this did not work for either mine or Syd's phone. Other passengers were also facing issues and the system had to be reset multiple times. Even the staff tried to get it working on our phones, but they were unable to. Eventually, they managed to get it working on one of their tablets, but there were only hot drinks and chocolate biscuit snacks left. Which clearly isn't sufficient for us on a now very, very long flight. The original flight was meant to be around 14 hours, but with all these delays we were closing in on 20!

Also, during the flight someone fainted, obviously, this cannot be helped, and the staff acted perfectly as they should. But it just added to the already hectic flight. I would just like to say that the crew did an amazing job on what was quite an eventful flight. Especially Chloe Lee, our direct cabin crew staff member, we chatted with her a bit, she had been up for over 24 hours and still had another 2 hours with a flight to Singapore.

Once landed, we passed through immigration, with the drunk guy a few rows ahead of us in a frenzy trying to get through. We made it through with no issues. We collected our bags and went to find our taxi.

There were two women sitting two rows behind us on the plane, with a child, who was good as gold by the way, and they too were waiting in the same place for their taxi. We joked about the flight and how we were all relieved about those three getting kicked off back in Gatwick.

They too were going to Chillax Resort Bangkok but had already booked their own private transfers. Otherwise, I would have offered them to come with us. I had ordered a van, as at the time of booking I didn't know how much luggage we would be bringing.

After about an hour's drive from the airport, we were taking down a dodgy side allay, which for our first experience in Thailand, was worrying. Thankfully, we noticed other holidaymakers here. We got our Covid tests, the lady pushed the brush quite high up both mine and Syd's noses, it gave Syd a little nosebleed. But she was fine.

It was interesting every time we got in and out of a building or taxi, just how hot it is outside. It really hits you instantly, just like walking off a plane in Spain, but a lot hotter. It almost takes your breath away!

The smog coming from the city in the distance was a sight to see. Although we were nice and cool in our taxi, it had fancy gold embroidery on the ceiling. During our ride, it was a real culture shock to see how different the people drive here! One that stuck out to us the most was a mother driving a moped with her daughter in the front. Neither of them wore a helmet, and the police didn't seem to care.

At the hotel, we checked in, the hotel staff took our luggage from the taxi for us, and up to our room! They also brought up our dinner selections. I had Thai basil chicken with rice and a fried egg, and Syd had Thai green curry with, again, rice and a fried egg. We both had these melon/pear type fruit slices, it was nice, Syd wasn't very keen so I had hers too.

We tried running a bath, but the plug let water through so the bath didn't fill up. I let reception know, and they moved us up a floor to a different room. The exact same room layout, just one floor above. While Syd was running the bath, I unpacked, noticing a pigeon nesting on our balcony - it looked as if it had been its home for many years.

After our bath, I noticed that our toilet had one of those bum guns, I didn't try it this first night as I didn't want to get it wrong. We went to bed soon after our bath, as we were both quite tired from the days of traveling. And we also couldn't do anything as our Covid tests had not come back, allowing us to go outside.

THITAREE'S KING, BUSES AND MILK

BANGKOK | DAY 3

12th April 2022

https://twobritsinasia.com/thitarees-king-buses-and-milk/

We started the day by checking our Covid results, thankfully both green, which meant negative, and we were allowed to explore! Outside our room, the staff had dropped off our breakfast ready for us to eat it. Syd had an American breakfast, and I tried the local curried porridge. I really enjoyed it, although putting the chili powder on it this early in the morning was a bit of a mistake, it was quite hot and my tastebuds had not adjusted to the spice levels yet. We ate this in bed, which is a novelty for us.

After breakfast, we decided to head up to the pool to check out the view and have a quick dip. The heat was intense and hit us as soon as we opened our airconditioned bedroom door into the hotel hallway. Instant sweat. We got into the lift and made our way up to the roof terrace; the view was amazing looking over the skyscrapers of Bangkok. There was an infinity edge to the pool, it felt as if you were floating above the city - was very special.

Once we were finished in the pool, we made our way from the hotel and started exploring to see the area around us. We found a shoe shop where I bought some sandals. I kept them on as we walked back to the hotel. I had planned on walking to the mall, which was about five kilometres away, but it was way too hot. Unfortunately, the left sandal was rubbing the back of my foot. So, I changed back into my socks and trainers. The sandal didn't cost very much, but I did want to wear local sandals while in the area.

Back at the hotel, we decided to get our first Grab to the Siam Paragon Mall. Grab is a mega app, like Uber, but all in one place. You can pay with it, order takeaways, have taxis, acts like a postal service, hotel bookings, and much, much more. The taxi ride was about 20 minutes and only cost 80 THB about £2. Very cheap, and we sat in the comfort of an air-conned car, taking in the sights of the city.

I had already pre-planned on meeting Thitaree (T), who used to be on my team where I used to work before doing this trip. We had planned on meeting at around 12:30 but we were about an hour early, so we decided to look around the mall as it was very hot outside.

There were lots of amazing smells and things to see. The ground floor was the food court, with a massive superstore in the centre. We walked in to see what the prices of groceries were like, again very very cheap! Near a quarter of the price compared to back in England. There was a massive shelf of dried noodles that Lawrence and I like to eat. I sent him a picture of it.

The next floor up was the luxury floor, with brands such as Fendi, Louis Vuitton, Channel, YSL etc. Syd wanted to see the prices of the LV bags, so we did. They were about the same price as back in London which surprised me. So we didn't end up buying anything in these shops...

Above this was a floor of cars, Bentleys, Aston Martins, Porsches, the lot! It seems their cars are actually more expensive here, the Porsche which we saw was about £250-300k with the same car (and modifications) being worth about £120-150k at home. This surprised me too.

The rest of the floors were a mix of things, like bookstores, surf shops, a complete range really. Right at the top, there were some chairs and a bubble tea stand. Just as we were about to order T messaged to say she had arrived, so we walked back down to the food court to meet her.

She brought her boyfriend, Wat, along with her. We decided that instead of eating in the mall, we would find an authentic

Thai restaurant outside, I say we, but in reality, we just followed Wat. His family has a house in the city, he knew a good spot, which we went to. I let them order what they thought best, and we shared everything. It was all very delicious, I couldn't tell you exactly what we had but from what I understand it was a papaya salad, some sort of pork rib soup, pork shoulder slices, catfish, some sort of sausage and some purple sticky rice, which came in this cute little warming pot.

After lunch we walked around some other malls, all the malls within an area are connected via bridges, keeping customers cool while shopping, instead of having to go outside in the heat. I was on the search for some flip-flops after my sandal fiasco earlier. Unfortunately, I couldn't find any that I liked the feel of, either too big, too small, or too loose. Not to worry - back on went the trainers.

In-between two malls outside there was a slip-and-slide sort of setup. The massive tarpaulin was soaked in soapy water, people were using skim boards and doing tricks with them. It was interesting to watch. T explained it was part of the early celebrations for Songkran festival parties tomorrow.

T needed to get something from the supermarket, so we walked back there. We saw some massive crabs and lobsters! There was some Japanese A4 wagyu sirloin steak for sale in the butcher section of the shop. I wish we were able to buy this back in England as easily as they can get their hands on it over here! Once T had what she needed, we went back to the food court and bought some Thai desserts. Syd really enjoyed these.

After, we walked back to Wat's car. He then drove us all to this famous milkshake spot, which I can see why it is famous, it was delicious! People were coming in and ordering over 20 bottles of the stuff and taking it home, to have as a cool drink later, as we consume soft drinks at home. We had ours with some toast, one had butter and sugar on and the other was plain with a Thai custard dipping sauce. Delicious.

From here Wat gave us a lift back to our hotel, I showed T the room and the pool upstairs. She really liked it. I asked her if she could help me take my sandals back or even just exchange them for a different pair. Back at the shop, the lady let me change them for a pair without a back (which is where it was rubbing before). She also gave me 50 THB back (the original price was 950 which is just over £20).

I gave this 50 THB to Wat as fuel money for driving us about, and he then drove us around the city showing us different well-known temples, government buildings, and a famous swing. During our tour, Thitaree was expressing to us how much she doesn't like seeing all the propaganda from government officials and the king himself. She said that the king is widely not liked now in Thailand, this is apparently because he spends so much of the people's money on himself. For example, renting out a whole hotel in Germany for him and his mistresses. There are a lot of pictures of the king all over the place, and not small either, some pictures are bigger than most houses in England!

She was also telling us stories about the old buses, how there had been a fire but the government still used the buses, even after they have been caught alight! Apparently, they just clean them up a bit before putting them back into service. This service started over 100 years ago and they are still using the same bus shells today! It was interesting to watch the buses, they don't really stop to allow you to get on or off, they just slow down a bit. I saw people use the time when they stop at lights to do the hopping on and off, which makes sense.

While driving around, we stopped off a few times and took some photos of each other in front of some of the temples. It was interesting to see the monks walking around the grounds. It was very peaceful. I had brought my brother's camera with us to take some more "professional" looking photos. I think they turned out great.

Once back at the hotel, T and Wat went on their way, and Syd and I went back up to the pool to cool off. While up there we got chatting with two others our age, a brother and a sister who had arrived earlier in the morning and had already got their Covid results back. They had come from Northern Island and were enjoying the heat too.

After our chat, we headed back down to our room and got ready for bed. Our dinner arrived, and both of us had gone for the Pad Thai, again eating this in bed as we were getting quite tired at this point. We also had the leftover mall desserts from earlier. I chucked a movie on my laptop, The Inside Job, and we went off to sleep.

SONGKRAN RUN AWAY

BANGKOK | DAY 4

13th April 2022

https://twobritsinasia.com/songkran-run-away/

A late start this morning as we were very tired from the traveling and yesterday's activities. It is the start of Songkran today, the Thai New Year festival. Usually, this is celebrated by water fights all over the city, so we were on a search to find some!

We walked to the infamously cheap strip that is Khaosan Road. It's only about a mile and a half from our hotel, but in the heat, it took us over 40 minutes to walk there. With stops for water and shade. While walking along the river we saw lots of fish. A man was feeding them which bought them to the surface. This made Syd laugh. We stopped and watched them for quite some time, along with some pigeons trying to get some scraps from the man's fish food bucket. I also saw another shoe shop where I looked and tried on some more flip-flops, but again the same issue. None really fit right, maybe my feet shape is unique in Thailand...

Once on the strip, we walked up and down, so many people trying to get us to buy stuff from them or use their tuk-tuk to take us to the "floating market" or some "special temple". I had heard about these types of scams, so we just carried on walking past them. We had started to get a little hungry so found a place to sit and eat. We had a portion of rice each and shared a chicken dish, some chicken noodles, and some Thai bread. The bread was a cross between a milk loaf, boa buns, and a French croissant.

The restaurant was designed like the skeleton of a boat, it was cool. I had tried asking around about the water fight but was getting mixed responses. It wasn't as busy as usual as people here still seem quite worried about Covid, having to wear masks everywhere, and most people are even wearing them outside. We find it too hot to wear outside though.

While eating, a few news reporters walked by, one even interviewed our waitress. I tried to ask the waitress what it was about, I think she was saying they were just reporting on why it was so quiet this year. After we finished our meal, it was around 2:30 pm and a few people had water guns, but it wasn't very busy at all.

Syd wanted a new dress, the first shop we went to was all too small for her. The lady running the shop tried helping her put it on, but it caused the strap to break. The lady was apologetic and didn't charge us for the damage. We moved on to another stall, where we found a dress Syd liked. This shop also had lots of different "designer bags" which were very good fakes, I didn't buy any though. I did however buy the dress for Syd and then we walked back to the hotel for a cool-off.

I had searched around online for a while, but it didn't look like anywhere was doing an organized water fight this year because of the Covid concerns still, which was a shame. There were some special events at a few temples though, so we got a Grab to Wat Phra Chetuphon. The entry fee was higher than a lot of the other temples I've seen, at 200 THB each (usually between 20-50) but still, this is cheap, about £5 each to go in. I think for locals it's free. It was well worth the money. Amazing Buddhas and other statues are made from what looked like gold and other precious materials.

From here, on the last-ditch attempt to find me a water fight, we took a Grab to Silom. In past years, it has been a hot spot for these parties. The taxi ride there was the hottest ride we had so far, as the driver had encased the front section with plastic for Covid reasons. This didn't let the air-con into the back. Syd felt quite faint after this. So, after getting dropped off we tried to get a bit of food and drink. I tried a "chicken" skewer that had just come off the BBQ. I don't think it was chicken, it may have been my first cat... I didn't finish it as it was quite gristly, with fatty and tiny bones. I tried to give the rest to a homeless man, and even he wouldn't take it!

We found a 7-11 and got a drink to cool us down. It can be hard to break the larger notes up while over there. I made up a slogan called "Joe's Travelling Top Tip" and my first Joe's Travelling Top Tip, to get change, is to buy one of these drinks, as they're about 20THB (50p ish). They're very nice and cold, and if bought with 1000 THB (or whatever high note) the cashier gives you plenty of usable notes for the street food. I think Syd thought I was silly for making up my own slogan. But I liked it.

Unfortunately, Silom was just as quiet as the other places. We walked up and down the strip trying to find someone who speaks English but with not really much luck. There were lots of massage parlours here, with happy endings... Syd didn't let me go in. While walking up and down the strip, I managed to take a lot of cool photos of the surroundings. It was a great juxtaposition to have the expensive modern skyscrapers and then the mass of electrical cables in the poorer areas.

Another Joe's Travelling Top Tip entered my head, if you go into a fancy hotel then it's more likely the reception staff will speak good English. We did just this finding the Pullman Bangkok, the receptionist explained that all official water-fight plans were cancelled this year. The same as last year because of Covid, with hopes that next year it will be back on again. That's a shame.

No worries, another Grab back to our hotel, and up to the pool to cool off, this time it was just us two up there, the hotel was very quiet. From here we then walked down our road to a street stall where we had two bowls of rice, a tom yum soup, pork and Thai basil, and a chicken noodle dish (Pad See Ew, which became my favourite go-to dish), all for 165 THB (just under £2 each). It was very tasty, the noodles especially. The stall was run by a couple, the man cooking on the main pan and his wife doing the prep work and cooking the rice. They were both very friendly.

There are a lot of these stalls, dotted all over the city. They do have menus, but you can also just ask for what you want, and if they have the ingredients, they will make it. We would then just sit and wait for the food to be brought over to us. It was a peaceful evening. Once we made our way back to our room, we decided to head straight to bed, ready for our temple adventures tomorrow.

TEMPLE TREKKING

BANGKOK | DAY 5

14th April 2022

https://twobritsinasia.com/temple-trekking/

I planned an early start today as the temple we were heading to this morning, Wat Benchamabophit, is usually busy, according to online reviews. I ordered us a Grab from our hotel to the temple. This was a 50 THB entry fee, which was fine. I had thought it would take about 3 hours to look around, but it only took an hour or so. Wat Benchamabophit Dusitvanaram, the temple's full name, is a Buddhist temple in the Dusit District. It is also known as the marble temple and is one of Bangkok's best-known temples. It typifies Bangkok's ornate style of high gables, stepped-out roofs, and elaborate finials

We were quite lucky as not many people had gone to the temple this morning, or at least not when we were there at 8:30 am. The temple itself is beautiful, red-orange roof with gold and white marble trim. Inside the main hall was a large golden Buddha, people were on their knees paying to it. We had to take our shoes off before entering the building.

There were big marble pillars holding up the outside roof, where there were 52 black Buddhas. This made a large courtyard, which was also empty at this time. It made for some really cool photos. Some of these black buddhas reminded me of a buddha statue my Dad had. He would have loved it here; I wish I could have shared it with him.

We walked around the grounds, through their grassy park area. It looked as though they were doing some building work here. No one was working on it at the moment, similar to in the UK, with weeks of having equipment up with no one actively working, and then a few guys do the work in the last couple of days. Apart from the work yard, the rest of the grounds were beautiful. There was also what looked to be a picnic tree spot, with a large statue of a buddha wrapped in a python. I'm not sure anyone can actually have a picnic here, but it would make a good spot to have one. We saw a few cats around, like in the other temples, they must be so hot!

A few monks patrolled the area but other than that it was very quiet. We saw lines of ants that had found a crack in the mortar within the building. They had formed a queue back and forth from their home. Clearly looking for food, but I made a joke to Syd that they were off to pray too, she wasn't amused.

There was a little stream going through the grounds, with little red bridges to cross over, with fountains in the water also. It was very picturesque, with some smiling buddhas along the stream edge too.

Once out of the temple, we found some shade. A lady next to us was selling live fish and eels. I was just on Grab to order us a car to take us to our next temple when an auto rickshaw (tuk tuk) dropped off some people. We bartered a price to take us instead, and he gave us the same price as it would have been on Grab, 80 THB, which was down from his original ask for 150 THB. There is a big culture of bartering here. It doesn't make much difference in the price as we are talking about a couple of quid here and there, but it's a bit of fun. Having this exchange every time is like a dance. The ride was great fun. Syd enjoyed the feeling of the wind! We were half lying down and half sitting up.

Once at our next stop, Wat Saket, we had both gotten quite hungry. We found a street cook who made us some pork noodle ramen, with thick rice noodles. It was so tasty and was only 60 THB.

We then walked into the temple and bought our tickets, which were 50 each, just like the one this morning. We walked all the way to the top. I think I saw a sign saying 385 stairs to the top! On the ascent, there were stops to take photos of the waterfall and the statues within. Also, there were lots of large bells which everyone was ringing. We did too! There was a massive gong that I hit, it was amazing to hear it and feel the vibrations in our bodies.

During the walk up there were also mists of water being sprayed, I am not sure what it was really for, but it helped keep us cool walking up the stairs. It might be for that, but also could have been watering the plants around the stairs. Under the golden bell was a golden buddha where people had left coins as donations to the statue.

Once we got right to the top, through a small staircase to the roof, there were amazing panorama views of all of Bangkok. Seeing the large gold bell close-up was quite something too! There were cyan-coloured statues surrounding the bell. It was interesting to see the different communities below with the skyscrapers in the distance. It was a dramatic scene.

We then made our way down and got another Grab back to the hotel, and back up to the pool for a cool-off and a bit of sunbathing. I popped down to our room halfway through briefly to pick up some water, as even though we were sitting in the shade at this point it was still over 35 degrees Celsius! We were up there for about an hour before heading down to our room during the hottest part of the day, with the air-con on to cool us down. Syd then Face Timed Harvie to wish him a happy birthday.

We started walking down our street to see if we could get a Thai massage, our corner shop where I had seen a few ladies out the front only had an old man standing there today, so we moved on. We got a Grab to Jay Oh Chula, where I had planned on having dinner, unfortunately, it was closed for the holiday season. Not to worry, it was cool to see the river next to the restaurant, with views of the houses connected to it.

I ordered us another Grab to get a taxi to Silom again as yesterday we saw loads of massage parlours. We found one we liked the look of and went inside, no happy ending for us though. We had two Thai massages; we were in there for about an hour and they only charged 500 THB (just over £5 each). Very cheap! Not as good as my physio back in England though, shout-out Tom! Also, the ladies were a bit rougher than I was used to, Syd said the same. But I can't really complain about pennies on the pound. Also, it was only me and Syd having massages at the time, which made for a fun experience, without the awkwardness of other people getting whatever they may have been getting done next to us.

We then got a Grab to Samyan Mitrtown, another large mall. There was an event because of Songkran. We were given free drinks (4 total in the end), and they were very sweet. Like Fanta but with even more sugar! We then had a (beef, maybe?) boa bao bun, dim sum, and some spring rolls all for a couple of quid. Canny go wrong! The event was very colourful, with strips of fabric bunting above us. There was also a stage at one end with different acts on it. Along with a host which kept walking around in the crowd asking people questions. They were happy to see that we had made it over from England.

As we had another early morning planned we decided to head back to the hotel. Quick cool down in the room before heading out to find some dinner. We walked down our street, and then down a little side alley, it felt very traditional, with people sitting, and relaxing on their doorsteps. There were laundry shops inter-mixed with massage parlours, food shops, corner markets, and all sorts. It isn't like in England where different parts of town would have different types of shops. Instead, everyone has just jumbled around altogether. It was nice, with much more of a community feel.

We found a food stall we liked the look of, it was the busiest one we had seen and smelt amazing. We had a portion of thin noodle mixed meat pad Thai, a chicken red curry, crispy fried pork, and a sweet and sour chicken dish all to share. It was all very tasty; we didn't finish all the rice as each (other than the pad Thai) came with its own rice. It was 210 for the lot, which is just about £5 for the two of us for a massive feast!

Once back at the hotel, Syd ran herself a bath, while I checked us into our flights for tomorrow's day trip to Chiang Rai to see the white and blue temples. We then went to sleep.

CHIANG RAI: WHITE, RED, BLUE, GREEN?

BANGKOK | DAY 6

15th April 2022

https://twobritsinasia.com/chiang-rai-white-red-blue-green/

A really early start this morning, waking up at 05:00 to get a Grab to the DMC airport, where we would be catching our flight to Chiang Rai. Airport security was light, as it is an internal flight. We only had to show our passports and boarding passes. No actual border security. We still had to go through a bag scan, but it wasn't as thorough as an international flight. Once through, we picked up a pastry and a little bottle of chocolate soy milk to have on the flight. It was beautiful to watch the golden sunrise over the airport and planes.

We have been seeing these little brown glass drink bottles around, not just in the airport but people drinking them all over. I decided to buy one at the gate, they look like cough medicine, smell like cough medicine, and taste like it too! It kind of tastes like a flat Red Bull, I text Thitaree and asked her what they were, and she said it's called M150, which is an energy drink. Which explains the taste.

It was interesting to see there were quite a few monks at the airport getting flights too. They seemed to be given automatic priority. Through separate lanes and first on the planes. They were sitting in the premium section of the aircraft too.

Syd and I sat right by the engine, which is cool to see over to the right of us. The take-off was a little strange, as once the front nose was up, there was a loud scraping sound at the back. Almost as if the rear of the plane had scraped along the runway. Around five seconds later, it was followed by a sharp bend to the right, even though we weren't that high off the ground! We were heading straight toward the airport terminal.

I must admit I was a little worried but put on a brave face for Syd. No one else seemed to be reacting to the noise and sharp turn, so I just went about looking at the views out of the window. Thankfully missing the terminal.

About halfway through the flight, we decided to have our pastries. They were very nice, they had cheese and bacon on them, a little oily but added to the flavour, and it was very doughy. Unfortunately, we couldn't have our milk as the air hostess came over and said we weren't allowed to eat or drink on this flight apparently. Not to worry, we had already finished our pastries and had our milk once we landed.

Once we touched down, it was very quick to get out of the airport, with no further passport checks. Literally from wheels down to being out of the airport was within five minutes. Very impressive. We got a Grab from the airport to our first stop of the day, Wat Rong Khun, otherwise known as the White Temple. It was about 25 minutes from the airport, we enjoyed the taxi ride looking at the fields we passed

When we got there, the entrance attendee said Syd's dress was a little too short. We walked along looking into some of the shops, she found one that she liked, and I bought it. It is a blue dress that was fitting for our final temple of the day. I think it looks quite Japanese; I like it too. She also broke another pair of sunglasses somehow (she had broken another pair on the flight over from England). She didn't drop them this time (or that I saw) ...

While walking back to the temple we saw some cones which had skulls on top of them, Syd took a photo of them to send to her mum.

The temple was amazing, like nothing I have ever seen before. Pearl white and magnificent! There were lots of different statues outside of the temple, all mystical type creatures. In front of the temple was a pond, which had different types of koi fish in it. On the bridge to the temple, underneath were statues of people's arms and skulls reaching up. And on the walls were diamond-shaped mirrors making the temple shine. This temple isn't used as a place of worship, it's more an art piece, and a tourist attraction, which is doing its job, as we are attracted.

It cost 100 THB to get in, which is double what it used to be, but still well worth it! This temple was originally self-funded by the artist making it, so paying a nominal entrance fee to support him to continue building it is fine. He started building it back in 1997 before I was even born! It's expected to be at least that amount of time again until it's complete!

In the temple itself was a very life-like wax figure of a monk sitting in front of a Buddha, we were not allowed to take photos inside, so I do not have a picture of it, unfortunately. After the main building, we walked around the grounds, along a walkway with millions of individual decorations hanging. They looked like the bit of metal that you use to help thread a needle, just bigger and tons of them! It made a cool wave-like effect when the wind blew through the walkway.

Further round the grounds was a large bell held up by a massive golden structure. Next to this were two swings that Syd and I sat on. Well, we took turns on just one of them, as the other swing was being used by someone else. There was a worker burning incense too which smelt nice and calming. There were also different statues hidden around the edges of the plot.

We carried on walking around to the golden temple. It was accessible by a golden bridge crossing, which we walked across.

This temple was dedicated to Ganesha, with a large statue of the elephant in the middle, at the top of the temple. There was a museum inside with lots of different paintings and large brooches. Syd really liked the look of one painting; I asked if it was for sale but unfortunately not. This is a real shame as I would have spent quite a bit of money on it, as it was beautiful. We found the same painting in postcard form and bought that instead.

Then we walked back towards the main temple, passing a wishing well in which we each flung a coin in, making our wishes. Then onwards to get some lunch, we stopped at a restaurant just outside the complex. We shared two curries and had rice each, Syd ordered the green chicken curry, and I ordered some brown ginger and chili pork dish (Hanglay). They were both delicious and only 60 THB each (about £1.50).

After that, we walked around to get some coconut ice cream which Syd had spotted earlier in the day. It was served in half a coconut shell, with freshly shredded coconut on top, along with peanuts and coconut cream. I really enjoyed all of it, Syd liked it other than the fresh coconut shavings, I think it might have been a bit too wet for her. She then had to pay 5 THB to use the toilet, which she almost tripped up the step on the way in as she was being cheeky with the tissue she'd picked up.

We then got a Grab to Wat Phra Kaew. This was more of a local place of worship, with no entry fee. There were two museums here, which we could go in and see the history of the area. One of the museums had a worker sitting and doing some cryptocurrency trading on his computer.

In the main building, there was a replica of the Emerald Buddha (which we saw the following day, near the Royal Palace). This one is made of Jade though; it was in a very green room. It was cool to see.

Syd was getting a little hot and bothered so we walked to the closest 7-11 to get a drink and more ice cream. We had a blue drink to match the next temple we were visiting, Wat Rong Suea Ten (The Blue Temple). We ordered a taxi which only took us about 5 minutes to the temple, I had expected to walk but it was about 15-20 minutes, and in this heat and not much shade in between, it wouldn't have been fun.

When we arrived at The Blue Temple, it was the hottest part of the day. I took some photos of the large blue statues and the white Buddhas. I also have some cool shots of the outside of the temple, and the other statues scattered around the grounds. Syd had found herself a seat under some shade while I was taking the photos. When I was finished, I walked over to her, and we both realized our tongues were blue! We took a picture in front of the main entrance with them out! We decided to get an ice cream each to help cool us down even more.

Once we had finished our little treat, we took our shoes off and then entered the building. The inside was also painted blue like the outside. The outside had golden trim around the edges, whereas in the temple it was more decorative paint, with pictures of the royals, elephants, and monks on the walls and pillars. At the back of the hall was a massive white Buddha, it was illuminated in blue from the walls and the blue carpet. We sat there for some time, noticing a smaller red Buddha on the left-hand side. Also, a bird managed to find its way inside, it landed on the big Buddha's head for a moment, I was too slow to take a picture, Syd thought it was funny.

We then walked out and looked at the market stalls by the temple. Syd wanted to get some more sunglasses, so we found a stall selling some. After much deliberating and messing about with some silly-looking ones, she decided on which ones she wanted, she went with a "Gucci" pair. I said to her that if these ones break, she won't get anymore (only half joking).

There was a cafe called Bike Coffee Bike Cafe, so we decided to eat there. I had some fried noodles and pork, and Syd had a nice glass of noodle chicken soup, both were very tasty. If I were to order again, I would have gone with the soup too as it was light but had tons of fresh flavour in it.

It was quite hot, so we decided to go to the airport early to sit in the air-conned hall. We bought a packet of pork scratchings, and a milkshake each. Syd had a chocolate Oreo ice cream and I had a caramel frappe. Syd dropped her new sunglasses at the airport, while we were sitting eating our snacks, she gave me a side eye to see if I had seen her drop them. I had... Thankfully they didn't break! We both giggled after I rolled my eyes.

On the flight back, during take-off, it made that shuddering sound again, and for longer this time. I checked and we were on a different aircraft, very strange. The landing was a bit rough too. Syd was complaining that her ears were hurting, mine were a little too. She reckons the plane might have been descending too quickly, as it was delayed getting to us (only by 30 mins). We landed 5 mins later than planned so the pilot had made up a good time.

We got our final Grab of the day back to our hotel; Syd was quite tired from the early start and three temple trips. It's been an awesome day trip though! I left Syd at the hotel while I popped out to pick us up some pork noodles, and two chicken skewers to share. By the time I got back, Syd was ready for bed. We were too tired and hungry, I forgot to take a picture of this meal. We ate these in bed and then went to sleep. With the plan to have a more relaxed day tomorrow.

THE EMERALD BUDDHA AND JAY FAI

BANGKOK | DAY 7

16th April 2022

https://twobritsinasia.com/the-emerald-buddha-and-jay-fai/

A late start today, as planned. The adventures yesterday were quite tiring, but we really enjoyed them!

We got up around noon and walked down to our local 7-11 to change some cash up as I had run out of the smaller notes. We then ordered a Grab to take us to Wat Phra Kaew (the actual Emerald Buddha).

Once we arrived, someone tried to get us to take their tuk tuk to a big Buddha. He was claiming that we wouldn't be allowed in the temple till 14:00 as prayers were going on now. This was total nonsense, so we just walked on. It is important not to fall for these scams, as they can take you miles away from the city, and then demand high payments to take you back.

Once at the temple entrance, though I was told I'd have to get trousers to go in, which was true, I thought I could get away with my shorts, which covered my knees. Not the case. They had a shop on site, but the trousers were about 200-300 THB, which isn't a massive amount of money (about a fiver) but relatively it's a lot.

We walked back to the street where there were clothes shops, we walked into one and they had trousers for sale for 100 THB or some to rent for 50 THB. I bought some blue and white elephant ones. I had thought later though how they could possibly track the rented ones. Unless you had to pay 150 and you get your 100 back once you return, I don't know.

Getting into Wat Phra Kaew was the most expensive yet, at 1,000 THB (just over £20). Still very much worth the cost though! It was the hottest part of the day when we arrived, I had originally planned to go in the morning, but we were too tired from yesterday, so we had changed the plans last night.

It felt like the hottest day today, probably from being out in the open next to these big buildings, with not much shade, as the sun was right overhead. Also, with my new trousers on, and putting some sun cream on just before leaving the hotel, I think my body was struggling to breathe. I was very sweaty!

The grounds of Wat Phra Kaew were very clean and well-kept. It was almost like Disneyland with the buildings being so extravagant. It was beautiful. All the trees seemed to be leaf perfect. It was cool seeing all the statues along the walkway in between the main temple buildings.

We first went to look at the emerald Buddha, as this is what the temple is famous for. There were restrictions on what and where we could take photos, but I managed to get a few cool ones where we were allowed. Once in the room itself, we sat on the floor for quite some time just admiring the immensity of it. The Emerald Buddha was placed high up surrounded by literally tons of gold. The building itself is covered in gold-coloured, mosaic tiles, with accents of sapphire blue and ruby red. There was some serious money being spent to make this place look the way it does.

It was interesting to sit and watch others praying to the Buddha. Some monks even came in and prayed in their own section at the front. There was always a police officer and some sort of guard near the emerald buddha, they clearly didn't want anyone to steal it! We then made our way outside and walked around looking at the other buildings within the grounds. All of them were very majestic, no penny spared that's for sure!

It was really special walking around the grounds, passing the royal house with the king's face painted onto the front. I was amazed at how close were able to get to the building. I doubt he actually lives here, it's probably more of a tourist attraction. It was beautiful.

We were starting to get hungry, so decided to go to Jay Fai for lunch instead of dinner later as we were close by. T had recommended we go here as it is one of, if not the only, street food stand in Thailand with a Michelin Star. We tried getting a tuk tuk, but they were all asking too much, I suspect because they had a good spot outside the temple to take people further for more money. I ordered a Grab instead, which took us there in no time. It was just a little too far for us to walk in this heat though, and, the break from the heat in an air-conned car really helps!

Once we got to Jay Fai it was only open for takeaway orders till later this evening when they opened the restaurant up. I didn't want to have a takeaway from here as I wanted to be able to try lots of different dishes fresh. So, we decided to get a taxi back to our hotel.

When we were back at the hotel, we had to do our final Covid tests, I am not sure why they needed us to do another test even though we were allowed to explore freely already. Either way, we did an NHS test first which we had bought with us, just to check we were fine, before doing the official one. Thankfully both clear! We had planned on getting room service for lunch, but after cooling off in the room it felt silly to spend three times more on something we could just get out in the street. They had offered burgers and spaghetti, but it seemed even more silly to order something like that when I could have that anytime at home.

We found a street stall we liked the look of, and both had a wan-ton dumpling and BBQ pork ramen with egg noodles. It was very tasty, and the cook was friendly and let me take pictures of her cooking. We gobbled this down, but by the time we finished, the lady had disappeared! We paid the stand next to her for when she would return, it was only a couple of quid for the both of us, with a drink of chilled bottled water too! This was only about 10 THB, which is less than 25p!

Back at the hotel, after cooling off again in the room, we decided to head up to the pool to sunbathe, swim and chill before our evening meal. We sat on one of the large circular chairs together. I had a swim, and Syd joined me for the last little bit. We then sunbathed for an hour or so before heading back down to our room to get ready for Jay Fai this evening.

At Jay Fai... or what I thought was... I had to run across the street to grab a mask from the corner 7-11 as Syd forgot hers. Back in the queue, just as we got to the door, I realized this wasn't Jay Fai... that was two doors down. I rushed down to see, but it was too late, already fully booked with two lines of people sitting outside waiting. I was a little annoyed as this may have been opened for lunch if I was looking in the right place! Oh well, we will have to come back tomorrow morning before our old city tour to come for breakfast.

Syd and I got to the back of the original places queue again. They seem to have a fast turnover so we weren't standing in the queue for long. We had a pad Thai each and shared a pad Thai wrapped in egg, it was a very thin omelette wrapped around the noodles. We also shared a bottle of fresh squeezed orange juice with large bits in it (basically mini slices of orange). It was all delicious! They arranged the prawns in a shape of a heart. It was quite expensive for what it was though, was about 10 times as expensive as the street food stands, I don't think it was 10 times as good. It was a nice experience though.

After dinner we walked down the strip, there were lots of different street stalls, all with higher prices than anywhere else. I'd guessed this was due to Jay Fai being down the road. People must go there and when they can't get in, they have to end up going elsewhere, since they aren't left with many options, last minute, they end up getting the overpriced street food.

Either way, we found a stall selling those mini green pancakes, the same as Thitaree had the other day in the mall. We got ten to share and ate them on the side of the road, they're very spongy and eggy. I really like them. After we scoffed these down, I walked back down to Jay Fai to try and book a table for tomorrow. They told me to come back early in the morning as they weren't accepting bookings since they were so busy. It was first come first served. So if we turned up at 09:00 tomorrow, when they open, we might be able to get in.

I ordered a Grab back to our hotel. This Grab was a tuk tuk, it was lit up with green LED lights. It was fun racing around the city in it blasting its music. We got into bed once we finished, and I finalized the plans for the Phuket section of our tour. And then we went to sleep, ready for our third attempt at Jay Fai in the morning, then the afternoon in the old city.

THE "OLD OLD" CITY

BANGKOK | DAY 8

17th April 2022

https://twobritsinasia.com/the-old-old-city/

We woke up a little late this morning as I was up late last night confirming the plans for Phuket. I had planned on hiring a car over there, but after using Grab so much in the city, and it is so cheap, I worked out that I would have to use over 1000 THB worth of Grab a day to make the hire car worth it. It does restrict us a bit in terms of moving the luggage around while traveling, as some of the stops I had planned were un-route to the best hotels. To overcome this, I moved some of the planned activities to the days which didn't involve changing hotels and moving luggage. This made it less stressful for us.

Once we were ready and "out" it was already 11:30, I thought to try chance Jay Fai, not with high hopes as they had said to come back at 9 am to try to get a table when they first opened. As expected once we got there, the queue was already building. I asked the lady at the front, and she said they were fully booked but we could wait if we wanted, but she couldn't give a time to how long it would take.

We stood there for about 10 minutes and there wasn't any movement, other than them letting a local group in. Maybe they had booked before, I'm not sure, but I asked the others who could speak English how long they had been waiting around. Most of them had been there since 9 am that morning, which at this point was 3 hours ago. There was no way I was going to wait that long for some noods! It's a shame though as I wanted to eat here, oh well, we will have to come back in the future.

Instead, we walked along the street for a bit looking for some-where to eat, the first place we went to was overpriced for a street stall. Instead, we decided to carry on walking a bit further, we ended up walking past one of the temples we had been to a few days earlier (Wat Saket, the big golden bell at the top of the mountain). Syd didn't feel like eating here again so we carried on walking a little further.

We made it over a bridge and found a stall we liked the look of. Both ordered the thick fried noodles and pork. I popped into the 7-11 next to it and picked up another one of those cough syrup energy drinks, and got Syd a cherry Fanta from the dispenser.

After eating we ordered a Grab to take us to the old city, Phra Nakhon Si Ayutthaya. The ride was about an hour, and cost 781 THB, which is £17.81, which isn't bad at all! A taxi ride this length and time in the UK would be over £100 (4,000 THB)! Syd had a little snooze to pass the time. We did have to pay an extra £2 odd when we arrived to cover the driver's charges for tolls on the roads, which is fair enough.

Once we arrived, I think Syd realized what we would be doing here, spending some time with elephants, her favourite animal! She was so excited when we pulled up that she didn't know what to do with herself, she even started to cry! She later said that she thought she was dreaming still, and once she realized it was real, she was just overcome with her excited emotions.

Since we were quite far out of the city, I asked our driver to stay around and I would pay him a holding fee, which he agreed to. It works out quite well as otherwise he wouldn't have been paid for his drive back to the city. We agreed on 50 THB an hour, which is just over a quid. He gave me his number and said just let him know when we are ready, and he will come to collect us to take us back. A pound an hour doesn't sound like a lot, but it's the equivalent of a meal out per hour and is considered a high rate for taxi holding.

Once we got out of the taxi we walked over to the elephants, we fed them a basket of courgettes, they were so very gentle taking them out of our hands. We were able to stroke their trunks while they took the food off us. We then went up a flight of stairs to be able to ride on them.

It was such a magical experience, the chair on top was a little sketchy but it was so much fun! It walked down past the old city's temples. Someone at the side of the road took a professional picture of us, which I bought later (both a hard copy and a digital copy) for about £3. I can't get over how cheap things are here. It really is eye-opening to how needlessly inflated the UK is...

Our elephant driver was very friendly, he had some local music on too which added to the experience. Some locals stopped to take some pictures with the elephant, they then paid it by passing the notes to its trunk, which it then passed it to the driver. Very cool.

A bit further down the road, some people had ice creams, about half-eaten, they gave the rest to our elephant. It was happy with that! Although there was a stray dog that scared the elephant a bit. That was a bit of a wobbly few seconds, but the driver got it back under control and directed it across the road. It's amazing how the cars stop to just let us pass, I suppose it's the same as the horses at home.

He took us to some great photo spots and even took some photos of us while turning around on the elephant. Very impressive. On the last stop on the way back out elephant had a poo, Syd found this funny. It was massive to be fair.

Once back on the hard ground, we explored the city further. Walking around the old, crumbled temples and buildings. We also walked along the lakes and over the bridges. We saw what I think is a Komodo Dragon or some other massive lizard. Syd originally thought it was an alligator! She said I hope we can out-run it if it comes for us, I said to her I only need to out-run you!

We saw lots of locals sitting and having picnics here, a group even had a fishing net and had caught something. They were clearly very local with no English so I couldn't ask them what fish it was. I wasn't sure what it was from looking at it. I should have got a photo of it, but I didn't think about it in the moment.

After a bit more walking, we found another temple with a large golden buddha in it. Further from here was the old palace, I took some photos and then contacted our driver to come to collect us. I sent him our location on WhatsApp, and he sent us a photo of himself so we could find him again. He was with us within a few minutes.

Once back at the hotel, I asked the driver if he was free to-morrow to drive us around as he was a quick but smooth driver and played good music. Which he was. We ended up using him as our personal driver for most of our time left in Bangkok.

Syd and I both went up for a quick swim and sunbathe, but because it was getting quite late and the sun was setting we didn't stay up there long. Since it felt a bit cooler, and we didn't really know what we wanted to have for dinner. We walked around the city for a bit, hopping to different street stalls and speaking with the chefs to cook us their favourite dishes.

These stalls do have menus, or you can just ask them to cook anything for you, but I wanted to try what the chefs liked to cook and eat themselves. We would order just one dish and share it and then do a bit more walking around the city and on to the next one. While the chefs were cooking our meal, we would try and talk to them, their English was about as good as my Thai, and I don't know much Thai. But they were excited to be seeing tourists again and trying hard to engage in conversation with us too. We did this about five times. I really enjoyed it. This was my fondest memory of the whole trip. It was real.

We wandered back to the hotel, on the way popping into 7-11 to pick up some prickly heat powder, which T had recommended to help with keeping our skin temperatures down. I also picked up a Thai-take on Oreos, the middle cream part wasn't cream though, it was green. I am not sure what it was made of, but it was sweet and tasty. After we had a few of these, we got ready for bed. I stayed up for a bit on my laptop messaging people, but Syd went straight to sleep.

THE TRUTH

BANGKOK | DAY 9

18th April 2022

https://twobritsinasia.com/the-truth/

Another later start today. Once we eventually got out of bed and ready, I messaged the taxi driver from yesterday to see if he was free to take us to The Sanctuary of Truth. He was. Before he arrived, we dropped some laundry off at a lady on the corner who quoted us 80 THB (under £2) for a medium to large load. I was happy with this price so agreed to come back later to pick it up and pay.

It was Easter Monday, so not much was open, not sure if that's just because it's Monday or because of the bank holiday. But they're predominately Buddhist here, so celebrating a Christian holiday doesn't make much sense. We found a shop that was selling wrapped bread with cream and one with sugar for 5 THB each (just over a penny) so we got two of these and shared them.

By the time we had eaten the first one our driver had arrived, so we had the cream one in his car. Syd wasn't a fan of this one, so I had it to myself. It's quite a drive to Pattaya, where the temple is, around two hours. During the drive it started to rain, it didn't last long and by the time we arrived, you wouldn't have known it had been raining at all!

Once at the sanctuary, we were luckily only about half an hour away from the next tour starting (unplanned). While we waited for the start of the tour, we explored the upper grounds. There was a lot of creepy crawlies which I took some close-up pictures of. There was also a farm section that we explored, there was a cute goat that was playing hide-and-seek with us behind the fence.

Shortly after we were called over to start the tour. Our tour guide, Lennie, handed us hard-hat helmets. These were to protect our heads in case any wood chipping were to fall from the carpenters putting up the sculptures.

Our guide took us through the factory where they make the sculptures, they're all hand-made taking weeks to months to make each piece. The whole sanctuary (which is seen as a museum locally) is made entirely of wood, with no nails or anything! She explained the techniques they use to lock the wood together. This was interesting to me, as some of my fondest childhood memories are in my Grandad's shed, with him, my brother, and me making random wood stuff together.

In this workshop, there was a scaled-down model of the main sanctuary. They would build extensions onto this model first to see how it would fit, before building it onto the actual building. There was so much wood being used, they needed to make the model first to make sure they wouldn't waste any of the wood by misplacing it in the real thing. It is like creating a proof-of-concept piece of code, before writing it in production.

Lennie then took a photo of the two of us in front of the museum before taking us inside. She talked us through the seven truths and what each story meant. In the centre there were pillars with two sides, one was the bad side and the other the good. The stories shown explained what the world is like if we are bad, and then the other side showed what the world would be like if are good.

Every wall inside the building was covered in carvings. I could see this becoming the eighth wonder of the world. The pictures didn't do it justice. The detail in these sculptures was insane. The stories they told were interesting too, the longer you looked at a piece the more you would see.

After the tour, we saw they had a pond which they could take you around on a boat. It was relatively expensive for what it was, so we decided not to do it. We will have plenty of time on boats while in Phuket!

Further up the park were some more elephants, which of course Syd loved! We bought a big basket of bananas to feed them. The owners even let us get right up next to one and stroke it. Syd really, really enjoyed this and was buzzing about it for the rest of the day, and probably will be for the rest of her life...

We met back up with our driver and he took us to the Lan Po Naklua market, which is a wet market. Yes, brave after Covid I know... but I wanted to see it. The plan was the get some food from here and then hand it to a street cooker to make a dish up for us. But the fish did really smell, so I went off that idea.

Instead, we decided to have some street food. To start we found a stall doing skewers, we shared some sort of fish ball in batter skewer (probably from the same smelly fish in the market, but oh well), a mini chili omelette skewer type thing, and a katsu chicken skewer (sorry Lawrence).

We walked a bit further down the main road, taking pictures of the street. Like Bangkok, there is just a mass of electrical and telephone wires everywhere. It must be impossible to diagnose if there is an issue. Maybe that's why it is like this spaghetti mess, they don't. Just put a new cable up every time.

There were not as many street-food stalls here as in Bangkok, which is to be expected. For one, we aren't in the capital, and two, there is that massive market, I'm sure most people just cook their own food here. We managed to find a ramen place and had a bowl each. It too came with some sort of fish; they were like dumpling balls. It was nice.

I think this place is like the Weymouth equivalent in terms of being right on the sea and having the "fresh" fish served up. And the truth of it is, I say "fresh", and apart from the smell, I do think the fish was fresh, some were even still alive! You can't get much fresher than that! I think the small came from it all being so close together and having no real cooling methods as we have in the West.

We noticed our driver was near where we had lunch, I asked if he wanted anything. But he said he was okay. We then got driven back to our hotel where we went upstairs to the pool to cool off a little. On the ride back Syd changed her background on her phone to a photo I took of her with the elephant. She was on cloud 9!

While at the pool a massive dark cloud filled the sky! The wind had picked up too and it started to spit a little bit. It then started to thunder and highlighting, I said to Syd it's probably best to get out of the pool and go back to our room. There was a strange light in the clouds, like a golden circle out of nowhere, it was cool to see, no idea what was causing it. But it wasn't safe to be at the top of this building on the roof terrace while the storm was about to start.

Back in our room, we noticed that the heavens had opened! It was quite something to watch, we opened our balcony doors and watched it for quite some time. Once it had died down a little, we decided to brave it to pick up our washing from earlier.

We managed to borrow an umbrella from reception and walked down the road to collect the washing. It was all nicely folded away and smelt great! We then walked over the river to find some food places, as a lot of the usual ones were closed, either due to the rain or because it was Monday, or maybe both.

Eventually, we found something that was open, we shared a soup of some sort and had a portion of rice each. I also ordered some roast pork, which was quite expensive for what it was, at 100 THB for a few slices. Probably one of the only things I can make at home for cheaper.

We then walked back towards our hotel, stopping at a roti (more crepe-like than a usual roti) stall and sharing one with Nutella on. Once back at the hotel, we packed ready for the next part of our travels, we were off to Phuket! We watched some Netflix in bed before going to sleep.

PINK CAB

PHUKET | DAY 1

19th April 2022

https://twobritsinasia.com/pink-cab/

We woke up late for our last morning in Bangkok. I had planned on grabbing some rice and a curry dish of some sort before getting to the airport, but it was getting a little too late. We would have had enough time, but I ran down the road and picked up some more of those packet bread rolls. This time I bought us a sugar one each and a coconut one to share.

Syd was sitting waiting in the lobby while I got breakfast. Once I got back to the hotel, I ordered us a Grab to take us to the airport. It was a pink one! The driver didn't have much room for our luggage in his boot. Only one of the large suitcases was able to fit in the boot, the other large one went on the front passenger seat. Our two smaller ones went by our feet. I had called our regular driver from the previous two days, but unfortunately, he was busy today with his family.

The driver seemed to be a bit of a nervous driver, taking ages to make turns, and pulling off very slowly. His windscreen was cracked at the top centre too! Also, he wasn't following his satnav. On the way to the airport, we drove passed a crash, it looked like someone had driven into the barrier. Not sure how it happened, there were a lot of police there though. Hopefully, no one was hurt.

We managed to get to the airport in time and checked in our bags. Syd's was a kilo over the limit after buying so many new sunglasses! I had to unpack some of her stuff and add it to mine. Thankfully we weighed hers first, otherwise, mine would have gone off on the conveyor belt. I had thought hers would be over as we packed the suitcases differently this time, filling hers first before packing mine. We then walked through the passport check, again since this was an internal flight, it was quick.

After walking to our gate, picking up a bottle of water and some more energy drink "cough syrup", we sat and ate the breakfast rolls I picked up earlier. Syd wasn't the biggest fan of the coconut one, so I had all the coconut, and she had the bread part. We then made it through the bag check, which didn't take any time at all. Before boarding the plane, we were given a bag of goodies to enjoy on the flight, this was a nice touch for a very cheap flight that was only going to take about an hour. We didn't end up eating the jam pastries since we were full still from breakfast.

On the plane, it had already passed the time it was meant to take off. There were a lot of kids on this flight, from a few months old up to about 4 or 5. I'm not sure why, our other flights haven't been like that. Annoyingly I had one right behind me kicking my seat. And another in front playing kiddie games on a phone or tablet of some kind, out loud...

The rest of the flight wasn't so bad, I had a little nap, not for long though as the flight was only about an hour and a half total. We came into land quite quickly, but we slowed down in time, as they always do! Our baggage was already on the belt by the time we got there, and there were no passport checks when we landed at all. So, we were out quite quickly, similarly to before with the internal flight, from wheels down to out of the airport within five minutes!

There were lots of taxi stalls trying to get them to use their taxis, but I just ordered a Grab. Annoyingly the first one cancelled on us for some reason, but another turned up minutes later to take us to our hotel. We were staying at the Pullman tonight, only for one night as we had a lot of exploring to do in Phuket. This was a recommendation from Issy, a good friend of mine, who had been here before Covid. It wasn't cheap, but for what it was, it was very well-priced, one of the most expensive on the whole trip but it was very luxurious. When we come back, I think I'll probably stay here longer and have more time by the pools.

As we were checking in, a member of staff brought us a bottle of lemon and mint water each, with a mini gift bag of masks and alcohol sanitary jell. We then walked back to where we had been dropped off, as that's where our cases were. We had to walk over a bridge which was over a pond to get there, it was very pretty. Back at our bags, the lady called for a buggy to take us to our room.

Syd and I didn't bother fully unpacking our bags, just taking out the clothes we would need for this evening and tomorrow. We sat on the balcony and ate the jam pastries we were given on the plane. They looked like sausage rolls; they were very tasty! After finishing these we got dressed into our swimming costumes, and we phoned reception for a buggy to come to get us to take us to the pool. They sent a car without doors, it felt like being on a rollercoaster bobbing about in it.

We enjoyed watching the sunset in the infinity pool, looking over at the beach and sea below. It really was quite fabulous! We could see some boats out to sea, they seemed to multiply as the evening went on. I wondered if they were fishing boats coming back home from their hard days' work.

We decided to stay here for dinner tonight to try out the fancy Thai food. We had quite a lot! A bowl of coconut, tomato, mushroom, and chicken soup, a bowl of duck curry with lots of different fruits in, like pineapple, lychee, grapes, some pea type things (not sure it was a pea though), it was quite spicy, I really liked it. It was a little too hot for Syd. We had a portion of rice each, along with a chicken teriyaki disk, and a spicy seafood salad. We also shared a portion of pad Thai. We even had a drink each, I had a local Singha beer and Syd had a Piña colada, which we ended up sharing, she liked it but just couldn't finish it.

Safe to say we were very stuffed after eating it all! It was a relatively expensive meal at over 2,500 THB, but really that's about £60, which for a luxury 5-star hotel meal, that big, with alcohol, is really a steal! It was interesting comparing the difference between luxury food and street food, and to my own Thai cooking. The Pad Thai and coconut soup were very, very similar to the ones I make at home, which is an ego boost for sure! They did taste different from the street stalls. Hard to say which was better, just different flavours. This meal had more subtle layered flavours, but the ones in the street are punchier.

We got a buggy back to our room, there were others in the buggy this time going back to their room. When it tried to go up the hill it stalled, it made us all laugh that with full bellies we must all weigh a lot more! When we got back to our room, we crashed on the bed trying to gain the strength to do anything!

Shortly after I needed the loo, so I got the strength to get up and go... About a week and a half in Bangkok on street food, and my bowels have been fine. One night in a fancy restaurant and it's Niagara Falls... What's that about then ay?!

Once back in bed we were too tired really to do anything else, we had planned on trying out the bath but neither of us could be bothered to run it. So, we went to sleep!

BEACH DOGS

PHUKET | DAY 2

20th April 2022

https://twobritsinasia.com/beach-dogs/

We had a bit of a lie-in this morning, not as late as some of our other days, but still not early. Checkout was 11 am, so we took it steady. There was a massive rainfall shower in our room which we enjoyed! Syd was more of a fan of the smaller more powerful head though.

After getting ready, we phoned for a buggy to take us to the lobby. We weren't due at our next hotel till after 3 pm, so I asked the receptionist here if they could hold our bags, and let us borrow some towels, which they agreed to.

We first made our way down to the beach below, on the way down we noticed some cabana-style beds overlooking the bay. The sea was electric blue, we were in paradise. On the steps down to the beach, we saw quite a large lizard! There were quite a few dogs on the beach, with no apparent owners. We think that maybe they are owned by street stall sellers. The dogs seemed to prove a useful service though, they would come and sit near people and if they saw anyone close to the baggage they would bark. I thought this was quite cool. Maybe they learned that if they did this, they would get a little treat.

Syd and I walked about a third of the way down the beach, watching out for the pine leaves which were like needles the trees had dropped. There was a cute swing in a tree, we decided to sit here with the shade from the tree, and the swing made for a bit of fun. We walked down to the water's edge, being mind-full of the little sand crabs scurrying along, there were quite a few of them!

The sea was lovely! Not cold at all, warm actually. The perfect temperature to cool you down out of the heat of the sun, and able to get in straight away without any issues. The tide was strong though, it almost knocked Syd over! She didn't fancy a swim; she just stood and watched me. I didn't go out far as the rip was quite strong. Syd thinks she saw a jellyfish, but I didn't see anything, not even any fish - other than a dead one that had washed up on the beach!

Back at the swing, we sunbathed out of the shade for a bit, before going back under the trees to get in from the heat. I walked up to the road to buy us some noodles and had just enough on me for some chicken nuggets on a stick, so I got that too. The noodles were more like a Chow Mein than anything else, quite sweet, but very tasty. The nugs were just the same as oven ones back at home really, they had been fried and were tasty with the noodle sauce.

We made our way back up to the Pullman, no lizard this time! We spent the next 3-4 hours sitting by the side of the pool, going in every now and then. Luckily no rain and the sun was hot! Both of us had burnt patches, which is a given for Syd, but a rarity for me.

We decided it was time to go and check in for our next stay. I tried ordering a Grab but for some reason, it wasn't letting me, I asked the lady by the buggies if she could order me a taxi to our next place, she phoned one up and said 600 THB, which I thought was a little steep for a 15-minute car ride, so I said would they take 500, which they would. Still relatively expensive for a ride like this, in Bangkok it would have been about 120-150 THB.

Once at the new place, it was out in the sticks. The concept was cool, there were 8 concrete boxes, four on either side of a pool, and a reception/laundry room. Unfortunately, our first room had an infestation of ants, which had seemingly made a nest under the bed. I phoned the receptionist back to look, he was in shock!

He started cleaning them up, but Syd didn't look too impressed, so I asked him if we could go to another room, to which he agreed.

Neither of the rooms had the air-con on when we walked in, so they were very hot. This room didn't have an ant infestation but there were still bugs crawling on the concrete floor. We didn't really have much other choice and we were only staying here for two nights so just gritted our teeth and went with it. I don't think being in the Pullman the night before helped, the contrast between the two was quite something.

We just took out the clothes we needed without fully unpacking, and decided to go for a walk, as it was cooler outside than in the room! We walked down the street looking for a BBQ place, which was recommended by the hotel. About halfway there I realized I didn't have my wallet on me, so we went back to the room to pick it up and then headed out again.

Once we got there, it was a BBQ buffet, but all the food was raw, and you had to cook it yourself. We weren't a great fan of this as all the meat was out in the open, with no covers and no apparent cooling to keep it chilled. There were also about 15 geckos on the wall behind the food.

We started walking back towards our room as we noticed some other eateries. We ended up at a local restaurant, it wasn't the best in the world and there were lots of cats about, even some further at the back were sitting on the tables where the food was being prepared. Since we were so far out of anywhere, there weren't any other options. We ordered a beef dish which came with rice and a fried egg, and a portion of pork wide noodles, which we shared. The beef dish was very flavourful.

While we were eating a frog jumped next to my foot, it startled me a little bit. There were also geckos here too, which the cats seemed to enjoy watching. While we were waiting for our food, I popped across to 7-11 to get some water, and some toilet paper as our room didn't have any. We had asked the receptionist for some but after he had left with no word from him in over half an hour, we thought we were not going to be getting any. It is so cheap from the shops anyways, and I can always bring it with us to our next stops.

Once we finished our meal, Syd had a craving for oranges, I went back into the 7-11 to try and find some. They didn't have any, and the only fresh fruits they had were some bananas, I didn't get them as they looked brown and looked to have been sitting around for a while. Back in England, Syd would have made banana bread out of them.

We tried a few more little local shops on our walk back, mostly they were just people's front rooms selling a few bits and pieces. We were also trying to look for some breakfast for tomorrow since we didn't want to chance the street stalls. But no luck, one shop tried offering us cigarettes, but obviously, we weren't interested in that.

Back at the room, even though I had turned the air-con on to the lowest temperature and "turbo"ed it, the room was still just as hot. We got undressed, but Syd put a pair of my boxers on, as I think she was worried about the bugs still. Once in bed, we watched the first two episodes of "Bad Vegan" on Netflix.

About halfway through the second episode, Syd had already fallen asleep, so I turned the laptop off and went to sleep too. Looking forward to our day tomorrow at the waterpark!

GETTING WET AND ONLY FANS?!

PHUKET | DAY 3

21st April 2022

https://twobritsinasia.com/getting-wet-and-only-fans/

We woke up early as we wanted to get some breakfast before the waterpark (Blue Tree Phuket) opened for the day. I slept well for most of the night, but it was hot, and the bed was hard.

Again, it was a struggle to order a Grab, and the fixed rate option I usually go for wasn't working. So, I ordered a taxi, still through Grab, but at a variable rate so you don't know exactly how much you will pay till after the ride.

It was an old man t who picked us up, he was very slow pulling away, and making corners. Also, when we arrived at Blue Tree, he was chatting with the security guard. All of this added to the cost of the ride, as it is time-based. I thought this was a bit cheeky of him. But clearly, this wasn't his first rodeo.

Once we got out of the car, I noticed on the Grab recent break-down that Grab charges a 100THB service fee here, in Bangkok this was only 20. Also, the taxi meter started at 35 in Bangkok yet started at 50 here. This surprised me, as I would have thought the capital would be more expensive.

Since I had bought our tickets online already, we were ushered straight in and given our wristbands. They were just paper ones like at concerts or whatever, but they had some sort of RFID (Radio Frequency Identification) chip in them, which I thought was quite neat. These are tiny devices that when put next to the correct receiver will open the locker for us.

We walked down the complex to get to the water park, picking up yet another pair of sunglasses for Syd as she has somehow lost her other pair... She thinks she left them in the taxi that took us from Pullman to our concrete room yesterday. Syd wasn't best pleased with my comments on her forgetfulness to the lady at the till. While at the shop, I also picked up a waterproof phone holder, which I could use next month while we are going to be snorkelling. I was going to wait till closer to the time, however, I thought it best to buy one here now so we could use it in the water park.

There was a place called the tree house, which we went to first to see what food they had, as last night's exploration for some breakfast to eat this morning had been unsuccessful. They didn't have any breakfast items per-say. The closest thing they had was a smoothy bowl, but it was quite expensive. Or they had burgers, which didn't seem right this early in the day.

We walked around to another restaurant; this one didn't even offer a smoothy bowl! But the guy at the till said that they don't really have "breakfast stuff" as we do back in England. Which, I kind of see thinking back to the meals we've had on the other days, mainly we just ate something earlier at lunchtime, and then had more food throughout the day. So anyways, we ordered something similar here, I had scrambled pork and basil with rice and a fried egg, and Syd had a big bowl of chicken fried rice.

As we were eating, we watched others come into the park and start going down the slides. It was funny watching people get launched off the big slides! I was looking forward to trying it myself! It never really got too busy at the park, actually, it was basically empty the whole day, which was nice as there was no queuing around for the slides or other attractions.

Once we finished and paid up, we hired out a locker for the day, using my wristband's RFID as the key to unlock and lock it. Once we stored our stuff away, Syd needed to make a quick trip to the loo, she somehow got lost even though it was basically a straight line.

After she found me again, we set up under some shade. She was a little nervous to try the big slides straight away, so we first went on to the smaller yellow ones. The first one we went down went 360 on itself, not upside down but round horizontally like a spiral. There were two ways down, both on separate slides. So, we picked a slide each and raced down. I could see Syd pass me on the way down. I heard her giggling like a mischievous child, it was nice to hear.

I don't think anyone has ever taught her how to exit a slide, so she swallowed a lot of water and was coughing and spluttering. But she enjoyed it, so we did it again. This time on the other slide. Next, we went on the straight slide, again there were two next to each other, we raced down them, and Syd won again.

She was then ready for the big launcher slide, there were four total, one small, two medium, and one large! Unfortunately, the large one was closed as they have had too many accidents on it, which was a shame. We tried the smaller one to start with, I braved it first!

It was really great fun! I landed fairly well on my first attempt. Syd somehow managed to spin herself around mid-air, locking her eyes on mine, I could see the look of fear on her face. She took a while to get back to the surface of the water so I pulled her up and pushed her to where she could stand up. Again, swallowing loads of water, coughing, and spluttering, but she was fine. She said she enjoyed it though but wasn't going to do it again.

I wanted to try the biggest one, but since it was closed, I had to settle with the medium one. It's only a couple more meters high, but the extra speed and the lip increase at the bottom really made a massive difference. I was flung far! The first time I did it I even make out a little "Woah" mid-air when I realized how high I was.

From here we tried the zip-line, which goes over basically the whole pool and into a cave on the other side. This was Syd's favourite part of the park. Mine was the big launcher slide! We had to jump off a tower on the zip wire which then took us into the cave. I jumped off first so I could be on the other side to catch Syd if she needed help getting off the wire. In the cave, after unclipping from the line, we walked up to the jump pads. There were two, the lower and the higher one. I started on the lower one, with the hopes Syd would follow, but she didn't feel up to it.

I climbed out of the water and back up the steps to see her. I wanted to do the higher one so I walked all the way up to do that, she wouldn't even come to the edge of that one, but she saw me jump off. I enjoyed the free-fall, it was quite a way up, not many people jumped off this one throughout the day.

After swimming around the cave, I met back up with Syd, and we then swam to the other side where there was a rock-climbing wall. It was a bit of a struggle to get out as the stairs were at an awkward position, this didn't bode well for our success at the rock climbing if we weren't even able to get out of the pool easily...

I managed to get out and then pulled Syd up. I tried the wall first, making it about halfway across, before running out of ideas about where I could go next. So, I jumped off the wall into the water, to let Syd have ago. She got one foot on but then didn't know what to do, so just jumped in the water from there. We then swam around to the ladder to get out of the pool, which was much easier.

We decided to have some shade time, so we moved our towels around the pool, finding a spot where we could see people jumping off the rocks and the big slide but still in shade. I tried sitting on a deck chair with cushions, but a woman came out and said I had to pay to sit there. It was 500 THB each, which seemed silly as we would only be there briefly. So, we found somewhere else. Still with just as good view of the jumps and still in shade, just no cushions.

A little while later Syd noticed some rubber rings. We walked over and as we were walking, I saw a SUP (stand-up paddle) board. I gave that ago while Syd was on the rubber ring. I've never tried it before, but I felt it quite easy, I was up on my feet quite quickly. We were on the water for quite some time, and as we were heading back, we saw a couple try and stand up too. The guy seemed a bit wobbly on the legs and didn't manage it, but the lady could. We then went back to our shade again for a bit.

We started to get a little thirsty and needed a cool-down, so we walked around trying to find ice cream. The first place we saw only did scoop ice cream, but we were fancying something a bit softer. As we were walking around, we saw the ninja warrior section, so decide to give this ago. It was great fun, it really made me sweat though. I enjoyed running up the vertical wall and lifting myself up.

Syd had found some mini bean bags to throw at a board with a hole in it. We played with these for a bit, and then next to that was an archery set (not real arrows but heavy-duty suction cups) which we tried too. There's loads of stuff to do here, including a decent skate park, basketball courts, etc.

By this point, we were really quite in need of a drink, I lead us back across where I had seen the softer ice creams. There were two flavours, mango and yogurt, unfortunately, the mango one wasn't cold enough so was more of a milkshake (I guess we were clearly having a fussy ice-cream day), so we opted for the yogurt one each. It came with chopped-up mango, a strawberry, and some mint leaves. It was very tasty. We also got a bottle of water to share.

I then wanted to go back on the SUP board, so I hopped back on one and paddled about. Syd took some photos of me standing up on it. I then wanted to go back on the big slide, so we headed that way. Syd didn't fancy it, so she just found a place in the shade closer to the slide to rest.

While I was on the slide again, I bumped into a couple from Essex, they were debating if they wanted to go down the bigger slide or not. I think I managed to talk them into it as they went down after I did. The guy, Billy, went down first, his back slammed into the water, it looked quite painful, but he said actually, surprisingly, he was all right. Then the lass, Tara, went down, a bit more graceful, but she said she had landed on her backside which was hurting.

They didn't fancy trying to go down on their front. I did explain that I found it better as I could lift my hands slightly off the slide, to then cause me to aquaplane. This allowed me to stop the spray from getting into my eyes. This also let me see where I was going, and how much I needed to rotate, while in the air.

I then went back to Syd, she wanted to go on the zip line again. We headed over and she went first this time. Once I had gotten to the other side of the cave, I wanted to jump off the rock again. I only went to the halfway up one as it was facing the way Syd was. I gave a little run and jump off to make it more exciting though!

Once in the water I swam around and got out to where Syd had walked to. We were feeling a bit thirsty again so headed to the bar. I saw the couple from the slide again, and we got chatting. It turns out they come to Thailand every year for 6 months in the winter, as it is where Tara's family is from.

We sat and chatted with them for about an hour, exchanging our Instagram's. Billy asked if I wanted to go for a cycle but unfortunately, they were heading home Monday (in three days' time from now) and we had already made plans up until Tuesday. But he said he'd let me know when he is in Bournemouth, and I can show him the Purbecks.

I then went back on the slide, this time with Syd filming me because Shaun (Syd's sister's partner) had dared me to do a flip off the slide, after seeing a video of me going down it earlier on Facebook. Which I managed to do, front and back flips. I had claps and nods from others around the pool watching. It felt good to perform again. Tara came to join me; she was still too scared to go down on her front but got two more jumps in on her back. Billy didn't fancy it again.

Once I'd had enough, we walked back to pick up our towels, and had showers, because we didn't fancy a shower at Ongla House, aka the concrete room. Once we finished this we started walking back, with the aim of grabbing some food on the way.

About halfway back, we stopped at a drinks stand called Mango, which is the same name as my Aunty Ann's local curry house, which Toby and I used to go to when we were growing up. Syd ordered a honey lemonade, and I ordered a brown sugar and honey milkshake. They were both very tasty, Syd wasn't keen on mine, but I was, so good job it was me drinking it! While we were here, Syd found out from a tagged picture on Instagram that Billy was quite well-known on Only Fans. And the Instagram he had given us was his private friends and family one. Fair play to him.

We carried on walking till we found a place that did noodles. It was quite a strange place, it looked like it was a barn from the mid-west of the USA or something. It was the busiest place we had seen though so we thought we'd go in. They had a lot of different options on the menu, so there was a lot to choose from!

We opted for a large sharing bowl, which had a hole in the middle, with lit coal inside it - keeping the soup warm. It was served with raw pork which was interesting, I suppose so you could cook it for as long or little as you like. We chucked all of ours into the soup pot, and the extra toppings that came with it, which were beef, bean sprouts, white onions, and some leaves of some sort. The pot would continue to cook this as the coal was still burning in the middle, while we ate a little bit at a time. It also came with a side of rice noodles which we could put a little in our small bowls each with the soup going on top. It was quite cute and very flavourful.

Once back in the room, Syd noticed a gecko run behind our toilet. Great... She was then too scared to go in, so I sprayed behind the toilet with the hose, and it came scurrying out. It then hid behind the mirror, but Syd was still too scared to go. So, I sprayed behind the mirror too. It then made its way to the ceiling, and then the bench in the bathroom.

I was too scared to grab it:
    1.) in case I killed it by accident, and
    2.) in case it gave me something I didn't want.

I phoned the guy at reception, but he took about half an hour to get to us. By which point we were near enough in bed, and the lizard wasn't where it had been when we last saw it. The guy came in nonetheless and sprayed the room around with vinegar, apparently, they don't like the smell.

Once he had left, Syd went to the loo, but wanted me to keep look-out... I did. I thought about pranking her by saying the lizard was under her feet. But rightly decided against that. I think she may have made me order a new room somewhere for us for the night.

We then got into bed and watched the rest of Bad Vegan on Netflix. Syd again fell asleep before the last episode ended. There wasn't much left of it, so I finished it and went to sleep. Looking forward to our next stay at the Blu Monkey Hub, with an actual working air-con and clean room! Looking back, we didn't take as many photos as maybe we could have at the park, I guess we were just so engrossed in the moment, enjoying it!

MONKEYING AROUND IN THE RAIN

PHUKET | DAY 4

22nd April 2022

https://twobritsinasia.com/monkeying-around-in-the-rain/

Luckily, we hadn't been eaten alive by the gecko in the night. We did have a lazy morning though because we were both sunburnt. Which was a first for me, to be this bad. Syd was still sleeping, so I was just on my phone doing some ETF trade purchases. Once Syd woke up, we got packed up and left. There was a cat resting under the table outside the door of our room: it looked very hot.

I ordered us a Grab to take us to our next hotel, Blu Monkey Hub Phuket. The ride was about 20 minutes, our driver was very helpful in loading our luggage into his van. There was plenty of room, I'd only ordered a car but was thankful a van turned up.

Even after our late start to the morning, we were early! Check-in was meant to be 3 pm but we were there just before 1. I had expected us to have to wait in the lobby area or in the communal working area until our room was ready. But the receptionist didn't say anything, simply gave us our room key. Happy days.

Once in our room, with a properly working air-con, we could cool down for a bit. This room was interestingly designed. It was all done in only black or white colours, which I really liked. It also had a balcony with Astroturf on the floor, but more strange, there was a bath with a shower head on! I was looking forward to trying it out!

After we cooled off, we both started to get a little hungry, as we had not eaten anything yet that day. While we were downstairs in the lobby area, we had seen the orange and apple juice were free for guests, so we had some. It was very sweet but nice to have some fresh vitamin C again.

We walked down the road to a 7-11 to try and find some after-sun. Next door was a pharmacy, but we went into 7-11 first. We couldn't see any after-sun the first time we looked. However, they did sell an orange with green skin, which looked interesting. Syd didn't fancy the oranges though as we had the OJ back at the hotel. We went next door to the pharmacy to get some after-sun, they only had aloe vera gel, and it was quite expensive for a small tube.

I saw there was a health shop across the road, so thought to try there. Unfortunately, they only had supplements and not any creams or gels for sunburns. They said to try 7-11 again, so we did. This time asking the cashier if they could help. There was a little section at the end of an aisle that we missed before. There were two types, a blue and a green one. Both were the same size and same brand, but the blue one was double the price. I asked what the difference was, but the cashier didn't seem to know, so I picked the cheaper one.

As we were walking back to our hotel, we had seen some food stalls. We decided on noodles with pork and beef (I think) it tasted kind of like liver if I'm honest. Either way, it was nice. Once we were finished, we then walked back to the hotel, having some apple and orange juice, along with a biscuit each. The apple juice was even sweeter than the OJ! Syd didn't like the biscuit, so I hoovered up hers too. They also offered free bananas, but they looked to have been out a while and weren't in the fridge where the drinks were, we gave them a miss.

Back in our room, we put the after-sun gel on. Syd had a little nap, and I was just cooling off and replying to messages on my phone. We then unpacked and rearranged our suitcases to get more organized after the last few days of living out of them. Once we finished this, Syd made us a hot chocolate from a sachet from downstairs, it wasn't the best so neither of us finished them. I think the milk powder was either not in date, or not milk.

I looked to see where Raya was, another Michelin guide recommended eatery, which Thitaree had also recommended to me. It was only about a ten-minute walk down the road, so I didn't bother with a Grab there. It wasn't too hot as it was getting later in the day, around 6:30 pm.

We ordered quite a lot at Raya, too much really, but I was excited to try it! We noticed it was cash only, I had 2,000 THB on me, which I hoped was enough, but I was a little worried it might not be. Annoyingly, just before we left the hotel room, I had thought about bringing some more cash with me just for the week but decided against it.

I had thought while I was there if it was over I could always just run back to the room quickly to pick up some more cash. But halfway through our meal, the heavens opened! I started to worry a little then, I didn't want to get needlessly wet running to and from the hotel.

We ordered a bottle of water to share, then also a sweet red drink for Syd and a sweet green drink for me. I couldn't tell you what the flavours were, just very sweet! For food, we shared everything, which was, fried chili squid, pork in pepper and garlic sauce, seafood noodles, crab coconut curry, fish in a traditional local curry sauce, fried pork bites, spring rolls, and some mango to finish (although I didn't order the mango, they brought it out for us on the house) ... I did say I ordered a lot.

It was all very delicious, Syd's favourite was the spring rolls, I liked the pork bites best. A guy came over to us once we had finished, he was dressed smartly with a clipboard. I think he may have owned the place. He was asking if we enjoyed everything, not too spicy (as we had left some of the spicier fish and crab dishes). We found the spice fine, it was very flavourful, but we were just stuffed!

Luckily when the bill came it was 1,960! Thankfully, no need to get extra wet from the shuttle run! I didn't ask for any change as our waitress had been very helpful all evening. I was thinking about ordering a Grab but as we were getting up another server handed us a brolly each. I asked how I would return them, and another lady (I think maybe the manager) said to just drop them back off whenever. Which was kind of her.

We then had a fun walk in the rain back to our hotel, with lighting and thunder overhead. It was an experience for sure!! The umbrellas were keeping our faces dry, but from our shoulders down we were soaked! It's not like English rain though, it was warm by the time it hit us, so it wasn't actually that bad. We were laughing most of the way back to the hotel.

Just as we got back a massive bit of lighting erupted right in front of us! I think this scared Syd a bit. Followed quickly by the loudest thunder I have ever heard. I think we were both glad to be back at the hotel after that! Back in our room, we stripped down and I put our wet clothes and shoes outside, on, and in, the bath to dry out during the night.

We were both stuffed! I went on the loo and again funnily after the fancy meal, my bowels weren't as firm as usual. I think it's probably down to stuffing myself too much, so "lesson learned" (probably not). We lay about in bed writing some reviews for the places we had stayed. We noticed the lightning outside of our balcony door, even though the rain had stopped the lightning lasted at least 3 hours after we got in, and probably more but we went to sleep. Syd was really looking forward to going to the aquarium tomorrow!

SHARK!

PHUKET | DAY 5

23rd April 2022

https://twobritsinasia.com/shark/

We woke up later than planned today, we had wanted to get to the aquarium at 10:30, but we were still in bed then! Unfortunately, our toilet got blocked while I was doing my morning business. We let reception know and they said they would sort it. While we were downstairs, we had some more orange juice and I ordered a Grab to take us to Raya to drop off the umbrellas and then onwards to the aquarium.

The Grab driver was strange as when we arrived at the aquarium, he was asking for an extra 300 THB in cash, which isn't how it works. He then followed us into the aquarium, but I told him he had to leave. Very strange. I rated him one star on Grab and let them know what had happened. Grab later contacted me and said he was suspended from their app until he underwent their further driving training program.

Anyway, once in the aquarium, we had a great time! Loads to see. Syd really does like her sea animals! She was loving it. We could also walk outside on a fly-over bridge, which they called the canopy walk, and look down into the tanks.

They didn't just have fish, they had reptiles too, and a few rabbits for some reason. The snakes were interesting. There was a massive python which I thought was cool because the programming language I'm most comfortable with is named after it.

We then went back to the ground floor and saw the black-tipped sharks. There must have been at least 50 of them in this massive tank. Next to them was a tank full of manta rays, one was coming up to the edge, playing with us, waving its wing and splashing us over the ridge. Further round the corner, there was an even bigger tank with bigger sharks and sting rays in!

There was a restaurant with a massive window into the pool, window is the wrong word really, it was a massive wall of glass! Before Covid this had been a fine dining place, I had tried to book a table for Syd and I to eat there. But now it's just a place for snacks, such as chips and American pancakes. We didn't get anything.

There was a tunnel off the side of the restaurant, they had used this for the expensive tables in the past to eat here in the evening. But now it's just a walkway, and a viewpoint to see other angles of the fishes. The tunnel led to a room full of jellyfish and starfish.

We then left to try and find some food in the mall before the feeding of the fish started in an hour. We first went to the top floor, passing Louis Vuitton, and the other usual luxury brands. I don't know how Syd does it, she always seems to be able to sniff them out somehow?! We didn't go in any this time as we had to get back for the feeding.

At the top of the mall were all fancy places, selling sushi, etc. I didn't fancy spending a lot on lunch as we had an expensive dinner planned for later. Also, Syd didn't fancy eating fish after seeing so many of them. While at the top we saw someone performing on a stage with judges in front. I think it was an improv Britain's Got Talent sort of show.

We went back down to the ground floor to the food court and looked around for what tickled our fancy. Most of the stalls were only accepting this special mall cash card. We found a stall that would take cash, at a good price too, they offered a plate of rice and two dishes for 50 THB. We had one of those each, and some pork skewers, and a mini bowl of tom yum soup to share. We both went for a chicken dish as one of our choices, Syd then picked a rice noodle dish, and I picked a chicken and chili one. It was all very nice.

By the time we finished our lunch, it was feeding time back at the aquarium. We started with the otters, they were doing lots of tricks, going around in circles, waiting, spinning in the water, etc. We then went on to see the penguins. They were just gathered into a huddle, but it was getting busier, so we headed down to the shark feeding spot to get a good view before everyone else came along.

We sat right in front of the black-tipped shark's tank. It was interesting to see they kept low in the tank, while the other fish in there kept higher up. Then once the food was chucked in, they swarmed the top and the other fish got out of their way! From here we went across the aisle to watch the manta rays feeding. This time the feeders were in scuba-diving equipment and went into the tank.

It was really exciting to see the feeders playing with the rays, holding their noses, and dropping the food in. They did this for a while, any dead fish that the rays dropped, the other live fish in the tank would eat the leftovers up. I wonder how they trained them all not to eat the live fish vs the dead ones they are feeding them.

There was about a half-hour break in the feeding. Syd and I sat in the restaurant catching up on messages while we waited for the big tank, with the big sharks in, to have their feeding time. About five minutes before the feeding started, we walked to the glass wall and sat in front of it.

Before the feeding started, they had millions of tiny little bubbles come up from the bottom of the glass window, acting as a curtain. It was cool as it made it hard to see through the glass, the two guys in the scuba kit were setting up the feeding stations in the tank. Once the bubbles stopped, the feeding commenced!

The two divers had long rods, which they put full fish on, and they then called the sharks over with hand gestures. The first few times they came over straight away. It was cool seeing them take the fish and then shake their head as you see in the movies with shark attacks. After they had a few fish each, I guess they were full, as they didn't seem interested anymore. With the divers calling them over, and even swimming towards them with the fish, they weren't biting.

Instead, the divers then started feeding the sting rays and other larger fish in the tank. They then moved over to the tunnel, where they fed a massive fish! It could have fed a family of four for a good couple of months! Once the feeding had finished, one of the divers took a photo with me and Syd behind the glass, it was funny. A lot of other people then copied us and did the same. Always been a trendsetter me...

We then got a Grab back from the aquarium to our hotel, where we had some more orange juice, apple juice, and even risked one of the bananas. The full works. It's just so nice to have some fruit again. There is lots of fruit here, but we can only really see it being sold on the food stands, and who knows how long it's been sat around there for, and how it was washed.

We stayed in the room for a couple of hours just cooling down and having a bit of a relax before the evening's activities. Luckily the toilet blockage had been fixed. I had a shower, I had thought about trying the bath on the balcony, but I really wanted to try and pop the sunburn blister on my shoulder, which would be cleaner in the shower. I couldn't pop it though, not quite ready, I might need to puncture it as it is a bit painful with the pressure of it.

Once we were ready, I ordered a Grab to take us to Leam Hin Pier. It was the same guy that drove us from the aquarium to our hotel a few hours earlier. He recognized us, he was a lot chattier this time. Thankfully it wasn't the driver from this morning who had followed us into the aquarium!

At the pier, we got a long tail boat over to Kruvit Seafood Raft, where we would be having dinner. It was beautiful seeing the mountains in the distance with the sun setting, the sky was orange. The boat ride only took a few minutes, but it was great fun!

The raft itself was quite sketchy, it was solid and felt safe, but there were gaps between the planks of the wooden floor. Not big enough to fall through, but definitely wide enough to drop your wallet, phone, or keys down. Syd gave me her phone as she didn't have any pockets, and she didn't want to lose it.

Yet again I ordered too much, but I just get too excited and want to try all these different flavours. We ordered a hot and sour seafood soup, it had squid, prawns, some other fishes, and crab in, parts of the crab with shells on too which was fun to use our hands to get the meat out. Along with fried chili squid, a spicy salad with fried crayfish (I think), a portion of vegetable fried rice, and then a massive fish which I forgot I ordered as it came out later than everything else. It wasn't just the fish that was big, all the portions were huge. We couldn't finish it all!

The bill came to 1,800 THB odd; I did have a lot of cash this time as I certainly didn't want to be stuck on a raft without having enough money. Although it turns out these guys accepted card payments. I paid with that, as the exchange rate was pretty good, and the card I use takes the most up-to-date exchange rate, with no fees.

We then got the tail boat back to the pier. I tried ordering a Grab but being so far out of town now, nothing was available in the reasonable price range. Luckily there were some taxis on the pier, originally, they said 400 THB, but they were just trying it on. I said no, 200, which they agreed to.

This guy's car was very fancy, it had those lights on the roof like a Rolls Royce Phantom. I asked him if he would drop us off at the 7-11 down the street as Syd wanted to pick up a nail file. We wanted some more of the aloe gel, but they had run out. We picked up some lotion instead.

Back at the hotel, we wanted some more OJ but the lady was refilling it, and we didn't want to be awkwardly standing around and then pounce on it as soon as it had been refilled. So, we just went up to our room. Syd had a shower and then was complaining her back was itchy, she kept putting different creams and ointments on. In reality, the more she thinks about it the worse it will feel for her.

I told her to have a cold shower to rinse it all off, and I put my cream on her back. Telling her to think about the fish we saw today to take her mind off it. That seemed to calm her down. We then shortly settled to bed, with the plan of going to the Phuket Baba Museum tomorrow.

SUNDAY FOOD DAY!

PHUKET | DAY 6

24th April 2022

https://twobritsinasia.com/sunday-food-day/

We woke up a little later than planned, only by an hour but I was told that the dim sum place we wanted to go for breakfast this morning ran out fast. We got up and ready quickly and made our way downstairs. After having some orange juice, of course, we made our way to Boonrat Dim Sum.

The plan for today was to explore the main town in Phuket and eat the local food. As a tradition here, every Sunday from 4 pm to 10 pm, there is a food street party on Thalang Road (Lard Yai). We have arranged to meet Thitaree's Mum, Ann, and Sister, Misora, there later at 6.

Our first stop, Boonrat Dim Sum, was about a 15-minute walk from the hotel. We walked through the town, passing the old police station and the first bank. There was also a cool pink-looking building with cartoon pandas on. Unfortunately, Boonrat had already sold out. Not to worry - we walked a bit further down the road to another dim sum place. We had planned on going there tomorrow for breakfast, but they still had some left. It was packed! There were loads of Grab food drivers waiting for takeaway orders too. We managed to get a table; I was then ushered to the front where I selected the dumplings we wanted.

It was a big metal casing with six doors on the top, the whole thing was basically a massive steamer. Inside each compartment there were different dishes, I could then pick whatever ones we wanted. Syd had to sit at the table to make sure it wasn't given to someone else, so I made our selections for both of us.

We had a right mix, including a fermented egg, Syd wasn't a great fan of this, but I quite liked it, the whites were purple and like jelly. The yolk tasted the same just a stronger, deeper flavour. We also had fish goujons which seemed strange as a breakfast choice, but they were very nice. We must have had at least 10 different plates, clearly not learning from my ordering too much... But actually, these were only small portions each, just single bites, so we weren't over full after, which is good.

Looking at the map, we weren't too far away from our planned lunch stop for the day. Since we'd done about half an hour of walking already it seemed silly to walk back where we had come from only to walk back here later. So, we decided to go there immediately and have something small to share instead.

I was a little worried walking there spotting that a lot of the shops at this end of town were closed. Thankfully the one we wanted, Mee Ao Gea, was open! We shared a bowl of their Hokkien Stir Fried noodles, and a milky tea drink to share. The noodles were nice, like a chow-mien, but with more sauce.

From here we walked back to the old police station and the first bank, which is a symbol for this part of Thailand. Lots of people stood outside taking photos of it. This had now been converted into a museum and learning centre, to understand the history of Phuket. It was free to enter and was informative. I'd recommend it to anyone. While we were there, we made ourselves a poster each with ink stamps of Chinese words. Mine went in the order of "Honour, Wealthy, Luck, and Go Higher". There is a lot of Chinese influence here in Phuket.

We then walked to a local street food stand that Thitaree had recommended to us. On the way we had seen lots of gold shops, we went into one just to see the prices. They were about 20% above the actual price of gold, but that's understandable, as they need to form it and make a profit. We didn't buy anything this time, but it was amazing to see all the gold in the shop. Also, along the way, we picked up a chocolate milk drink from 7-11. A massive cup for 25THB, which is less than 50p. It tasted like chocolate Oatley milk back home. Delicious.

The street food stall, Soi Lhor Rong, who is known for its variation of a spring roll, pork soup, noodles, and the famous Phuket dessert Oh Aew. Unfortunately, they weren't doing the spring roll today, but we ordered everything else. The dessert is a bowl of some kind of jelly, with red kidney beans, topped with tons of crushed ice and some sort of red sweet syrup. I quite liked it; Syd really wasn't impressed so she let me finish it.

We then started to head back to the hotel, with all this food and the massive drink of chocolate milk onboard, Syd really needed the loo. And quick. We were about 20-30 minutes walk away from the hotel at this point. She said she could hold it, so I didn't order a Grab, and we started walking back.

About 2 minutes later she proclaims, "I need to go!" I asked a local shop if they had a toilet she could use. They said yes, but unfortunately, they didn't have any toilet paper, only the water jet. Syd hasn't been using the water jets at the hotels, so she wasn't too confident in using them. So, we carried on. We then walked past the 7-11 again, I popped in here to ask if she could use the staff toilet. They agreed but they didn't have any toilet paper either. I suppose, looking back, we were in the store we could have just bought some for her to use. Anyways, after the second failed attempt, Syd says again that she can hold it.

Walking back past the gold shops, I thought it would make for a good souvenir if we bought some of the gold from Thailand. We went back into the gold shop we had been in originally. I saw

TWO BRITS IN ASIA

at the back they had little square nuggets. Syd liked the look of some heart earrings with rubies in them.

We got talking to the lady behind the desk, I asked if they had any other patterns. She said they had another new shop further down the road, that wasn't open yet, but she could show us. So we went into this new shop, it was very luxurious. They had a lot more selection here. I found a card of gold I liked the look of and kept that to the side. The earrings Syd liked were in this shop too, but she found another set that she liked the look of. These were small, hooped earrings with golden beads at the bottom of them.

In total the gold weighed 1.9 grams, and the shop was selling at about 3,400 THB per gram. Since we were buying two items, and this shop hadn't officially opened yet, they gave us a deal for 5,500 for the two. Which is about £125, for reference, raw gold in the UK at the time was worth £48.42 per gram.

We were happy with our purchases and made our way back to the hotel. Syd ran straight to the toilet, she gave me the "news flash" that her business was massive and that she was now tired after the ordeal! This made me laugh. While she was in the loo, I lay on the bed to cool down. The maid hadn't been yet, but about 5 minutes after we got back she knocked on the door. I told her that I'd find her once we were out of the room again, which wouldn't be long.

5 minutes later, I found her again, and Syd and I popped downstairs while she cleaned. Thankfully Syd's massive poop didn't block the toilet like mine yesterday! While downstairs we had some more apple and orange juice, along with a banana each. We're really going to miss this feature at our next stay!

We sat by the open doors to the pool with a large fan pointing toward us. We had taken a bottle of water from the fridge too, which we drank. I walked up a flight of stairs to see the meeting rooms, they were quite cool. I like the idea and design of this hotel, which was four-star, and acted like a central "hub" (hence the name, Monkey Hub) for people to come and communally work alongside each other.

Once the room was clean, we headed back up. We spent a few hours just lounging around and cooling down from the hectic day of walking and eating. Syd had a nap while I was on my phone replying to messages and watching some videos.

We had a bath on our balcony, it was great fun. Syd ran the bath. I got in first, then she got in facing away from the balcony, towards me, so the outside world wouldn't be able to see anything. But Syd decided she wanted to turn around and see the outside world while she was in the bath, it was a novelty!

After our bath, we then got ready for the street party, Syd wore her new earrings. I took my camera to the main street, where the food stalls and party were. It had passed 6 and I realized we hadn't arranged a place to meet Ann and Misora. It was very busy, and I didn't know what they looked like so I phoned Misora, to arrange a meeting point.

There was a lot going on: different performers on the road, tons of different food stalls, with clothes and souvenir shops at the top. It really was a party atmosphere like a community-based car boot sale, with an emphasis on tasting great food and having a fantastic time.

We walked back to the golden dragon to meet them. It was starting to get dark, so I wanted to run the camera back to the room to save carrying it around all night with it being so busy. Ann and Misora had got us a bag of local goodies, which was really kind of them. I took this back to the hotel with me too while dropping the camera off.

When I got back, all three of them were watching a break-dancing street performance. I stood and watched it with them too. I was sweating quite a bit, after power walking to and from the hotel in the heat, because I didn't want to keep them waiting.

After the performance, we walked past the clothes and orna-ment stands, towards the food and drink stalls. We first had a sticky rice package, wrapped in a banana leaf, with lots of dif-ferent things in the rice, such as pork, and dried fruits. Ann had recommended we try it, as well as the traditional syrup drink we had next. It tasted like a root beer. It was very refreshing.

T's family owns one of the main houses on the famous strip. They rent part of the downstairs out to a shop and the other side to a café. They were renovating upstairs. They also own some other property in the town. It was great to see them creating and also helping these local businesses.

Further down we saw some fried chicken, which we wanted to try. It was like Wagamama's tori kara age (fried chicken bits). Ann and Misora had some fried oysters with pork crackling, they let us try some, and it was very tasty too!

Next, we had a Japanese pizza, which was basically a thick pancake wrapped around itself with shredded cabbage inside. We had ours topped with sausage, their sign said chicken and ham, but we think they meant chicken ham slices. We weren't sure what it would be like, so we just went with sausage.

A few stalls down were selling mini chicken and pork satay sticks, so we bought some of those too. It came on a large plate with lots of peanut sauce! We stood and watched another break-dancing performance while we ate them.

Syd then saw the desserts she likes, back from when we had them in the mall with T and Wat back in Bangkok; we got a mixed bowl of sweet and savoury ones. We found out the white part is egg whites, almost like soft meringue, and the ribbon toppings are egg yolk or coconut depending on which ones you have.

We then saw a stall with 100s of gyozas, we had a box of differ-ent types to share, spinach, pork, vegetable, and prawn. Opposite this stand was a building that looked like it belonged in Paris, it was very pretty. We took a picture outside it.

Further up the road was a dessert shop, we sat outside as it was packed in there. I had a traditional local dessert, which was similar to a rice pudding, but it had black rice and light purple ice cream on top, I'm not sure what the flavour of the ice cream was, it was sweet and refreshing though. Syd had their take on an ice cream Sunday, it had mini chunks of brownie and wafer in it, and it too was very nice.

We then headed back to the hotel, saying goodbye to Ann and Misora. It had been a great evening, but I sure was stuffed again! I never learn... It all tastes so good though!

We both got straight into bed and replied to our messages before heading to sleep.

CERTIFIED WARRIOR

PHUKET | DAY 7

25th April 2022

https://twobritsinasia.com/certified-warrior/

We started the day early because we wanted to head to Boon-rat Dim Sum. On Google it said they were open but I checked on Grab food and which said closed. We chanced it anyways. Unfortunately, it was closed, so we walked back to the main street. A lot of other shops were closed because it was a Monday. We found an Indian-inspired place, so we had breakfast there. Syd had a chicken curry soup with noodles of some kind, like a Tom Yum, and I went with a chicken and Chinese kale with thick rice noodles (Pad See Ew).

Syd couldn't finish her soup as it had a lot of harder ingredients in it, such as chunks of ginger. I helpfully finished it for her. We then ordered a roti, which is what this place is known for. We had it with banana and chocolate, it had an off-white sauce over the top. We were trying to think what it could be; I think it was most likely ghee, it was sweet and salty at the same time, very rich, I liked it.

Back at the hotel, we packed up and cooled off on the bed with the air-con on full blast, as we plan to have a fairly full-packed rest of the day. When we checked out, the receptionist asked where we were heading next, which was the first time any of the hotels had asked that. Either way, I ordered us a Grab which took us to our next stop, the Shanti Lodge, the cheapest of the stays. At just £10 a night for the two of us.

When we arrived, the lady at reception was very friendly, she got some other staff to help take our bags up to our room. We just put them in and headed straight back down into the same taxi to take us to Wat Chaitharam (Wat Chalong). This is the most famous temple in Phuket. It was very pretty. Although after seeing the temples in Bangkok a few weeks earlier, especially the Emerald Buddha, this temple was dwarfed. We've been spoilt!

The first building we went in was three stories, the first two were full of different golden Buddhas. The middle floor looked like it had some water damage from somewhere. The top floor had jewels encased in a glass room. People had pushed money through the gaps in the glass doors to pay their respects and donate to the monument. We could also see the big Buddha up on the mountain from here. Our plan for tomorrow is to go see it up close.

We then walked back down the stairs, the first step on the top flight was strange. It was about a third of the size of the other steps and had an angled drop on it. We think this was to keep any water out from the top floor (which was opened up into a court-yard almost), which might have been added after the damage was caused to the middle layer. This is only our guess though. On the way down we saw some lotus flowers which are the same as the ones Syd had tattooed on her arm in England. She wanted me to take a photo of her next to them. I obliged.

It was beautiful seeing the other temples hidden in the trees and the mountains in the background. On the ground floor of this building, we saw a cat resting under the stairs, laying on the cool floor. Since each temple was so close to one another, I didn't bother putting my shoes on each time – so I was running and jumping over the hot tarmac to get to the next one. It reminded me of when I was younger (much much younger), when we were on a family holiday in Tenerife, the sand was so hot my Dad did the same movement across it!

The second building had incense burning, with three statues in. What we noticed walking between the buildings, was China or porcelain flowers embedded into the tarmac, they were pretty. It seemed they were also building a white temple here too, not as extravagant as Wat Rong Khun, which we saw a week and a half ago. This one had a grey centre, I quite liked the design.

Following the path around, we found another building. This one had air-con in, so we cooled off in here for a bit. There were three life-like monks in the room. Syd couldn't tell if they were real or not, I could see they were fake, but I jokingly said, "are you real" to them, of course, there was no reply. Syd claims she thought she saw one blink. She must be blinking mad!

Out of that one and into the main building. People were placing gold leaves onto three Buddhas in the centre of the room. There were others rattling sticks around, a stick would fall out. They would read it and then do something. I'm not sure what the sticks said. It must have been some sort of praying. There was a lot of construction noise from the new building being built. It's funny, wherever in the world you are, there is always someone with a jackhammer disturbing the peace somewhere...

We then walked over the road to the older temple, but this was closed. So, I put my shoes back on and walked over to see if any of the taxi men standing around would take us down the road to the Tiger Muay Boxing camp. Most of them were there waiting for their previous rides to finish with the temple. One guy quoted 300 THB to take us there, but it's only a 5-minute drive. He was claiming it was at least 15... Grab was saying about 100, I told him this, and he dropped to 200, but wasn't budging off that. So, I ordered a Grab.

Once it arrived, it was our first woman driver the whole time we had been here. She had a nice car, she reminded me a bit of Aunty Ann really, blunt and to the point, bordering on rude, but softening up once she got talking. Once we arrived at the camp, she gave us her card and said to phone her anywhere in Phuket for a taxi. This was helpful to have as I've explained earlier Grab isn't as reliable here as it was in Bangkok. We did end up using her a lot for the rest of the time we were in Phuket. We know her as Miss Kamonyupa.

When we arrived at Tiger Muay Thai Boxing and Mixed Martial Arts, we noticed lots of famous people had trained there. I did know this, hence why coming here. It's arguably the most famous and prestigious MMA fighting training camp in the world. With most UFC (Ultimate Fighting Championship) world titles training here.

Even while we were booking our session, there was someone who had clearly been fighting all his life. He had the big bulging ears of years of scarring. He was going to be staying at the camp for the next month straight.

We had a 1:1 hour session, each with our own private trainer. It was great fun, learning different punches, elbow strikes, and knee and leg kicks. It was about 40 degrees Celsius heat, so it was hard work. We were both sweating a lot! It was much needed after all the food we had yesterday. We had to stop every ten minutes or so for a water break.

After the workout, I wanted to see if I could buy some gloves as a souvenir, but they didn't have the design I wanted in my size. Not to worry. Looking back, I was never going to wear the gloves so I should have just got the design I wanted. Oh well.

We walked to their on-site restaurant and shared a chocolate muffin and a blue Gatorade instead. We just sat there for a while cooling off under the fan and recuperating from the workout. Syd only took her ring off halfway through the workout and thinks she bruised her finger in the first half (later on the following day it was fine just a little bruised). But she did have a big bruise on her knee!

The plan was to stay here till dinner, as the restaurant we were going to tonight was only down the road. However, we were both still sweaty (even though I'd taken my top off). So, we decided to head back to the lodge and have a shower. I messaged Miss Kamonyupa, to come and pick us up, which she did.

Back at the hotel, we lay on the bed for a bit trying to cool down. There was an air-con unit in the room, but it didn't seem to do anything, there was also a fan above the bed which was at least moving air onto us. After about an hour of just lounging around, we had a cold shower each, the shower (and toilet) was outside, in a private roofed courtyard area. This cooled us down.

We walked down to reception while waiting for our lady to come to pick us up again. While we were down there, we had some water and were chatting with the receptionist. She had come over from the Philippines when she was 18 and had stayed ever since (I think she said she was 34 now).

I said that our air-con doesn't seem to be doing much, and another worker walked by and said, oh yeah that room's air-con is broken. The receptionist had not realized this as she had only started here a few days ago. She said we could do a test and have both air-cons on in the rooms, and whichever room was the coolest when we got back, we could have that one. Which was very kind of her.

Our evening plans were to eat at the restaurant, Mor Mu Dong. It was all outside, with the tables and chairs covered by canopies. The reception and kitchen were in an actual building though. It was quite big, with different seating areas all over the place. Thitaree had recommended this place to me as it was very well known to locals, there was nothing else out this far. T said her family has been coming to this restaurant for generations!

We had a wide selection of different dishes, all recommended by T. The servers brought us out some mixed fruits and a chili dip to start. Our favourite dishes were the fried prawn fish cakes, pork bites, and the stuffed fish (which was stuffed with meat, we had no idea how they stuffed it). I had some blue rice, which tasted like normal plain rice, Syd had mixed vegetable rice which was nice.

We also ordered a black octopus, which was served in its own ink, it was very very black, and stained the plate, our mouth, tongue, and teeth! It was nice, just tasted like a normal octopus, but richer. Syd wasn't a big fan of it, she prefers fried octopus, and this was more either grilled or steamed, it was hard to tell. It could have been raw for all I know.

There were two dishes both of us weren't fans of, some sort of seaweed soup with prawn paste. It was just a bit too sea-like for us. And another dish of seaweed, but this seaweed was a stem with 100s of tiny balls on it. It felt quite funny when biting down on it, with it popping in our mouth. It tasted ok, but the after-texture of the slime in our mouth was very off-putting, very much like phlegm. There was also a plate of different vegetables with a strong prawn mini soup in the middle. This was a bit strong for us too.

The waiter could see that we hadn't touched those dishes much, and with limited ability to understand what we were saying, a table next to us was able to help translate. We had tried to ask if we could change those dishes for some more pork bites and prawns. But they said once it's been served there isn't anything that can be done. This is a different culture to what we are used to in England with food that we don't like the taste of, usually the chefs will do what they can to make you happy (within reason).

Before the table next to us helped with the translation, I tried to call Thitaree, but she didn't answer. About 5 minutes later she did call back, I explained to her why I'd tried to call, and she said to pass her over to the waiter and she'd try to explain. The same answer was given, once it's served there's nothing they can do. Not to worry we were full of what we had eaten, and also had a lot of food yesterday so we weren't going to go hungry.

After eating we walked around the grounds a little bit. Seeing the massive kitchen, they had and the live crabs waiting to be cooked.

Our taxi driver said she had to pick up her daughter from the airport so wouldn't be free until later in the night. Instead, I ordered us a Grab back to our hotel. We had thought about stopping off somewhere for some more food in case we get hungry during the night. But I remembered we still had the gifts from Ann and Misora, so we could eat those if needed (which it wasn't).

The new room was much cooler, so they moved us into that room. Thankfully it was literally the room next door so wasn't any hassle. As we were only staying here two nights we hadn't really unpacked much anyways. This new room was at the end of the terrace, so we had an extra window too, looking out over the pool.

We got ready for bed and started a movie on Netflix, 14 Peaks. It was about a Nepalese guy wanting to climb the 14 biggest mountains in the world, within 7 months! We got halfway through, just as he summited Mt Everest, before turning it off and going to sleep.

TAXI MAFIA

PHUKET | DAY 8

26th April 2022

https://twobritsinasia.com/taxi-mafia/

Both of us woke up early this morning, awoken by the heavy rain. We stayed in bed; Syd fell back to sleep while I was on my phone just chilling. We had a few of the snacks from Ann and Misora for breakfast. I did a bit of ISA investment paperwork before we got out of bed.

Thankfully by the time we got out the door, the rain had stopped. We made our way walking up the road to a shopping centre called Lotus. The plan was to have KFC, as we had seen it yesterday while driving past to go to the temple. I wanted to see what the differences were here compared to England. The walk there didn't take long, maybe 10 minutes, but it was a bit sketchy as there wasn't any pavement, and it was all dual carriageways. Luckily there weren't many cars, we only had a few honks.

At Lotus, there was a car wash outside with lots of cars that had been dropped off for them to clean. Inside there were loads of little stands around the outside walls, and a supermarket taking up the whole back half of the warehouse-style shopping centre. We walked round till we found the KFC.

However next door was a sushi/buffet place called Shabushi. It was a similar concept to Yo-Sushi in England, where plates of food would move around on conveyor belts around the tables. But instead, the food was all raw, including the meats, and you'd have a big bowl of soup (with a divider in the middle, as you could have picked different flavours) which was on your own personal hob to cook the foods.

It was just over 400 THB each, I think it was 419 (which is just under a tenner). This let us have unlimited food and drink, for 1 hour and 15 minutes, and then every subsequent 10 minutes was 20 THB per person. But that wasn't needed! We had so much food! They had a sushi section too, with fresh sushi!

We kept picking lots of different dishes off the belt. I mainly went for the meat (obviously), some fish and prawns too. I also had a little bowl of rice noodles, then remembered the number 1 rule of a buffet: the establishment MUST lose money when I'm eating there, even if it makes me physically sick (which luckily, I wasn't, this time...)

Syd had a slightly more conservative selection, which included veg thrown into her mix, along with a healthy serving of meats and egg noodles. She also tried some bacon, which I didn't get around to having. It was quite an interesting concept of cooking the food how you liked it. Like that BBQ place, we saw a few days ago, but that was just a little too out in the open for our liking, with no food standards.

Another section offered fried gyozas, chicken bites, prawn bites and fried mackerel. They'd run out of the tempura prawn sticks, so I had to wait for 10 minutes for them to refill, but this gave me a much-needed break.

The last area had bottomless (soft) drinks, and next to the drinks machine, were four flavours of ice cream: chocolate; vanilla; lime; and green tea (Syd wasn't a fan of the green tea one). Syd had two bowls of the ice creams while I was waiting for the prawn sticks to replenish.

After I'd paid up, we waddled back to the hotel. There were a few spits of rain, but very minimal, and if you'd have blinked you'd have missed it, as it was over within literal seconds. Once back at the hotel, we flopped back down on the bed, exhausted! Syd had a nap while I replied to messages.

Later, we decided we had gained enough strength to go see the Big Buddha at the top of the mountain. I tried messaging our taxi lady, but she was two hours away with another client, so I ordered= a Grab. The drive up to the mountain was about 20 minutes, and it was steep. I'd love to try to cycle it one day! Nearly at the top was an elephant sanctuary. This made Syd smile.

Once we got to the top, the diver asked if we wanted him to stay around, I had said we didn't need him to as I thought I could just get another Grab later... Oh, how I was wrong...

The view was amazing. We could see for miles around, basically, most of southern Phuket could be seen from here, along with a lot of the islands off the coast and towards Krabi. There were lots of boats in the water, and when it got darker, we could see all the green light boats on the horizon again, as we saw at Pullman on our first night in Phuket. We were also able to see the other mountains further north, with that mountain haze around the peaks. It was very pretty.

Syd had seen a monkey sitting on a roof, and then another one on the stairs up to the statue. Further around there were a whole bunch of monkeys, including baby ones too! They were very cute, but there were signs everywhere saying not to feed them as they bite. We kept a good distance from them. There was a monk walking past the monkeys, but he must live here, and they must be used to him.

At the bottom of the stairs, Syd wanted another picture with her buddha tattoo this time, next to the massive statue behind her. Once she was happy with the pictures, we climbed the stairs up to the Big Buddha, Syd counted 100 steps to the top. It looked to of been made of marble as there were workshops dotted around the site with marble tiles in the same shape as the ones up on the Buddha. We could walk inside the base of the Buddha. There were flags up from all different countries, we found the Union Jack and I gave it a touch. Syd then touched me as I touched it as she couldn't reach up to it.

Around the side of the Buddha, I noticed the ears had holes in them. Interesting. There were also bells around the perimeter, massive too! We tried pushing them, but we could only move them a little because they were so heavy! As it started to get darker, we decided to make our way back down. I tried ordering a Grab at first, but no one would take our ride.

I had seen further down a few people holding taxi signs, so I asked them if they would take us down. They were asking stupid prices, double what I paid to get to the top. I tried bartering with them, but they weren't budging much. I tried Grab again. Luckily someone accepted instantly, and they were already at the top of the mountain.

We walked over to his car and got in. What happened next shocked us though. The taxi people surrounded his car shouting at him for picking us up, there were about 5 of them. He seemed quite scared; he asked us to get out. I stayed half in this guy's car while I spoke to what seemed to be the leader of this taxi ring and said sternly, I wasn't going to use his taxis as they were charging too much. And then got back in our car.

I told our driver it was time to go, and he drove off. One of the taxi people took a picture of his car. Very strange. He was clearly shaken up by the exchange, he explained that they were a taxi cartel, and they were not happy that he had picked us up. But it wasn't his fault as it was a Grab service. He also had someone else waiting at the top for another ride. Unfortunate timing, as they phoned him as we'd only just left the top of the mountain. He pulled over and tried to talk to them on his phone.

He was clearly in a state after what had happened on the top, and we just wanted to get back to our resort at this point as it was pitch black on the side of a mountain. I touched his shoulder and said it's okay, we're only down the hill, which at this point was about 5 minutes away. He carried on and dropped us off. Just before he did, he phoned his next passengers trying to explain to them to walk down from the top a bit, so he didn't have to see those taxi scammers again. He was struggling with English; I took his phoned and talked to his next passengers for him. I explained to them what had happened, and they were okay with walking down slightly to the elephant sanctuary, to make sure our driver was ok.

We sat at the on-site restaurant and ordered a plate of chips, our first plate of chips since we arrived, I think they were only Mc-Cain's oven chips. I couldn't decide what else to have, as in truth wasn't too hungry after everything we'd had at lunch. I asked the friendly receptionist what her favourite was. She said the chicken masala curry and the chicken burrito were favourites of hers. We ordered that too. The curry was delicious, very creamy and came with those pancake-like rotis. The burrito was just as good, but by this point, I was stuffed! I lounged out on the sofa I was sitting on for a good 20 minutes, with the complex owner's dogs coming up and getting attention from me. I paid up and then we went up to our lodge.

As we were going up, the owner noticed Syd's burnt back. She said to go into her garden and take some of her aloe vera to put on Syd's skin. She said that when her daughter comes to visit, she mixes it with her sun cream, which we thought was a good idea. We took an arm of the plant, someone was playing the guitar outside her door too, which was nice. They said they had come from South Africa to start this business. It is something that appeals to me. I don't think Syd could move this far away from family though.

Back in our room, we put the fresh aloe jelly from the plant on each other and let it dry before getting into bed. By the time we got into bed, it was too late to watch the rest of the 14 peaks tonight, so we will save it for another night. We also hadn't packed up yet for tomorrow's check-out, but we were so stuffed and tired from yet another day of eating shenanigans, we went straight to sleep!

MEN STROKING THEIR DOLPHINS, LUNCH HIGH, AND HALF-NAKED WAITRESSES

PHUKET | DAY 9

27th April 2022

https://twobritsinasia.com/men-stroking-their-dolphins-lunch-high-and-half-naked-waitresses/

I woke up this morning with a lot of mini spots on my inner right arm, where my elbow joint is. I took some photos of them and sent them to Mum. But it was 4 am in England at the time so I wasn't expecting a reply for a few hours. We packed up the room and checked out, leaving out suitcases at the reception behind the sofa I sat on last night, which they said we could do for the day, while we went to our show.

Our taxi lady was already sitting waiting for us. She drove us to the dolphin show. Once we arrived, I showed them my ticket, unfortunately, I had bought the wrong ticket. I'd bought the ticket for Thai nationals, which was cheaper, but we weren't allowed that ticket. Not to worry I just paid the difference. While I was spending, I also upgraded our seats to the front row.

We then sat on the blue chairs outside waiting till 11, the start time of our show. I bought us some popcorn for 50 THB. They only had salted, I was hoping for caramel, but since I didn't know they had popcorn until about 20 seconds before ordering, I wasn't too upset.

We were then shown to our seats, dead central front row. We were given splash suits (thin raincoat mac type things). I put mine on, but it was way too hot. So, I took it back off again and put it around my legs as Syd had done originally. This was still too hot for me, so I just wrapped up my backpack in it, to try and at least keep the bag dry.

To start with there were two seals performing with a lady. They were very strong and had amazing balance. They even swam with the dolphins as well, one of the seals even got on the dolphin's back and waved, while the dolphin swam around the arena.

When they were done, the main event started. There were now two other guys with the woman performer. There was 6 dolphins total, and each performer had two that they were with. They did all sorts of amazing tricks, such as twirling around in all different directions. They sang for us and even had the performers on their noses pushing them quickly around the arena, and even catapulting them out of the water and into a dive at times.

The dolphins even made a painting that had a red heart in the middle. We thought this was quite cool, but then the speaker started an auction of it. It was quite awkward as not many people wanted to bid on it as we all had the same thoughts of this doesn't feel right. Either way, a family won the bid for their child, and the show went on. We thought this was a bit cheeky.

A family in the audience who was bidding on the painting, but didn't win, one of their daughters was invited to the stage. She was given a hoop, along with the dolphins and they all spun them around together.

One of the male performers, who looked to be having the most fun playing with the dolphins, every time he went past this family, gave them an extra splash. Which made us all laugh. This same performer even danced with the dolphins in the water. He clearly cared a lot about his two dolphins even when we weren't meant to be watching him, as the others would be doing something. He was sitting stroking his dolphins.

It was amazing to see the dolphins jumping so high, hitting balls from the ceiling. Jumping over rods, and through hoops. We did have ethical reservations about coming to see this show. It is branded as the best in Asia, and I could see why. The animals all looked well cared for, so we were glad we had come to see them.

Once we got out, soaking wet, we found our taxi driver again, and she took us back to the lodge to pick up our bags. It didn't take us long to dry off in this heat! She then drove us to our next hotel, the Secret Cliff Resort. This hotel is back on the west coast of the island. It was right above Karon Beach (just south of Patong beach, which is the most infamous in Phuket, for many reasons...)

We needed a buggy again for our room, this time it was like a golf buggy. Syd sat on the back, while I sat in the middle holding onto the luggage to make sure it didn't go flying off. It was only a short ride across the road to our sea-view villa. There were steep hill climbs for our buggy to get up. Syd almost got flung out of the back of the cart at one point as she didn't realize how steep the hills were! We weren't going very quick, and she just jumped back in. The driver didn't even realize.

After changing our clothes, since we were still a little wet in our undergarments, we - lounged on the bed to cool off for a bit. A little while later, we called reception for a buggy to take us down to the lobby then we set off exploring the rest of the resort for a bit. It is on the side of a cliff, meaning there was a lot of walking up and down different parts. There were two pools there, a restaurant, and the lower part of the resort looks to be getting a complete makeover.

Once we finished our exploration, we found a table looking right down onto the beach. There was a circular chair that Syd liked the look of, so I took some photos of her sitting on it with the sea below. We were high above the skyscrapers below as we really were quite high up on the cliff. Talking of high, I saw a bowl of marijuana drying in the sun on one of the tables. I later saw a menu with said leaves as part of the food. We didn't have any of this!

When we sat down there was only one other couple eating, which goes with the trend of a lot of these stays. There still aren't that many people traveling yet. Anyways, the waiter brought over the menus and moved a fan to direct its air at us. I ordered pork noodles and Syd had chicken noodles. But when it arrived, we both had a bowl of vegetable soup, with a bit of meat. It was nice but we only had a few mouthfuls as we realized there weren't any noodles in it. So, it wasn't what we wanted or ordered.

I found the server and pointed to him again what we wanted, as there were pictures on the menu of the dishes, and he changed them for us. There was a bit of deliberating about what had happened. Different servers came over with the menu to try to figure out what had gone wrong. Very strange.

Either way, when we came to pay, they didn't charge us for it. But the water was 40 THB each, we had two, which is a lot, usually at other places those bottles are 10 each. And then when I came to pay the bill, the lady at the till didn't ask if I wanted to pay in GBP or THB, and just guessed GBP. This is not the case as it charges me more to do that. The card I have can be used anywhere in the world at local rates, with no fees. Meaning I was charged for this in GBP, paying their card machine's worse exchange rate and a fee!

Thankfully the manager was there and seemed to tell her off for not asking and paid me back in cash the difference. It wasn't much, around 13 THB, but it's more the principle, and we were already kind of fed up with answering the same questions over and over again about the menu fiasco! Looking back at it, I should have just kept both dishes and let it go. It's such a minimal amount of money, I must have been hot and bothered.

We got a buggy back to our room to cool down, as the rash on my arm was getting worse in the heat. I think it is a mix between a heat rash and the cheaper lodge we stayed in for the last two nights. Mum had messaged me back while eating, she thinks it might be eczema, but this wasn't like my usual eczema, it wasn't dry and scabby. But instead, prickly, and itchy, which are side effects of heat rash. I had Googled a few example pictures of different rashes, and this looked the most like the heat rash ones. I decided that we go out for dinner later, I'd look for a pharmacy to see if they have anything for it.

After a bit of chill time on the bed with the air-con blasting, a cold shower, and some of the snake powder the rash had gone down a little bit. But it was still itchy. Either way, I ordered us a Grab to take us to Patong, where we were going to Hooters for dinner. I had dressed similarly in a white top, and short orangey shorts. Syd had no idea at this point what Hooters was.

The Grab I ordered wasn't a fixed-price one, as there weren't any of those around. The meter in this taxi was going up quicker than I'd ever seen any other! When we were close, there was a road blockage for some road works, it changed his satnav to double the time in the car. I asked him to pull over and we could walk the rest. As it was still possible to walk through this closed road.

On the way to Hooters, we stopped off at a bag shop that Syd liked the look of. The lady took us to the back room where there was even more! They were quite expensive, but good quality. We said we'd have a think and come back later. We had noticed a pharmacy down the road too, which we went to as I was running low on my Cetraben cream. I should have packed two really. Unfortunately, the pharmacy was closed.

Syd quickly realized what sort of restaurant Hooters is, she gave me a half-jokingly tut and eye-roll, she enjoyed the food nonetheless! We shared a plate of boneless wings (basically just chicken bites) with ranch dressing. Syd had a burger with blue cheese, and I had a Texas BBQ melt burger. They both came with fries, and I ordered a side of American cheese sauce, as Syd has been wanting to try that for ages. I also had a Singha beer, and Syd had a Mojito.

We were both fairly stuffed afterward. I felt a bit awkward asking for a photo with them, even though I'd intentionally dressed the same. So, I just paid up and we went on our way. Going into different pharmacies (which by the way, there are tons on this strip), but unfortunately to no avail. We saw there was a Boots, but this was closed too at this time. We planned to go back tomorrow and see if they have any of my creams.

I felt kind of annoyed that I didn't get a picture with the Hooter ladies, especially as they were very kind to us and I was dressed like them. So, we headed back to get a picture with them. On the way back Syd went to a few more bag shops to look. She wasn't too sure what she wanted so we carried on. We went back to the original shop too, but the price was just a little more than we wanted to spend. But if we change our minds, I'm sure they'd have plenty in stock.

Back at Hooters, I asked if it was okay for a picture, and they laughed and said of course. They rounded up a few of the waitresses and took a picture of me with them. They also took a picture of me and Syd together with the backdrop of their poster. It was very kind of them to do this.

I then tried to order a Grab back to the hotel, but nothing was available, and the estimated price for a metered taxi was 5 times the price it should have been. Unfortunately, our taxi lady said it was too far from where she was for this little journey, which is fair enough. I asked a tuk-tuk driver if he would take us back. He originally said 300 THB, which was a little more than what I wanted to spend. I said 200 THB, and he tried moving to 250, but I was fairly stuck on 200. I started walking away and then he gave in to the 200. I've always been a master negotiator.

This was a larger tuk-tuk than back in Bangkok, it had actual seats, well two benches, they were along the walls facing each other. The driver was blaring music the whole way up the mountain and taking corners very quickly and sharply. It was a bit sketchy going up this steep cliff that quickly if I am honest.

Back at the hotel lobby, we got a buggy back to our room. I think the driver must have misheard us as he took us to the wrong villa originally. For some reason, Syd got off the buggy, and when he started going again, she was only half on, and she was hopping along behind it. She wasn't hurt, well only her ego, but she laughed it off like a champ.

After being dropped off at our correct room, we went in and got ready for bed. We don't really have many plans for tomorrow, other than we have breakfast "included" here so we want to see what that's like. And we will head back down to Patong Beach, and probably buy Syd a bag, knowing what she's like...

THE SECRET BAG ROOMS

PHUKET | DAY 10

28th April 2022

https://twobritsinasia.com/the-secret-bag-rooms/

We woke up quite early but didn't go to breakfast till later as we were enjoying having a lie-in. We didn't have any hard plans for today, just that we wanted to go to Patong Beach. There had been lots of rain in the early hours of the morning, which kept waking us up but we were able to drift back off to sleep.

Once we finally got up we called for a buggy to take us down to breakfast. We waited about 5 minutes, but nothing showed up. This was strange as it's about a 20-second crossing over the road. I decided that we'd just walk over as the rain had stopped for now.

At breakfast, it was a buffet-style selection. They had some strange chicken sausages, the same as the ones on that Japanese pancake we had at the Sunday food party. Along with ham which had been boiled (very strange), some fried rice, and a thick noodle dish. Like the one I ordered last night, just with less meat in it. They also had a selection of fruits, I had a bit of dragon fruit, some cereals, bread, and juices.

We had a plate of hot food each to start, then Syd went back for 4 slices of bread to make into toast. She had lots of jam with it! I decided I'd have another plate of rice and noodles, this time with a fried egg on top (I had not seen the eggs earlier). I thought it best to fill up on the included breakfast, so we don't need to spend so much at lunch, even though it's so cheap it's just my habit...

When we got back to the room, the rain had started again. There were slight breaks but not for long. I looked on the weather apps, all saying different things, so they weren't much help. I thought it was best to wait an hour or so, as it was a thick cloud overhead, and up in the mountains, we couldn't see the tops because of the cloud. Syd wanted to head out after waiting around, so we did. I had grabbed the two included handheld brollies from the room, almost forgetting them just nipping back in to get them before the door closed.

I ordered us a Grab to the front, but there wasn't any fixed price available, so I went with a metered one. However, when we got in the car, it didn't have a meter in it. I thought this was strange, and what was even stranger was the driver asked to see my phone, seeing the estimate Grab had given (which is always way higher than it actually is).

When he dropped us off, I stayed in the car asking him how much he would tell Grab it would be, as how can he know without having a meter? He put 300 on the form, which was three times what the fixed price would have been. I told him to change it to 100, which he did, as he clearly knew he was in the wrong and was just trying to short-change someone. It wasn't a lot of money, but it was the principle.

As soon as we stepped out of the car, the heavens opened. Thankfully I had the brollies with us! We walked across to a side street, where we found a place to stand and stay dry. It was next to a restaurant that had a pizza oven, half of which was used as the brickwork to the building. It was hot to the touch, so I told Syd to move away from it as I knew she would have burnt herself standing so close to it.

After about 5 minutes, the rain hadn't stopped or even eased, and a talkative Pakistani man let us sit in his restaurant. He told us his stories of having six girlfriends here in Thailand, but how they only want money and not real love. He went on about his fiancé in New Zealand, who wanted him to move over there, but he didn't want to. Apparently, they got into this big fight, and she might not be his fiancé anymore. He seemed like a nice enough guy, but I certainly don't have the same outlook on multiple girl-friends. One is enough for me to handle!

He had moved to Thailand a few months earlier, working with his brother (they looked like twins) in this restaurant together. His brother is the chef, and he looks after the front of house. Syd wanted to get a taxi back to the hotel as it was so wet, but after her wanting to come down to the beach in the first place. I said we should at least stay till the rain clears now. Which I had no idea how long this would take, but I could start to see some blue sky so I didn't think it would be long. Luckily, I was right.

Finally, the rain calmed down, so we walked on, thanking the guy for letting us sit and stay dry. We carried on looking at differ-ent bag shops, which like yesterday all had "secret" back rooms. These were air-conned; I suspect so you stay in there longer. The quality of the fakes here was very very good. Down to the button details too. Syd wasn't sure which one she wanted, so we carried on, as these were more expensive than the ones in Spain but are clearly much better quality.

While walking along the beach promenade, everyone con-stantly bugged us, asking if we wanted a taxi, tuk-tuk, massage, jet ski ride, parasailing, you name it! Literally as one leaves you alone another one pounces. We haven't had this anywhere else in Thailand this bad! Of course, wherever you go, they always ask if you want a taxi, and in Bangkok, there's the classic floating market scam. But this was relentless!

There were lots of bars on this main strip connecting the beach and the town. They were mostly empty as it was early in the day, and they were still cleaning up from the night before. There were a few street stalls out selling fruits, which was ironic as they were in front of kebab houses and bars.

We walked back to Boots, but unfortunately, they didn't have my cream. We looked at lots of different moisturizers and creams, all of which had loads of additives and smelly stuff, which would just irritate my skin more. Also, they didn't have the purified water, which I need as the normal water (aqua in ingredients) causes my skin to dry out more. We found this one brand, Cetaphil, which had purified water and no additives. It didn't have paraffin in, which my usual cream does, but everything else looked like my Cetraben. The names are similar too.

When we walked back up the steps, a swarm of tuk-tuk drivers, at least 7 or 8 of them, all asked in unison "tuk-tuk taxi?". I laughed and waved them all off. I think they were laughing too; I couldn't really tell as I had my brolly up still. But the rain had basically stopped, so we put them away and walked to the beach. This time along back towards Hooters, looking at more bag shops on the way.

Because it had been raining so much, the roads had stayed wet. It made for interesting reflections of all the lights and signs. I took some cool photos while we were here. It was funny seeing people on their peds with the same thin mac-type coats we were given at the dolphin show to keep us dry yesterday.

Syd was still undecided about which bag she wanted, so we went to the beach and paid for two loungers while she was contemplating. The loungers were 100 THB each, including an umbrella for the two of us, for the day. No one was sat there yet, and I probably could have bartered them down lower. But I thought it was a fair price, so paid it without hassle.

We went into the sea a few times; it was good to have the shade of the umbrella when we were out. Also, it was good to be off the sand with a cushion. However, lots of people kept coming up to us, trying to sell stuff, at least once every 5 minutes! It wasn't as bad as walking on the promenade, but still noticeable, and annoying.

I ran across the road to the shop twice to pick up some water. The first time I came back with a tube of steak Pringles and a new drink I saw. It's called a C-Vit. It was the same size as the M-150 (medicine bottle) energy drink, but it had a clear glass. This flavour was pomegranate. We shared it all, this new drink was nice, Syd liked it, which is good as she's not a fan of the medicine one. Syd also finished one of her books while we had this relaxing time on the beach.

One of the girls, who were part of the family that was placed next to us, had a fake bum, boobs, and lips. Syd said she looked like a shelf! Thankfully they didn't hear us! The mother and her, both had foot massages on the beach next to us. A lot of skin was taken off their feet, I'm not sure how hygienic that is to have such fresh skin on the beach.

I noticed a jet ski was stopped in the water, without anyone on it. People were running and jumped onto another jet ski to get it back but didn't seem like they were able to start it. They waited for it to drift back into the beach, before putting it on a trailer, which went on the back of a moped.

Like the other beaches, this one too had dogs on. It was funny watching them playing with waves. The dogs then started barking at two sus looking men, they were trying to shut the dogs up, but it caused more people to look, so the men left the beach. I think those dogs are really protecting the beach, and it's cool to see.

We left the beach a few hours later, after putting on some of the new creams. Of course, there was more bag searching while we were looking for dinner. The prices here are defiantly higher than in the other places we have been in Thailand. Not crazy expensive, but relatively high. We found a place that would do us a plate of noodles each for 200 THB (about double Bangkok prices). Syd had a classic pad Thai, and I had a pad Thai with thicker noodles, as I really like their texture.

The bars had now turned into strip clubs, with signs of the infamous ping pong show, Syd didn't let us go and see it. No idea why not... The bars and clubs had started to fill up now, and the people who had earlier been asking if we wanted to go on jet skis etc, now turned into asking us if we wanted to see these shows or shoot guns down a range.

A very strange place this Patong. I'm sure it is a very different experience if you were single, or at least, acting that way... There were lots of massage parlors with the girls sitting out front, all with their breasts basically on show. Also, in the bars, there would be girls just sitting alone at tables waiting for people to go over to them. Syd's certain she could tell which were ladyboys or not. I'm not so sure you could tell really. There were a few which were obvious, but I think some hide it well.

Final bag searching, refining down which one Syd wanted. There were loads more bags in the secret bag rooms than on show in the shop. I'm unsure yet if the best ones are at the front or kept at the back. Because they could pull you in with nice-looking ones at the front, or even real ones up front. And then sell you the cheaper fakes in the back room. But also, they might be keeping the expensive ones off the street to avoid getting robbed, as they're behind lock and key.

We were back at one shop and a secret room that we'd been in earlier today. Syd tried on two different sizes of the same bag. Figuring out which one she wanted. We had been in the room for over an hour! They were good quality, and the shopkeeper even went off to get the paperwork for them, including a Chanel "Card of Authenticity" with a serial I checked online that matched. Quite impressive really.

He wanted quite a lot to start with, 4,000 THB, which is about £100. I ideally wanted to be paying no more than 1,600 (or just shy of £40). But after a lot of "playing the game", he really wasn't budging off 2,000 THB. My final tactic, to at least make the deal sweeter for us, was to find a purse we liked. I saw a Christian Dior one, in the same style as a bag my mate Lydia tried to get in Tenerife a few months earlier.

I got 2,000 THB cash out of my wallet, and handed him the purse and the money, as he was holding the bag. He shoved the purse into the bag and said, "our little secret". He probably wasn't meant to do it, but I'm sure he wanted the commission of the bag sale. Thinking back on it, I probably could have got a deal with both sizes. Oh well, at least Syd has a bag she wants, and Lydia will get a new purse once we're back as a traveling gift from us.

Our taxi lady was half an hour away as she had just dropped someone else off at the airport. So instead, we got a tuk-tuk back to the hotel. I asked the driver's friend first to take us, but he wasn't budging from 150 THB (after saying 200 first). Ideally, I only wanted to pay 100 tonight, as it was still relatively early on, and the tuk-tuks hadn't really started moving about yet. As he was sitting there doing nothing anyways.

This driver was crazy! Honking each massage place. Swerving all over the road, it felt like we would tip over! Halfway through the ride he stops and asks if we wanted to listen to music, which would be an extra 200 THB! The cheek of it, of course, I said no. He turned off the speakers to the back and tried to play music in his cab. But he was clearly having issues with that as he kept hitting the amp...

So much so that he missed our hotel! Syd and I had both realized this at the same time. We started banging on the window of the cab to let him know. He spun it round and apologized, explaining about his music system not working so he missed the turning. I gave him the 100 and told him he was a crazy driver, he laughed and then shot off.

We asked reception if we could change our beach towels, as they had gotten wet and a little sandy from the beach earlier. The receptionist said to come back in the morning. The night staff never seem to know what's going on.

Anyways, we got a buggy back to our room, Syd was very happy with her new bag. I had a cold shower and put on some more of the new cream and finished getting ready for bed. We are planning on going to the other side of the cliff tomorrow, to Karon Beach. With Syd still buzzing from her new bag, after packing it up ready for the beach tomorrow, we went to sleep.

SADDLING A STRANGER

PHUKET | DAY 11

29th April 2022

https://twobritsinasia.com/saddling-a-stranger/

We woke up to our alarms this morning at 8 but didn't get out of bed till about 10. We heard the groundskeepers sweeping outside, it sounded like they were in the room! Once we were up, we didn't bother phoning for a buggy, we just walked across the road to breakfast.

I didn't take my phone today to take a picture of the food as I thought it would have been the same as yesterday. It was not. They still had the weird chicken sausages. Along with a different noodle dish, and a new dish of pork, onion, and pepper dish. It's a strange combination for breakfast. But since we were having it later, we saw it as an early lunch and ate quite a bit to save having to find something for lunch later, like we did yesterday.

While eating breakfast we saw a mother cat and her two kittens walking around the grounds. It was very cute. We saw one of the workers try to give them some water, but they didn't seem interested. It had also started to rain, luckily it didn't last as long, or wasn't as hard as it was yesterday morning!

Back in the room, we cooled down a bit from breakfast. We wished Toby good luck via text as he was off to the hospital this morning for a Flexi-Sigmoidoscopy.

The rain was on and off for the next hour or so, it was strange because the skies were blue. Once it had stopped for about 10 minutes, it looked like it was properly clearing up. I had another cold shower to get ready for another day down the beach. This time the other side of the cliff, at Beach Karon.

My heat rash wasn't looking as inflamed today, so I didn't have any antihistamines. However, the new cream and lots of snakeskin powder were put on to keep it cool. Syd put the rest of her P20 sun cream on, but it seemed to have a weird yellow tinge to it. Either way, she finished the bottle which luckily just ran out as she was finished.

Our washing bag was almost overflowing so I decided it was best to try and find somewhere to get that lot cleaned. The hotel was charging per item, and expensive too. Whereas the local shops charge by the kilo. Between 40-80 THB per kg usually, which is for a wash, dry, and fold, I can't complain really.

Once we were ready, we walked back across the road to reception, to pick up our new beach towels. While picking up the new ones, I tried to see if there were any Grabs about. Nope, not even the metered taxis. I asked reception to phone for a taxi, but they quoted 300 and she wanted us to pay her. It seemed a bit suspicious, since Karon is much closer than Patong beach, and that's been a maximum of 200 THB either way. Usually just 100.

I phoned a few taxi companies, all saying about 150-200, which I guess since they're not close, I'd need to pay for their time to get here. I thought it was still a bit much for such a short journey. I messaged our taxi lady, but she was on the other side of the island at the airport and would be at least an hour. I decided we could just walk down.

I carried the laundry, the big water bottle, and my bag on my back with my spare clothes, the new cream and snakeskin power, and the camera. Syd had her new bag with sun cream in it, her new book, a change of clothes, and a few other little bits, along with the Tesco bag with our new towels in it.

Just outside our hotel, and onto the main road (as there were no footpaths down to the beach), there was a sign that said 1km to Karon. I thought this will be all right as it's downhill the whole way. We set off and hit a climb straight away. Oh. Right. Not to plan... Thankfully, it was over fairly quickly, and we had a water stop at the top. The rest of the way was downhill. Stopping a few times for some water again.

It wasn't 1 km to the beach, but two. Interesting everywhere but where I had applied the snakeskin powder was sweating. Whereas the places I had put it on were perfectly dry and cool! I guess that proves it really does work! No idea what's in it, I doubt it's actually snakeskin. It's very much like talcum powder in consistency, it smells nice too, fruity, and flowery.

Once we got to the beach, we decided to get some loungers and an umbrella again. Since it was only 200 THB, the same as yesterday, and it was a great investment at Patong Beach we went ahead with it. It wasn't as busy down here, and no constant badgering either. This town seemed to be more just for locals, it was nice to be away from the hustle and bustle. There were still a few people walking on the beaches trying to sell stuff, but nowhere near as many.

I still had our massive bag of laundry on my wrist. I asked the beach porter (not sure what the official term would be here actually?) if he knew anywhere to get it washed. He said yes follow me. So, I did.

I left Syd on the beach with our other bags and followed the guy. He took me to his moped, so I straddled over it behind him, and off we went. It was great fun, a bit sketchy mind, one hand on the handle behind me, and the other holding the washing close to my shorts so my phone didn't fly out of my pocket. It felt good to have the wind in my hair again. It felt like I was out cycling over the Purbecks again! I've missed that.

We tried a few places, but they were closed. He found one that could only get it done by tomorrow afternoon, which was no good as we were leaving to go somewhere else tomorrow morning. Luckily just next door, they were able to do it by 6 tonight. I asked the guy if he'd be able to bring me back at 6, which he said he could. We had 4kg total and this shop was charging 60THB, so 240 total. This was about £6 which isn't too bad, and it's one less thing to worry about. It would have cost 5 times that back at the hotel!

On the ped again, this time both hands on the rail. I took a quick video of us going along which was funny. A little difficult to put my phone back in my pocket, but I managed it. Back on the beach, Syd had set up our towels, had got out her book, and was ready to go in the sea. We both went in. The current was stronger than yesterday, the waves were bigger too.

Syd was a little nervous to get in, but it got less strong the further I went out, so I swam back and walked her through the rough part. I think she was a little worried that she'd drink too much of the salty water. I was having a great time. Diving through the waves, jumping over them, and just bobbing about. Reminded me of when I was back in Lyme with Lawrence playing The Wave Game ™.

Once back on the beach, I wrote some investing tips for Toby's mate. I then walked over the road to a 7-11. The first one I tried was closed, I went into the pharmacy next door to see if they had anything, but they didn't. They also said that the 7-11 had been closed for two years. No worries, there's basically one on every street, so I walked back to the beach and went down another road.

I didn't have any shoes on as I only thought I'd be going to the one across the road. The floor was hot, and I kept trying to find shade bits to walk on. Then I'd do a bit of a jumpy fast stride where there was no shade. At this 7-11, I picked out a drink for each of us, cough medicine for me and a similar C-Vit drink like yesterday for Syd, a large bottle of water, and some Pringles.

Originally, I had picked up a large tube of the sour cream and onion flavour, but for some reason, it didn't scan. The guy at the counter gave me three smaller tubs of sour cream. I asked if I could swap one of the tubs for a plain salted one, as I wasn't sure which Syd would prefer today. He agreed.

I thought I could give the third tub of the sour cream one to the guy as thanks for driving me about. But just as I got back to the beach, he tootles off somewhere, I hope he comes back! Oh well, I let Syd choose what she wanted, she did want the sour cream too. Which just left the plain salted ones. We ate our mini tub each, had our drinks, and shared the water. Syd read a bit more of her book and I just chilled.

A bit later Syd thought she could see someone far out to sea, I couldn't see anyone. I got my camera out and she tried to zoom in on it, but it was blurry. After a few attempts, I was able to see what she was looking at, I tried zooming in with focus. It turned out to be a buoy, just bobbing in the sea, it did look like a person's head though, or even a seal.

We went back in the sea, Syd didn't stay in for long, she was just cooking off. I stayed in a bit longer as the waves were bigger now. Another traveling couple was in the sea too. We were all laughing as bigger ones came as a surprise.

Up at the loungers, I moved them more into the shade as the sun had moved around a bit. I started to need the loo so walked towards the beach entrance, the porter was back now. I handed him the Pringles, which he was very thankful for. He told me where the loo was, which was thankfully only just over the road. They had a strange stairway on the outside which led to nowhere and a mini quarter pipe, which was half falling apart and splintering.

Once back at the loungers, after speaking with Toby's friend earlier about investing, had gotten me in the mood to make some trades myself. What a place to do it! Right on the beach! After some trades, I got to speak to Toby about how his day was at the hospital. He said they had to take the happy gas off him as he was having too much...

We were just on the loungers for the rest of the afternoon in the shade, as we had both started to get a little pink again. Syd had put some more sun cream on but the spray had gotten on her sun-glassed. It made up both laugh. At about quarter to six, the guy walked over and said we will go in 5 minutes to pick up the laundry. I said "okay" and popped back over to the loos before going. This time it looked like a group of local people had met up for some make-shift volleyball in the carpark. Once back at the beach, the guy was waiting for me, I got on the back of his ped again, and off to the laundrette we went. I paid the lady and was then driven back to the beach.

I had 500 THB note in my wallet, which I tried to get changed up at the laundrette, but I don't think the lady understood me. So, I tried changing it with the guy. He thought I was asking how much he wants for driving me, but he didn't want anything. I explained I wanted five 100 notes for my 500. He laughed as he realized what I meant and swapped them over. I tried giving him one of the 100s, but he wasn't having it. What a kind man! It was lovely to see his genuine kindness of him going out of his way to help me today.

We packed up, again saying thank you to the guy, and went on our way. First looking at the food street stall stands. However, none of them had tables and chairs, and they were only giving the food out in polystyrene boxes. We carried on walking, up the street on the way towards the laundrettes, as I had seen a few restaurants up this way.

Nothing tickled our fancy, although we had stopped off at a fruit stall as they were selling some durian and mangosteen. This seemed to be a bit of an elusive item here, as every hotel would state that they are not allowed in the rooms. Being treated almost with the same severity of fines as if someone was taking drugs or partying in the rooms.

I asked if I could only have a little bit to try, and the lady agreed. The durian didn't have a bad smell like I had been reading. It tasted quite nice, a mix between a pear and a mango. The mangosteen I had was a little past ripe, (I think, but I've never had one before so who am I to judge), it too was very sweet. I liked it. If I see some again, I'll try to get some more to compare.

We then walked back towards the beach to maybe give the food stalls a try again. On the way, we saw a place we liked the look of. An old fella was chopping what looked like some sort of apple (well a whole box of them). Syd had a yellow chicken curry, which had potatoes in it! I think this was our first bit of potato on the Asia part of this trip. I had a duck Penang, there wasn't much meat, but it was full of flavour. We also had a portion of boiled rice each and shared a bottle of water.

They brought us out some complimentary pineapple and watermelon. Like how we have bread in England at the start of a meal. It was quite expensive at 390 THB for all of it. Again, this is less than a tenner, but relatively speaking... Outside of the restaurant, they had a little beach shop, which of all things, sold petrol. The petrol was in what looked to be old rum or wine bottles. Safety isn't at the top of anyone's priority list here.

Not far down the road, we saw some tuk-tuks, we weren't far from our hotel, about half the distance than when we were in Patong. So ideally, I didn't want to spend more than 100 THB on the drive back to the top. The first driver quoted 200 and didn't seem to want to budge at all. I then moved to the next one, but clearly, the first driver had shouted something to him, so most of them down the line were saying 200 and not budging...

The last guy in the line, who was younger than the rest, and was working on the LEDs on his tuk-tuk, had moved from 200 down to 150. I stuck at 100, but he didn't want to do it for that. We met at 120. Which is fine really as I didn't fancy walking back up the cliff.

His car made a right racket, I think it was due to the poorly installed induction kit, trying to sound like a turbo but instead sounding like a dying weasel! We saw a few police cars on the side of the road with their lights on, we couldn't see what they had stopped for though. It's strange to see police pulling someone over, they're usually lenient with the things that go on here.

Back at the hotel, just as we arrived a buggy driver was walking across the lobby. It looked like he had just woken up from a nap as he was a little wobbly in the legs. Well, either that or had a bit too much to drink...

Once in our room, I had a cold shower, and Syd had a normal one, just to get the remaining sand off us. The last thing we wanted was to get sand in the bed, as it's horrible to sleep with! After our showers we packed as much as we could, looking forward to our most expensive hotel as part of the Thailand section of this trip!

NOT VERY GRACEFUL

PHUKET | DAY 12

30th April 2022

https://twobritsinasia.com/not-very-graceful/

We kept the curtains open last night because there was a lot of thunder and lightning which we wanted to watch. This meant that when my morning alarm went off it was already bright in our room. We stayed in bed for a couple more hours before getting up for breakfast.

Again, we walked over to breakfast and didn't bother with the buggy. This time I brought my phone to take a picture of the food. It was different again today, still with the same chicken sausage, but also today they had French toast (it was lacking a lot of egg though), some chicken (not much of that either) chow mien dish, and some ham and vegetable fried rice. They must have been running out of supplies!

I had two plates, the first with the "French toast", some noodles, and the rice with a fried egg on top. I had some type of syrup over the toast which was nice. On my second plate, I had some more noodles, and rice, this time with two eggs. As I was walking back to our table the lady brought out some more of the noodles, with lots more chicken in them. I took some of the chicken and added it to mine. I also added the syrup over the noodles which went really well together surprisingly.

Heading back to our room, we didn't bother getting a buggy back from breakfast, but we did see a lizard on our walk back across. We did our final packing and had a cooldown and relaxed on the bed, Syd actually had a nap. Once we were ready to leave, I messaged our taxi lady to come to pick us up. While we were waiting for her to come we got a buggy over to the lobby and checked out.

When our taxi lady arrived, I don't think she saw us as it looked as if she was going to pull off again and go further down the road towards where our room was, but we were already in the lobby. I knocked on her window and she reversed back in. I gave her the address of the new hotel and we were on our way!

About 5 minutes before we arrived, her GPS died. Luckily I had a signal on my phone so just used my Google Maps to get us the rest of the way. There was a big steep hill to get up to the lobby. She put her car in manual mode and drove up very slowly. I think she didn't think we would make it up. Thankfully we did.

Our room wasn't ready yet at this new hotel, Crest Resort & Pool Villas, to be fair we were three hours early. I asked if we could leave our bags at the reception and use the pool while we waited. They were more than happy to let us do this and brought us some complimentary blue coconut drinks. I really liked it, Syd, not so much. I finished hers.

There was a lot of AstroTurf around the grounds, and wood around the pool area. It was very hot to walk on! Even the half a metre from our shaded loungers to the pool burnt our feet! The lady behind us noticed Syd's shark tattoo and complimented her on it.

The first time in the pool I basically just flung myself in as my feet were burning from the wood. Once surfacing, I said, "Well that wasn't very graceful!" I got a few laughs around the poolside. Syd joined me too, but she walked to the steps and lowered her- self in. She wasn't in for long because she was sun burnt from yesterday.

I stayed in a bit longer. There was a pool inflatable Lilo on the side. I asked the people next to us if it was theirs or if it belonged to the hotel. It was theirs. They said I could use and keep it, since they were leaving in a few hours. I let them know that we were only staying one night but thanked them nonetheless!

I had forgotten my goggles; well they were in the suitcase at reception but I wasn't that fussed about it. Slightly annoying though as I'd forgotten them the two previous days when we were down at the beach too! The whole reason I brought them was for these pool and beach days.

The receptionist soon came out and said our room was ready. I just went with her to see where it was and left Syd at the pool with the day bags. I had asked the lady while we were walking if any of the pod villas were available, but unfortunately, they were fully booked. In fact, she said the whole hotel was full! This is different from everywhere else we had been staying. Not to worry, our room was amazing anyways!

We had our own pool which we could access from just outside our balcony doors, with loungers and jets attached too! Not as many jets as my hot tub at home, but nice to have some again! The room had a separate massive rainfall shower and bath. When I told Syd, she didn't know which one she would want later! Maybe both! There was also a big picture window connecting the bathroom to the bedroom which gave a view of our pool, over the side of the cliff, and onto the sea below.

I walked back to the pool and showed Syd to the room, we took our day bags with us. Our suitcases shortly followed, brought to us by the hotel staff. Back at the main pool, we chilled for the rest of the afternoon, going in and out of the pool to cool off. Re-applying sun cream after, trying to be more sensible now. The main pool wrapped around the hotel building. It was a massive pool! All with infinity edges.

Syd started to get a little hungry, so we walked to reception to drop off our pool towels. While we were there, we noticed a sign for a BBQ that evening on the sun terrace, with live music. It was 700 THB each, which is quite expensive relatively, but we were quite far away from the town. I didn't think any Grab food delivery would have been still warm by the time it arrived. Either way, we decided it would be a nice experience to get all dressed up posh to have a fancy meal on the terrace.

Back at the room, we got into our own pool, and I sat on the submerged jet lounger for a bit. It was nice to have the massage on my back again! I then ran a bath for Syd. I added the flower heads and petals, which were on our bed, into it. We then got ready for the evening meal.

Up on the terrace, it was beautiful. It was like being on the set of Love Island. There were lights overhead on wires, with modern rattan furniture. The sun was setting over the mountains in the distance, this made a dramatic orange sky for the clouds to play in. It was truly stunning; I am so glad we did this.

The live music was really good too, they sang English songs but with their own slight twist. There was a lot of food selection, not just BBQ stuff either. There were some traditional Thai dishes too. Strangely there were some Italian options too, clam spaghetti and some pizza slices.

I tried a bit of everything, Syd didn't eat all the barbecue stuff because she was worried that the chicken might be slightly undercooked. It seemed fine to me, maybe some parts were a little pink. She filled up on a lot of ice cream though!

After dinner we walked across the top of the roof, finding man-made "nests" which had lights around, they looked nice. It seemed they had a wedding room with a beautiful view of the sea and the beaches below, with the mountains in the background. It would make for a very special wedding spot.

Walking back to our room, we saw a pool table, so we had a few games. Syd had never played before, so I went a little easy on her. But I still won both games. Even after potting a few of Syd's balls for her.

Back in the room, we were both fairly stuffed from dinner. We had planned on watching a movie, but Syd's sister called so Syd spent some time on the phone with her. I was just watching some YouTube videos.

Once Syd was finished on the phone, we both went into our pool again in the dark. It was much chillier now, amazing how quickly that sun warms up the pool! We stayed in for about half an hour before Syd became too cold and wanted to go in. Which we did.

We got ready for bed, which was massive by the way! And drifted off to sleep.

GAMES DAY AND THE CAPE

PHUKET | DAY 13

1st May 2022

https://twobritsinasia.com/games-day-and-the-cape/

We woke up a little later than planned today. I had wanted to go into our own pool this morning before breakfast but there wasn't enough time now as we had to get to breakfast before 10:30 finish. Then also needed to pack up when we get back from eating as we were only staying here the one night because this hotel was fully booked because of how unique it was. Which was a surprise as the rest of the places we have been in have been mostly empty!

There was a big selection for breakfast, fresh salad, an attempt at an English fry-up (without any sausages or bacon, but ham instead), some leftover food from the night before, a few other curries, rice, thick noodles with veg and egg, patisseries, cheeses, hams, and a few other things. Syd started by having a few pancakes, with tons of Nutella! She also had a mini pain au chocolate and a cinnamon roll but she wasn't a big fan of the roll. I had some noodles, topped with an extra fried egg, a selection of dim sum, and a bit of roti, it wasn't as pancake-like as the ones we have had elsewhere, fresh, with the locals.

We had a second plate each, Syd opting for rice and chicken curry, and myself opting for some more noodles, another fried egg, some more dim sum, and a few mini cupcakes. I also had a pink drink the second time, I couldn't tell what it was, I think it was lychee and something. Syd stuck with the orange juice and a glass of apple juice. Someone at breakfast over from us was really going to town in their mouth with their toothpick. It made Syd giggle.

Back in the room, we chilled on the bed for a bit, letting our food go down. We finished packing and called reception to check out. Someone came to pick up our luggage while we made our way to the lobby. After checking out and paying for last night's meal, we got some pool towels and headed for the main pool. It was cooler this morning, so we decided to go and play with the big chess.

In the distance, we could see the rain coming down quite heavily on the sea. It was coming our way, bit by bit. We managed to finish our chess match (I won) just as it started spitting. We went back to the loungers and took our stuff in. Not wanting to get wet we walked downstairs to the games room and had a few games on the pool table again. Syd was getting better, but I still won them all, other than one game, where I accidentally potted the black too early. Doh!

The rain had stopped so we decided to go back up to the pool for another dip had remembered my goggles today! Big win! After our swim we just rested on the loungers, Syd was reading her book and I was replying to messages. There were a few helicopters circling above and over the sea below. Red ones, unsure if they were looking for something or if they were private tours.

We spent most of the afternoon up by the pool. We had another game of chess, which ended the same as the first... While playing we had some more of the snacks from the Ann and Misora tuckbox When we finished playing, we had another dip then dried up and played another game of pool. We didn't have time to finish this one as our taxi lady was outside waiting.

The hotel staff loaded up the car for us and made a joke saying see you tomorrow. It made us all laugh. On the drive to our new hotel, we passed one of our previous ones, the Secret Cliff Resort.

The plan was to go to the new hotel (Navatara Phuket Resort) first to drop our bags off. But the sun had already started setting so I asked Miss Kamonyupa if she could drive us straight to the Cape. Which she did. After dropping us off, she waited in the car park while Syd and I walked up the road to the viewpoint.

There were a lot of cars and people here, it's clearly a very popular spot. We then found a gap in the wall with some stairs going down onto an old dirt track. This led us all the way down to the bottom of the Cape. We both had a few close calls with slipping! Luckily no actual tumbles though.

Near the bottom, we saw a monk standing and watching the sunset too. We could see a lot of boats out in the sea. Kayaks and paddle boards too. A few of the larger vessels were party boats and we could hear their music blasting. It was quite cloudy so wasn't the best sunset, but still, lots of beautiful oranges in the sky. We made our way back up to the top, getting quite sweaty I must add. There was a pretty shrine of elephants at the top of the climb.

We found our taxi lady again and went to our hotel, which was only down the road. After checking in and having a bit of cool-down time on the bed. We looked at what was available to us on Grab to eat, but nothing tickled our fancy.

I asked reception if I could hire a ped for the evening, but he said it was closed for the day. I wonder if it's a contractor that comes during the day to hire them out. Anyways, instead, we walked down to the beach and found a restaurant. The first place we tried was full, a good sign for them, but not so good for us. We carried on walking further into the town. The drivers were passing us quite quickly, it was scary because there wasn't really a footpath here either.

We found a nice place right on the beach, it had bamboo furniture, and a little private bamboo shack that we sat in. I had a pad Thai, Syd had a spicy chicken noodle dish (which wasn't very spicy), and we shared some fried prawn cakes, these were delicious. The table behind ours had someone on it that looked like an old neighbour of ours, Dean. It wasn't him, but we do wonder where he is now, we hope he is ok.

Once we had walked back to our hotel, we unpacked what we needed for tomorrow, and got ready for bed. I'd asked our taxi lady to pick us up in the morning at 11:15, to take us to Rassada Pier. We are looking forward to our Phi Phi island-hopping adventure!

PEE PEE?

KRABI | DAY 1

2nd May 2022

https://twobritsinasia.com/pee-pee/

After sleeping through both of my alarms this morning, we woke up not too much later. This meant we didn't get so much of a lie-in before getting up for breakfast. This bed was the comfiest we had slept in so far. It was very soft.

At breakfast, there was a little buffet of cereals, bread, and croissants. Along with a fridge with dark purple juice (not sure what it was, but it was very tasty), orange juice, milk, and a strawberry smoothy. I had a glass of purple juice and orange juice, and Syd had a glass of orange juice and the strawberry smoothy.

For the main breakfast, it was ordered off the menu, as much as you liked, and cooked fresh. I had two fried eggs, an eggs Benedict (but on bacon, not gammon), extra bacon, beans, and a waffle with maple syrup in a cool-looking glass with a glass cap on it. It almost looked like a miniature whisky bottle. Syd had the same without the two fried eggs, she had extra beans and a few slices of cheese. She also had some French toast, but she couldn't finish all of it, so I had some. It was much better than the other French toast we had the other day.

We then had some banana cake each, I'm not too sure what the difference between this and banana bread is. This one had banana sliced long ways on the top. It was served warm and was nice. We then had a brownie each and took two more for a traveling snack on the ferry later. It was a big breakfast...

Once back in our room, I had a shower and got all packed up. There wasn't much to pack up as we had only arrived here about 15 hours earlier. Our taxi lady said she had to spend the day with her daughter now, but instead she would send her boyfriend. He arrived in a London taxi-style car. The meter was going up quite fast though and started at 150, which is very high compared to usual. When we got to the pier it was 515 THB total, which was on par with Grab, when I looked, to be fair.

We signed into the boat reception desk, dropped our bags off, and took a seat. About half an hour later, we were called to board on the speed boat. It left on time, it really was a speed boat! We sat right up front! As we were leaving the harbor Syd asked when we would leave, not realizing we already had (she couldn't see over the side of the boat). But as she said this the captain must have heard as he put all the engines on, and we were flung back! We were off!

The ride was just under an hour, it was warm, it was nice with the wind blowing at us. About mid-way, there was a bit of rain, but it wasn't too bad. In certain parts of the ride, we sailed past flags in the water with different colours, I'm not sure what they are for. I'd guessed maybe telling the captains if there were any rocks underneath or for direction purposes. The last 10 minutes were the roughest, it was fun jumping off the waves and crashing back down. A French couple, with their three boys, were enjoying the airtime too!

We started at Phi Phi Don, the main of the five islands within Phi Phi archipelago. I'm not sure how to pronounce Phi Phi, some people were calling it pee pee? But I'm not too sure. On the pier, we waited for our bags to be unloaded and then walked down the pier. We had to pay 20 THB each to get on the island. It didn't look like Thai nationals had to pay, thought this was a bit cheeky after already paying the boat ticket, but oh well it's not much, about 50p.

We found a guy with our hotel sign on and walked with him down the street waiting for our porter. We stood right outside

McDonald's and opposite Burger King. It is a shame to see that even on a remote island there are these fast-food chains. We had been waiting about 15 minutes and no sign of our porter. The guy with the sign was looking around frantically for him but to no avail. In the end, he took our suitcases for us to the hotel, which was only a 5-minute walk up the road anyways. There aren't any cars on this island as it is too small.

At the resort, we checked in, but the first room seemed quite prison-like: small, and with no wardrobe space. I phoned reception to ask if they had any other available rooms, and they said I'd have to upgrade which cost more. If we were only here for the night or two, I'd of sucked it up, but since we are here for 4 nights I thought it best to upgrade.

We were shown two different types, a private bungalow, or their superior suite. The bungalow was the nicest and they were the same price, so we went with the bungalow. It was only an extra 2,000 THB for the whole stay. I paid by my card so had to pay their 3% fee, it seems random when it must be paid or not, I think it might be down to what contracts the hotels have with their payment providers. Either way, it was only about an extra £48 odd for the whole 5 days, which back in England we would spend on just one takeaway. This was well worth it for the difference in the quality of the room.

We cooled off on the bed for a bit, before heading out to the swimming pool. There were rooms with balconies onto the pool, but unfortunately, these were all fully booked. There were two pools. One at ground level, and then another one above some of the rooms. We went into the bottom pool first; it was a spiral design. There was a decking over the deep end, I was a little worried to go underwater near it in case I came up under it and couldn't get out of the water far enough to breathe. Again, safety is not really on anyone's radar here.

The top pool was warmer, it wasn't heated, but the pool flooring was a lighter colour than the downstairs one. This caused the sun's reflection to warm the water up more. This one was in a shape of a large, squared horseshoe. Once we were finished, we dried up and walked back to our room. We unpacked and sorted Syd's case out as she had just been throwing (she says "folding") her clothes in! Once I repacked for her, there was about 2/5th more space in there for her! She goes, "Oh, more room for gifts..."

We decided to go for a walk down to two of the main beaches on the island, they are very close to each other, similar to the road to Portland in Dorset. Since Phi Phi Don island is only thin in parts, the beaches were basically opposite each other. The island is quite grand, with towering cliffs on either side, with exposed rock but also very tropically green. There was a lot of over-growth on them. I bet a lot of this island has never been walked by a human, there are probably species here that no one knows about.

There were cats and dogs on the beach here, Syd made a good point about wondering how they could have got here. I'm not sure, maybe someone brought them over at some point, and now they just repopulate themselves. As there are no apparent owners for these dogs and cats. There were also two huge birds flying above us, I'm not sure what they were, maybe eagles of some sort.

There were a couple of people running on the beach, the island isn't very big, so this must be one of the only places to run. We talked to a few of the tour stands asking for their prices, and they were all about the same. We're not too sure if we want to go on one yet as the weather hasn't been 100% this last week.

We started walking back to our hotel, looking for somewhere to eat. Passing a place that was nearly fully packed, it had a beautiful view of the sea and the mountains behind. It had live seafood out the front too. We carried on walking a bit closer to our hotel, but there wasn't much else. One place we walked past only had one couple in, this did have a better view, but we thought if it's got that good of a view and basically empty, then the food must be rubbish.

So, we walked back to the busy place. Luckily there was space for us. I ordered some thick noodles and chicken, and Syd had a chicken yellow curry, with rice. While we were waiting for our food, two cats came and sat next to my chair! I've flown halfway around the world to get away from mine begging at my feet, and now these damn things are here too! They weren't sitting by anyone else. I must just give off a vibe cats like... I don't know?!

Even when our food arrived, and throughout the meal they sat next to me. The food was very nice, I'm sure we will be back here later in the week as I want to try their hot seafood salad. While walking back to our room, we checked out where breakfast would be tomorrow, it was at the tiki bar in the complex. This had access to a private beach. There were a few swings on the sand and some long tail boats in the water. We sat on the big swing for a bit, seeing a shell crab walk towards the water. There were also bottles with flames coming out of the top all over the place, some were for light and the smaller ones to keep the mosquitoes away. They were effective at both.

We noticed a sign saying there is going to be a fire dance show later in the evening. Which we planned on going to later. Back in the room, I did some ETF ISA documentation, finishing just in time to watch the show. We walked back over to the beach and sat right next to them on a wooden canopy. We shared a Lipton Lemon drink and watched the show.

Near the end of the show, we were asked to move as they were going to be doing some more extreme moves. I'm glad we did move as there were a lot of sparks going right where we had been sitting! A few people from the audience also got up and had a go. I didn't fancy it myself, and neither did Syd. It was an exciting performance.

Once back in our room, we got ready for bed. Then started watching the first Pirates of The Caribbean. As Johnny Depp and Amber Heard's trials had been going on and it got us in the mood to watch some of his stuff. We only got halfway through before Syd started drifting off, so I turned it off and went to sleep myself.

VIEWPOINT

KRABI | DAY 2

3rd May 2022

https://twobritsinasia.com/viewpoint/

We were woken up quite early this morning (5 am) by the prayers going on next door in the mosque. They didn't last long, and we went back to sleep fairly quickly. Once up properly at about 8ish, we got out of bed slowly making our way to breakfast. Everyone had the same thing: you just chose how you wanted your eggs, fried, scrambled, or as an omelette.

It came with vegetable rice, half a chicken sausage, a slice of ham, and two bits of toast with butter and jam. We had some orange juice too. It was such an amazing spot to have breakfast: close to the clear water with the backdrop of mountains and palm tree forests. Exactly how anyone might imagine paradise in their head. And we were here!

A few other groups came down for breakfast later. They looked like they had some French toast and Syd said she saw croissants too. I'll have to ask tomorrow how we can get that. On the way back from breakfast Syd spotted a large worm of some kind, she proclaims that she is now David Attenborough!

Once back in our room, we cooled off for a bit, trying to figure out what to do for the day. I saw that there were a few viewpoints up in the mountains, letting us see the island below. So, we got ready and made our way to the top!

At first, we walked along the seafront, which was the long way around. However, the road quickly transformed from a concrete path, into a gravel lane, which rapidly became just a thick bush. We decided to turn around and find the stairs, the quick way up. The word quick is misleading here, it still took us about 20-25 minutes to even get to the first viewpoint. There were 333 stairs in total (I think, I might have counted wrong in the heat). We were both very sweaty.

We had a few water breaks on the way up, passing chickens, and even a massive pet lizard! There was a reservoir which we walked around; although it was a little low on water now. This was because Thailand only has about a six-week window of the year where they would have monsoon weather. This would then re-fill the stores, however, the monsoon season was expected to start in a few weeks, which meant they were at the bottom of their last year's stores. We also passed a gym, but no one was using it, certainly, it would be hard work to train in this heat.

About halfway up the climb was a restaurant which we stopped in just for a breather, we didn't get anything though. In the later stages of the climb, I had Syd in front of me walking up the stairs. That way I could catch her if she fell backwards. Thankfully this wasn't needed. A further 15 minutes and we were at viewpoint 2. Literally, moments before we got to the top, the heavens opened!

Luckily there was a cafe at the top, which we went into to dry off. We had a Fanta each, I had an orange and Syd had a strawberry one. Both were very refreshing. The staff gave us a towel to dry off, which was kind of them. We sat here for about half an hour to three-quarters an hour, for the rain to pass. Syd had a little nap while we were waiting.

Just as we were leaving another couple walked into the cafe, also soaking wet. I asked if they got caught in the rain too. They looked confused and said no - we're just sweaty! We all laughed; they headed back down the cliff shortly after. I paid the lady at the till, and then took some photos of the top viewpoint, with the island below and Phuket in the distance.

Looking down at the island from up here was amazing! Really jaw-dropping and a must-see for anyone on the island. It was only 30THB to have access to the pathways which is worth every THB! We got chatting with a lady from Germany while sitting on the ledge at the top. She asked if I could take a picture of her, which I did and in return, she took one of me and Syd. There was also another group of girls at the top, which made for a cool photo, so I took some photos of them too, looking out over at the island below.

The descent down was much quicker than the climb up. Syd's left leg started shaking near the bottom, I think her muscle needed some more oxygen. I told her to breathe deeply and slowly, and the shaking stopped. There was some construction work going on and a cat was sitting on a digger cleaning itself. It looked like the cat was going to be doing the construction work.

Further down the road, we found a local place called Garlic 1992 as the name suggests they cook with a lot of garlic and have been open since 1992. We ordered "a few" dishes to share. Some spring rolls, crispy noodles and chicken with brown sauce, and a chicken Penang curry which came with a portion of plain rice. We won't need much for dinner now!

Back at our hotel, they hadn't cleaned our room yet, but then I remembered the porter yesterday saying something about if I wanted the room cleaned, I had to let reception know. So, we got changed into our swim stuff and headed to the private beach. On the way popping into reception to let them know our room needed cleaning.

I remembered my goggles! We set up on some lounger chairs, which were free as they were part of the complexes, and then got straight into the sea! I saw a few fish, Syd didn't want to get her hair wet, even though she already had from the rain earlier...

Either way, she didn't put her head under the water to see the fish up close. We spent the rest of the afternoon sitting on the beach.

At one point a cat walked past and weed on one of the other lounger chairs next to us. It made us glad we had put our towels down first. We didn't go back in the sea again as the tide had gone out and once it goes out it's then flat for ages so you can't swim it's just ankle depth the whole way. Like Weymouth beach back home in Dorset, but even further!

Back in our room, it had been cleaned but our card to turn the power on had been removed from the cardholder. This was slightly annoying because it turned the air-con off. Not to worry I ran down to reception to let them know the cleaners had taken it. They gave me another one and I went back to our room, it cooled down again quickly.

We got ready for our evening, wanting to book a snorkelling tour for tomorrow. We headed back to one of the guys we spoke to yesterday, as even though it was slightly more expensive, there was breakfast and lunch included in that tour. It was also an early start so the other boats wouldn't be around yet, which worked in our favour.

When we got there, the couple from earlier on the climb were there too. Syd didn't recognise them at first, as she had been half asleep when we saw them earlier. The fella recognised me first before I did. They too were booking the same early morning tour as us. After we paid, I wanted to get me and Syd some rash vests to keep on while snorkelling to help protect us from the sun tomorrow.

We only walked a few shops down before we found some we liked. After buying them we then headed back towards the hotel. We decided to go back to where we ate last night, we really enjoyed it there, and I wanted to try those other dishes!

This time we ordered a little bit more (I know we were only meant to have a smaller dinner, but ya know... it is what it is...) We shared the spicy prawn salad, it was very tasty, almost syrup-like, a bowl of vegetable and egg fried rice, and some grilled orangey red fish which the owner (I assume, she had that authority) had recommended. She let me pick which one I liked the look of, then weighed it, so they knew how much to charge me.

I'm not sure what the owner said the fish was called, after looking on Google it looked like a Red Snapper. The chefs would cook it, how ever we would like. The owner recommended it to just be simply grilled with some butter and a chilli dipping sauce. This is what we went with, it was very tasty! Beautiful. I had a ginger ale to drink, and Syd had an Orange Fanta. Thinking about it, this meal was up there on some of the best food we had in Thailand. The fish was so fresh and cooked perfectly, and the view of the mountains and boats in the distance was magical. It really was amazing.

Halfway through eating our fish, there were a few raindrops. We moved our table under the cover and continued to eat there. A cat (different from yesterday) came up beside me again. This time putting its paws on the table, it must have smelt the fish! I told and gestured to put its paws down, which it did. I'm not sure if we are allowed to feed them or not. We didn't as I'm not sure the restaurant wants to encourage their begging, which might annoy the other customers.

After I paid up, I said thank you to the owner and chefs, letting them know that the fish was very tasty and that it was a good recommendation. We went straight back to our room since we have an early morning tomorrow, and we didn't go to the fire show tonight. We got ready for bed and watched the rest of Pirates of the Caribbean, before falling asleep.

SWIMMING IN SHARK INFESTED WATERS, WITH THE SHARKS!

KRABI | DAY 3

4th May 2022

https://twobritsinasia.com/swimming-in-shark-infested-waters-with-the-sharks/

We woke up early this morning, both thanks to my alarm and the prayers from the mosque. After getting our bearings, we got ourselves ready for the day of snorkelling we had planned. We only saw a few other people while walking through the town this early in the morning. Usually, it's hard to walk on this strip as it's so busy! It was interesting seeing it so empty.

On the way to the meet-up point, we popped into a 7-11 to grab some water and snacks for the trip. We were getting fed while on the adventure, but just in case we thought it best to bring something else too. Once we got to McDonald's, the meeting spot, we were given a form to fill in for our lunch choice. It was either chicken or vegetable fried rice. We both picked the chicken option.

We were then ushered around the corner, where we would wait for the others. There was tea, coffee, and Thai donuts. We didn't have any tea or coffee, but we did have some Thai donuts! They were like churros but with smooth edges, and in the shape of the letter H. We said hello to the couple we had bumped into yesterday. It was beautiful with the early morning mist coming off the sea, with a row of the classic traditional Thai longtail boats lined up on the sand. Idyllic.

Once everyone had arrived, there were about 20 of us including the crew and tour guide, we walked down to the pier and got on the speedboat. We took off our shoes before getting on the boat, they were placed in a wash bucket and placed under the boat for safekeeping. This was to keep the boat clean. Our tour guide, Tipper, welcomed us all, and she gave us a quick run-down of what we would be doing today.

The speed boat really sped up once we had left the harbour, Syd and I sat right at the back. It had two 250 HP Honda engines. Our first stop of the day was Maya Bay. It was featured in the Leonardo DiCaprio film, The Beach. Neither Syd nor I had seen this film, but the beach was beautiful, nonetheless.

There were black tip sharks here, we could only get into the water up to our knees. There is currently a three-and-a-half-year ban on swimming enforced in the bay to help the coral and fish repopulate. We could see massive schools of little fish along the bay, with the sharks swimming through and eating them, it was fascinating to watch the fish move around the sharks to avoid getting eaten. Not every fish was so lucky... It was amazing to be so close to the sharks. Syd was in her element! They were literally just feet away. We took lots of pictures.

On the walk back to the boat, we saw a massive spider and its web! It was the biggest spider I have ever seen in the wild, it must have been at-least 10cm! Once back at the boat, the captain washed off our feet with a bucket, removing the sand, as we got on. This, again, was to keep the boat clean.

Next, we went around the island to our first snorkelling stop of the day. Syd put a life jacket on to help her float. She wasn't too sure how to use the snorkel at first, getting confused that she couldn't breathe through her nose. Some others in the group had seen a bigger shark, but it had swum off by the time we got over to them.

After getting back on the boat, we made our way down Pi Leh Bay (Pi Leh Lagoon). Tipper took some photos of me and Syd standing at the back of the boat. Before mooring up for us to jump off the boat on one side, or snorkel on the other side. I started off with a back flip off the side of the boat, it got a few looks and the guy from the viewpoint yesterday gave it a go too. His was a bit wonky so I gave him some pointers till he was able to do it properly

While snorkelling this spot I saw my first sea urchins, they looked very prickly, and not something I'd like to stand on! Thankfully the water we were in was quite deep so no chance of standing on them. I dove down to get a closer look at them though, it was cool to see them up close.

From here we had a drive-by viewing of the Viking cave. No one other than workers are allowed in the cave anymore. This is to protect the birds that are there, they create nests with their spit! The workers collect and sell for massive expense, between one and two grand (GBP) per kg! It is called Viking cave as apparently there is an ancient painting in there of a Viking ship.

The tour guide gave us all the knowledge that she knew about it and made a joke that if anyone had any questions, they could use Google. As we were leaving, she then handed around some pineapple slices for us all. Syd had a bit of hers then gave the rest to me. They were refreshing after being in the salty water.

We were then driven to our next spot, Monkey Beach, which as the name suggests had loads of monkeys on. They were very cute. They watched us as our boat reversed close to their cliff-face caves and trees. The big boss monkey sat on the top branch looking down at us. There was a tiny baby monkey too!

With our leftover pineapple, we were able to feed them. They were very gentle! When they yawned you could see their fangs though! I wouldn't want to get bitten by one that's for sure! Two of them had a squabble on the rope, and one fell into the water. It swam back to the cliff and ran up it, only its ego hurt.

The captain chucked a plastic bottle of Coca-Cola up to the top monkey. He knew how to open the bottle, he seemed to really enjoy it! They had shaken the Coke up first to make sure it was flat before throwing it up. Once the monkey was done, he dropped the bottle back down to us. We were able to feed the monkeys by hand, being very careful to stay away from their face, but handing them the food and stroking their hands, which they seemed to like.

The boat then dropped off the people who were only doing the half day, back on the main island. Our lunch was also brought on-board at the same time, and we headed for our next stop, Bamboo Island. The ride over there was quite rough. Syd, I, and the other couple were up the front bouncing about with all the waves!

I got on my knees and faced forward toward the oncoming waves. Being able to brace myself and use my knees as spring dampeners. Also, I was able to let the others know when a big wave (which caused bigger drops) was going to come. Giving them time to brace themselves also. There were times when we were all airborne! It was great fun! Syd had taken a sickness tablet already, I had not, thankfully we both felt fine.

There were a lot of boats on Bamboo Island when we got there but our driver managed to squeeze in between two other boats. It was quite the ordeal and took some time with the help of the other two boats' crew. There was a bit of boat crashing and crunching, but nothing serious. I don't think those other boats should have been there at that time, as once we arrived, they all left fairly quickly.

Our tour company is the Local Phi Phi Island Tours, and I wonder if they have priority over the other tour companies coming from Phuket or Krabi, since this is their island. As when we were at Maya beach, we were the first there before the crows, and even while we were there, not many other people arrived.

Anyways, after our chicken fried rice lunch, we dropped our rubbish off on the boat and picked up our snorkelling gear. I also picked up Syd's rash vest too for her to put on. We walked along the beach, where we bumped into Tipper, we dropped off our water, phone, and sun cream with her while we went for a swim. The island is only tiny, you could see the whole thing from the beach, and could cross it in about 2 minutes of walking. Our stuff was safe, but it is just a habit.

About 10 minutes later she needed to go back on the boat for some reason, so she put our bits next to the other couple's stuff. We got talking with them again. I showed him how to drive underwater with a snorkel on, and how he doesn't need to lift his head out of the water to start breathing through the pipe again.

On this beach we finally learned their names, her name was Freya, and he was Elliot. They were both very friendly, they were traveling for 5-6 months. Taking it day by day with nothing really planned. Quite impressive if you ask me. Personally, I prefer having things planned to save having to worry about it. But I can see the appeal of it being so free to just change your plans last minute.

Back on the boat, we had the music blaring, heading to our final two stops. These were great snorkelling locations. Lots of tropical fish, and the captain was feeding them with some leftover rice. I think I might have kicked a few by accident, but they seemed ok. It was great to look the fish in the eyes and swim with them so close. Syd had got in, but after spotting a jellyfish she shot back into the boat. I think it spooked her a little. Before she left though, we saw a spiny rockfish, which is much more dangerous than a jellyfish, and she was fine seeing that. Those spines can kill you.

Onto the final spot, Syd did get back in the water which was good. She stayed in longer at this spot, really getting the hang of snorkelling. After she asked if we could buy some snorkels, so tomorrow's task is now to find some kits in the shops. We made our way back to the pier, and said our thanks, leaving a hefty tip, as we really enjoyed the day.

Back at the hotel, we had showers, first with our swimming stuff on to get as much of the salt water out as possible. I didn't want our new rash vents to get all salt crystallized overnight. They were a good purchase and did really help to protect our shoulders today.

We then both had a nap, I had one for an hour and a half, while Syd was out for about 3 hours! I think the early start, all the swimming, the sun, and the excitement of seeing the sharks really knocked her for six! I woke her up as I didn't want her sleeping too much and messing up her sleeping pattern.

Realizing that we were now both hungry, surprise, surprise, we got ready for our evening meal. We went to the posh restaurant that the porter recommended on our first day. We had a table right on the balcony, looking down at the sea below, the town's lights, and the mountains in the distance. There were a lot of mosquitos, big ones too! I asked the waitress if she could bring us some repellent spray, which she did. That seemed to solve the problem, but I had been bitten a few times before the spray arrived.

We watched as a wild dog was scavenging on the beach below. He was playing, well trying to catch I think, the crabs. Flinging them about to kill them before eating them. It was interesting to watch, I didn't think dogs would eat crab, but I suppose if that's what the food choice is here for them, that's what they eat.

Speaking of eating, me and Syd ordered a seafood tom yum, steamed soy and ginger sea bass, and some vegetable fried rice (with a fried egg on top) to share. Along with an Orange Fanta for myself and a strawberry Fanta for Syd. We had already had a fair bit of pop today, as the boat had unlimited Coca-Cola and water. We only had one each, but that's still a lot for us...

The food was really nice, Syd enjoyed the tom yum. The sea bass was nice, but I must say the grilled fish yesterday, with just a bit of butter and a chili dipping sauce, was nicer. I couldn't pick the one today, which I could yesterday. It was still tasty though!

We walked back to the tour shop, as we had forgotten to get Tippers number since she took some photos of us. The guy at their counter recognized us as he spoke with us yesterday, and he gave us her number. We had a quick cool-down in the room, before going off to watch the light show again.

It wasn't as good tonight; they were dropping the throws. Also, there weren't as many people watching. We left before it finished and headed back to our room. We were tired after our full-packed day anyways. By the time we were back in our room, Tipper had sent us the photos she had taken, we thanked her again for a great day and then went straight to bed.

NOT OUR DAY

KRABI | DAY 4

5th May 2022

https://twobritsinasia.com/not-our-day/

I woke up around 8 this morning. Syd had an extra hour or so before she woke up. Because we were both knocked out from yesterday's activities, neither of us heard the prayers this morning. We got up and made our way to breakfast.

This time we asked for a menu, but the waiter didn't understand. He just kept asking how we wanted our eggs cooked. I tried explaining that we had seen others with different breakfast items than us on the first morning. Syd asked for pancakes, I was happy with the same as yesterday.

When her plate arrived, Syd just had just one tiny American pancake, with two bits of toast. It did come with butter and jam, but she didn't look too impressed with the size of her portion. For some reason, I also had the same, but mine came with an omelette, half a chicken wiener, and a slice of ham. No rice though, which is what I had asked for extra of.

We saw the table in front of us had a portion of rice so I asked the waitress (who seemed more able to understand us) if she could bring me a bowl of rice too. Which she did, along with another bowl of rice for Syd, and another plate with more toast, another pancake, and two fried eggs... No idea what was going on. But we ate it all, including the fruits they brought out (watermelon and pineapple again). We had two orange juices each too.

Syd couldn't finish all her rice, so I finished it for her- of course. A group of "trust fund" girls (you know the type...) sat down behind us. One of whom had an annoying dry continuous cough. I thought about leaving one of our Covid tests on their table for her but I didn't. We went back to the room to cool off and decide what we wanted to do for the day. We both felt like having a chilled day on the beach today. So that's what we packed up for and set off shortly after we sun-creamed up.

We saw some snorkelling kits in a shop, and the store lady sold us two pairs for 500 TBH (after some haggling). We made our way to Loh Dalum Beach, which is the main swimming/sunbathing beach on the island. However, there weren't any sun loungers or umbrellas on the beach. We had found a row of about 10 or so, slightly back off from the beach, still with sand but behind a thin row of bushes. We decided to set up camp here as the bushes were giving a little shade, which was better than nothing.

After setting up a guy came over asking for 100 THB per lounger, which is fair enough and the same price as we had paid before. So, I coughed up the funds and got our new goggles and pipes out of their cases. I could see once I had gotten them out of the packages that they weren't the best quality. I persisted though and we went in the sea, Syd didn't bother bringing hers along.

They worked for about 20 seconds, but then water started coming into the glasses, and into the pipe. This is obviously less than ideal, so I took them off and gave them to Syd while I just splashed about without them on. Back at the loungers, we noticed there were a lot of ants about, and we were getting bitten quite a bit. This mixed with the shade not actually being shade made us decide to move on.

We offered our loungers to a fella and his family, who had been arguing the price with the chair guy. Turned out he had already paid but thanked us for the offer anyways. We took the snorkels back to the shop. There are signs in all these shops saying, "NO REFUNDS", but it was the same shop we bought the rash vests from the other day. I explained that I was drowning while using them. So, she did give me my money back, which was decent of her.

For some reason we then decided to have lunch, I'm not sure why. I thought Syd had said she was hungry, I certainly wasn't. It turns out she hadn't said that, but I'd already ordered for us. Oh well. We shared some flat noodles with chicken and some vermicelli noodles with seafood. I enjoyed both, Syd wasn't a big fan of the sauce that the vermicelli noodles came in.

We had also ordered some fried chicken tendons, thinking they'd be like fried chicken strips. Well maybe they were meant to be, but these weren't. They didn't taste like chicken, and they were basically just gristle and bone. Not enjoyable, we had literally less than one bite each and left the rest. It may have been a cat, canny confirm. I also popped into the corner shop to grab us a bottle of water. I saw the same snorkels we bought in the shop earlier here, I asked how much they were. The cashier said 399 each, so I did get a good deal on the ones earlier, shame they didn't work.

We decided to cut our losses and walk back to the hotel. We spent the rest of the afternoon at the top pool area. The same group of "daddy's money" girls came up around halfway through. They weren't being considerate of their noise level to the other people trying to have a peaceful relaxing time up here. They won a few disapproving stares from the other guests too, but I don't think they cared.

The girl with the cough sat right next to us. Syd suggested that we could go down to the bottom pool, but there wasn't any shade down there, so we stayed up top. Luckily, they didn't stay up near us for long.

Once the hottest part of the day was over, I decided to go down to the bottom pool as they had cushions on the loungers there. Since the sun had gone down a bit, I wasn't too worried about the shade. There was a blow-up swan in the pool too, which I played about with. However, I noticed that this pool was dirtier than the top one, with lots of bugs and grass cuttings floating on the surface.

After staying down there for an hour or so, we headed back to our room to get ready for our evening meal. We decided on walking into town to find a cheaper side-road place as we weren't too hungry after all the other food we had already had today.

We found a nice little shack and ordered a few things to share. We had seen they did sticky rice on the menu, but they had run out, so we ordered a plate of pad Thai instead. I also ordered some prawn cakes (which originally the server thought they had run out of, but thankfully they had not), a yellow curry, and a hot octopus salad for us. So much for not ordering too much... Again...

We had the pad Thai first; it was served on a banana leaf. The octopus salad was quite spicy, Syd couldn't eat it so I had it all to myself. It was served with mint, I enjoyed it. Syd ordered herself a mango ice smoothie, which we ended up sharing. It was very refreshing. The yellow curry was very yellow. We wondered how they got it so yellow; it was almost neon glow in the dark! The prawn cakes came with some prawn crackers with their rims being different colours. These were our first prawn crackers in Thailand.

After dinner, we went looking around a few of the shops, as Syd had seen a style of half trouser half skirt, she liked the look of. Unfortunately, after trying one on, the style didn't really suit her. She looked at a few other items. But similarly, they were all designed for the local stature, which didn't fit Syd well.

Back in our room, we decided to put on the next Pirates of The Caribbean movie. We got ready for bed, Syd packed her suitcase, and we started watching it. Getting about halfway through before Syd felt sleepy, so I turned it off and went to bed too.

KIDS ON BIKES

KRABI | DAY 5

6th May 2022

https://twobritsinasia.com/kids-on-bikes/

We started the day rather lazily, in no real rush to get out of bed, as checkout was at 11:00 and our ferry wasn't till 13:00. Once we did eventually wake up, we walked over to breakfast. Intrigued to see what we would get served today. Thankfully it was the lady waitress who was on our table again this morning.

I asked for a bowl of rice and an omelette. Syd asked for some French toast and pancakes. Mine arrived first, I got my rice, but also some toast and a pancake, but no butter or jam like before. Since it's fairly usual for the food to come out at different times, Syd and I have just been eating as soon as whoever's food hits the table. This way it saves any critters landing on it, and also prevents the food from going cold while waiting.

By the time I'd finished mine, still no sign of Syd's, this was strange. Mine did come on two plates, the rice being separate from the rest, but the lady did confirm it was all for me. Syd ordered hers again, but only got two small slices of French toast, and no pancake! We did have two bigger glasses of orange juice and a glass of water each today though. Along with our usual fruit.

Syd was obviously still hungry after only such a small breakfast. I made a joke that the ants and mosquitoes biting us during breakfast had more to eat than her! There was also a cafe on the complex, it had a cool thread art of a boat in the café. It reminded me of my Aunty Susan's tapestry she did. While in the café, I bought Syd a croissant with a sachet of chocolate sauce. She enjoyed this. It seemed the ants liked these patisseries too since there was a long line of them walking to the counter!

Back in our room, we both prepared for the day's travels. I packed my suitcase and Syd did some final packing herself. I then took the bags down to reception while Syd got our towels ready on a bed by the pool. I was able to leave our bags at reception and made them aware of our ferry leaving time. They said they'd get someone to take our luggage down to the pier for us to save us the struggle, which was nice of them.

We spent the morning by the side of the pool, not actually getting in as we didn't have anywhere really to change. We could have made it work if we really wanted to, but we were just enjoying the rest. It did start to rain a little, but thankfully that didn't last long, and also we had a cover over the bed we were lounging on, so we didn't get wet.

On the way to the pier, I took a few photos of the long-tail boats with the camera, while Syd walked with the luggage porters. They had to have a run-up to get our luggage up the hilly part of the route. At the pier, I gave them a good tip for their effort. I tried to find us a drink, but nothing tickled my fancy. On the boat, the luggage was all packed up at the front, and the passengers at the back, so I wasn't able to gain air on the waves this time. There were two crew members holding the luggage down in the rougher parts of the water. Luckily nothing went overboard!

The boat made a few stops before getting to our island, Koh Yao Yai, first stopping at the mainland (Krabi). At the stop before ours at Koh Yai Noi, a little boy was busy eating his sausage and didn't realise where we had stopped. As we were pulling away, I think he suddenly realised, because he ran to the front of the boat. The captain laughed as they realised this was his stop. They pulled back in and then handed him over to some workers on the dock. Everyone on the boat had a giggle about this, as we continued over to our island.

There was a taxi already waiting for us as soon as we got off the boat with my name on it. They drove us to the south of the island where our hotel was, GLOW Ellixir Koh Yao Yai Resort. The ride took about half an hour, there isn't much on the island, just a few shops, and a school, that's about it.

On the drive, passing the school, a ped with three boys drove past us, and when I say boys I mean all under double digits! They were giggling when they passed, and the youngest put his middle finger up to us, playing about. We laughed as they went past.

After checking into the hotel, we were shown our room. We have our own villa again, right next to the pool. It's a nice room, with an outside shower. It's also got a cool netting over the bed, I assume to prevent the mosquitoes. The bed itself was on a plinth, it was quite stylish. Syd was a bit hungry so we decided to go see what was about.

We started by walking down to the private beach. There were lots of sand crabs running about, and a few shell crabs. Syd found it funny watching them all scurrying around. We could see Phuket in the distance from here. Further down the beach was the resort's restaurant, it was open but no one was in there. So we carried on walking.

Making our way towards the town, on the way we saw another massive lizard, it may have even been another Komodo Dragon. Syd pretended she was David Attenborough again... pointing to it and pretending it was a crocodile. From the drive down we knew there wasn't much about on this island, but luckily at the top of the road from our resort, was a place we could eat.

We sat down and shared a large vegetable fried rice and a red curry. It was very tasty. We also had a strawberry smoothie to share, which was very, very sweet. Syd really enjoyed that. Once we paid the lady, she said they also hired out peds here. I asked how much, she said it was 200 THB a day (24 hours) which is less than a fiver. So - it's gotta be done, I didn't even bother bartering with her.

I've never driven one myself before, she called over some guy who gave me a quick guide. When I say quick, I mean quick, and when I say guide, I don't mean guide... I had no idea what was going on. He just pointed to the bike, and that was about it... They let me try it out before I committed to hiring it. I really enjoyed it. I wasn't the best at turning so I needed to get used to that. It was a little low on fuel so I took it down the road to try and get it filled up.

The shop had said the fuel was about a minute away, but I had passed it as it was like 10 seconds away. After about 3 minutes, I thought to myself I must have passed it as I was now out in the middle of the wilderness! There had been nothing but trees for the last mile or so. I turned back and saw the shack, they were selling the fuel out of bottles, it made me laugh, they filled her up for me. Only cost us 45 THB (basically a quid).

On the way back to the restaurant, where Syd was waiting until I got more used to it I realised that the owner had jumped onto her ped to see where I had got to. Syd said they were all joking about when I pulled away, and I'm not surprised! I paid them the 200 and Syd, then got on the back and we went for a little ride a few miles down the road.

Everyone could clearly see we were new at it. Giving us waves and head nods. It was really great fun. I could hear Syd laughing the whole way behind me, in between her telling me to slow down... I wasn't going too quick actually, I normally cycle faster than what I was doing. When she got her confidence up I sped it up some more.

It was interesting that I didn't have to give my name, or any form of ID, or even a credit card etc. No paperwork was signed it was just cash, and no insurance either. Bit of fun though eh? We did have helmets that we put on, we're not stupid.

Back at the resort, I parked up and we walked back to our room. We unpacked and then chilled on the bed for a bit before heading back to the resort's restaurant to see what they had for dinner. But it was overpriced and there wasn't much on the menu anyways other than the basics which we didn't fancy.

We decided to take the bike out for a spin to find somewhere to eat. There really isn't much here, we didn't want to go back to the same place we had lunch just hours earlier, so we kept going. We found somewhere else not far up the road, but the lights weren't even on when we first arrived. There were two ladies sitting at the entrance who turned the lights on when we arrived. But again it was fairly expensive for what it was, and no one else was there.

After making a few wrong turns, which added an extra couple of miles onto the journey, and not finding a single restaurant. We found the main 7-11 on the island, with the plans of just getting a few snacks and heading back to the room. Thankfully there was a restaurant next door, it was fully packed though! Not surprising as it was the only one we had seen open for the last 5 miles.

Next door was another one that was packed too, but thankfully there was a table hidden right in the corner that was available. We sat down and the waitress brought over the menu. It seemed to be more of a family place where friends come to eat rather than tourists, as there were no prices on the menu. I asked how much the pad Thai was, as this is a generally good indicator of how expensive a place is. Anything under 100 THB is normal. I can't remember what price she told me, but I am not even sure why I asked, we didn't have much choice anyway.

Syd ordered a Tom Yum chicken noodle dish, and I ordered a spicy chicken curry, that was literally the name on the menu. I ordered a side of rice too to fill out the meal. I had asked for a jug of water and some glasses with ice, as I had seen the other tables with it on. But apparently, they had run out of both the jugged water and ice. So, we were left with warm bottled water... I said to Syd I should have gone across to 7-11 to pick up a large cold one.

Either way, the food was really nice. The chilies in mine were extremely hot. The first bite I had of the chili, I knew I was in trouble. I started coughing straight away. But managed to swallow it. My mouth hurt for about 10 minutes after, and I continued to sweat the rest of the meal! I didn't eat any more of the chilies.

We also ordered butter and condensed milk roti, which we shared. It was very nice. But while the lady was making it, obviously a local, or a family member turned up and was given a jug of water... and then later one of the kids went into their cool box and got some ice out! The lady caught me seeing it and gave me an embarrassed smile and laugh. Not to worry, it was only 200 THB for all of this, which we can't complain about.

While eating, there was a little boy, about 3, who was playing hide and seek with us. He kept hiding behind the kitchen curtain and showing himself again. We were all laughing. It was very cute. There was another table with a group of local lads, about 6 of them, it looked to be their meet-up spot.

After dinner, we popped into the 7-11, where we picked up a tub of Pringles and a bag of peanuts. Then headed back to the resort. Going a bit faster on the way back as Syd had started to feel a bit more comfortable on the back of the bike with the speed.

Once we got back to the resort, we put our helmets under the seat, although unfortunately, I now wasn't able to lock the seat. I thought I must have put the helmets in a different position. But even after taking the helmets out, the seat didn't close. All it needed was a slam. After a few attempts, someone from reception came out with a light. It was good to see they were checking on strange noises. I managed to lock it shortly after and we said hello to them, and walked to our room.

We got ready for bed and watched the rest of the second Pirates of the Caribbean, which we started a few days ago. Once this was finished, we went to sleep.

IN SEARCH OF A TOUR

KRABI | DAY 6

7th May 2022

https://twobritsinasia.com/in-search-of-a-tour/

We started the day relatively early, as breakfast is only served between 7 and 10 here, whereas the other places have been around 6 till 11. No worries, once we were up we walked over to the restaurant and sat down. Only one other couple and their kid were there. I don't think this island is particularly well-known yet.

The breakfast selection was quite good. It was menu based, and we could pick whatever we wanted off the menu. Syd went for yogurt and an omelette with everything they had (other than mushrooms, she did her usual "I don't have mush-room on my plate" joke). She also ordered fried tomatoes and baked beans but didn't end up eating the beans as she didn't like the taste. I thought they tasted all right.

I ordered pad Thai, with chicken and prawns, it had some tofu in it too. I also ordered some fried potatoes, but they were more baked with a bit of seasoning on them. We shared a basket of toast with different jams. I had asked for pineapple jam, as I'd never had that before, but they must have run out because it came with butter, strawberry jam, orange jam, and Nutella (which Syd liked of course).

We also had a plate of fruit each. Syd only ate the watermelon on hers, she tried the dragon fruit but said it was too seedy... I gave her some of my watermelon slices, so at least she was getting a bit more in her. Along with the watermelon and dragon fruit, it also came with pineapple.

There was a dog hanging about, we had seen him on the beach yesterday. He kept coming around the tables while we were eating. We didn't mind, but the waitress kept trying to move him on. We later found out that it was a stray, it did look very skinny.

Once we got back to our room, we chilled for a bit trying to decide what to do for the day. I was in talks with the James Bond tour guide I had planned on using. He told me that he would need to be paid in cash, but I didn't take enough cash with us to pay for the trip that way. I also didn't want to take it out of an ATM because the exchange rates on those machines are rubbish, and they charge a fee too! Unfortunately, he didn't accept card payments, PayPal, bank transfers, or even crypto. So I decided that since we had the bike, to go exploring around the island to try and find someone and their boat to take us. Full of this plan, we got ready and left.

We first saw a tour shop just down our road, he was charging 5,000 THB which was 2,000 less than the original tour. But also, he didn't take card payments. So I said we'd come back later if we couldn't find it elsewhere. He said we might have better luck in the north of the island back at the main pier. So off we set!

It took about half an hour to forty minutes. I only got lost a few times (it might have only been once actually) and stopped for fuel about halfway through. Getting it again from a side-of-the-road shop, out of an old Coca-Cola litre bottle. When we got to the pier we first went all the way down to the bottom. The first guy we spoke to didn't really speak any English so couldn't understand what we were asking. Thankfully his friend walked over, he knew what we were asking, and he phoned someone for us.

I was on the phone with him for about 10 minutes. He was charging 5,500 and he would accept a bank transfer. He did, also, offer a speed boat instead of a long tail, but that was 16,000 THB (about £400). I took his number down and said I'd message him later if we decide to go with him.

About halfway down the pier, we found someone else, who initially said 6,500 THB but then after speaking with the guy who gave us his phone, said 3,500. He didn't seem to really know what was going on either, and Syd didn't have a good feeling about it so we didn't go with him either.

At the bottom of the pier, we noticed a sign for tours so we stopped, just as we did two lads on a bike passed by. They stopped and called over someone else, who phoned a lady whom I spoke to. She too was asking around the 6-6,500 mark, again, cash only, so we moved on from here.

Heading back towards where I had made a wrong turn, I saw a sign to another pier. We went down there. It was basically empty, with only three boys playing about in the shelter, who didn't speak a word of English. An old man who spoke even less English... and some people in diggers working on the pier. We decided to turn around and head back to the hotel.

On the way back we saw another tour stand, but no one was there. We stopped at the viewpoint on our way back. Driving half-way up with the ped. It was a very steep hill, it scared Syd a bit. But I've cycled steeper so was able to control the bike fine, telling Syd to keep leaning forward otherwise she'd fall off the back. We walked up the steps and looked over the sea towards Phuket. It was beautiful. I walked on the balcony part, but Syd was too worried to walk on it. I could see the big buddha from up here.

After taking some photos, we stopped for a water break A massive black hornet-type thing flew right toward my glasses, and then towards Syd. It spooked us both, so we walked back down the steps and carried on our journey.

We did take a detour to a busier part of the island. There were two larger hotels here which had clearly attracted other businesses. Three places offered tours down here. Two of which were cash only and were around the 6-6,500 mark again. The third, which did take cards apparently as there were signs outside for visa etc. But no one was in the shop! I called the number on the sign. The guy that answered said he would be there at 6, so we said we'd be back later to speak with him.

Heading back up the road, we saw a drinks shop with a sign for 20 THB per drink. So, we stopped and had one each. Syd had a strawberry and soda, which was very, very sweet. I opted for a chocolate and caramel, which was nice, and funnily enough, wasn't as sweet as Syd's strawberry one! They had a lot of ice in both which cooled us down. He was also selling some sort of Chinese buns and some dim sum, but it didn't tickle our fancy.

Back towards the hotel, I made a final detour to another pier that I had seen on the map. I went the wrong way to start with and ended up on the beach with the bike. Thankfully a local boy explained how to get around to the pier, so we did. Again, it was fairly empty. Two girls were playing at the end, they couldn't speak English either and I think they were laughing at our accents. They were only young.

At the start of the pier, there was a shop. I asked if they did tours, the lady phoned someone and then a guy came over. After much deliberation, they agreed on 5,500 for the tour, and they accepted card payments too. But at the end when I was confirming everything, I showed them a picture of James Bond Island, just to make sure, and they looked as if they didn't realise that's where we wanted to go. They still said yes to that price, but Syd wasn't feeling too confident about it, so we moved on.

Finally heading back to the hotel, we passed the first tour shop again, but the guy wasn't there this time. We went into our resort's reception, where they had a sign-up for a tour too. But they were charging around 7-7,500, which was the most expensive. We decided not to go with them.

Back in our room, we chilled for a bit. We tucked into the Pringles we bought yesterday and finished the last of the snacks from Ann and Misora. We then spent an hour or so by the pool. Seemingly moving every bit of pool furniture around until Syd was happy with where we were lying down.

The pool looked like it was underfilled from not being used and the sun evaporating it. A good half, to a full, foot below where it should have been. Either way, it was nice to cool off, but there were quite a few bugs floating on the surface, so we didn't stay in long. While Syd was sunbathing by the pool, I popped back to the ped rental and paid another 200 THB to keep it for another day.

After getting back in our room, we dried up got and ready for our evening meal. We decided to go back to where the two larger hotels were situated since there was more choice there. So off we went. Stopping for some fuel on the way. This one was more expensive at 48 THB (the others being 45) for a bottle. And I had to fill it up myself, which the others had done it for me!

The first place we stopped at was very busy and also quite expensive, so we carried on further down. The next place looked okay, but it was empty. The third place was lit up the most and had a few people in, and the prices were good too. So we stopped here, "just right ey, Goldilocks" I joked to Syd.

We ordered some Thai fish cakes to share, I had a chicken, prawn, and basil dish with a side of steamed rice. Syd had a chicken Massaman curry, which came with rice too. We had planned on stopping off at the main 7-11 to pick up a drink, but I had forgotten. The drink stand from earlier had closed, so I ordered a coconut to drink, and Syd had a mango smoothie. It was all very nice, but it did take a long time to get the food out to us, about half an hour. Which in Thailand is a long time. Usually, our food is on the table within 5 minutes of ordering.

There were a lot of bugs here. One of which was a May bug that had somehow got itself stuck inside a fan! There were a few cats around too. They looked very skinny. I had a lettuce leaf so I dropped that to see how hungry they were. They turned their nose up at it! Interesting... I dropped some of my coconut flesh too, wasn't interested in that either. So we then dropped some of Syd's chicken. At first, they weren't too sure but then scoffed it down.

Heading back to the hotel, we stopped off at the 7-11 to pick up some aloe vera gel, since Syd had burned her shoulders thanks to the day of riding on the back of the ped. We also picked up some more toothpaste as we were running low. Some more Pringles too, along with some mosquito spray as those too were getting low on the supply front.

Once back at the hotel, we got ready for bed. The shower here is outside. A frog sat watching Syd have her shower, which freaked her a little bit. But the frog didn't move the whole time!

I noticed that I had a fairly bad looking, very itchy, bite on my right side, just below the hip. I'm not sure what it was. It might have been a spider bite. It looked like a mosquito or some sort of other allergic reaction to a bite this morning, like any of the other bites we've had here. But this one now looked a lot worse. I took a photo of it to monitor it. I then put on some bite cream and put a blister plaster over it, to keep me from accidentally scratching it in my sleep.

We finished getting ready for bed. We are planning on going to try and find a laundry shop tomorrow while we still have the bike. And maybe (if Syd is feeling up to it), give Syd a go at driving the ped. She seems a little hesitant at the moment. But we can see what happens. We then started watching Pirates of the Caribbean three. It wasn't long till we felt drowsy and went to sleep!

BUBBLE BUTT

KRABI |DAY 7

8th May 2022

https://twobritsinasia.com/bubble-butt/

I woke to my alarm this morning and spent about an hour on my phone watching some YouTube videos. Syd had this extra hour in bed. She said she had been up in the night because of the thunder and rain. I can't remember even hearing any. She said we spoke about it in the night, I certainly can't remember that.

We got up and went for breakfast. The family whom we saw there yesterday, were nowhere to be seen today. But instead, a new couple who had been checking in yesterday while we were asking about the James Bond Tour at reception. We sat at the same table as yesterday for breakfast.

Both of us ordered yoghurt today, and another bowl of toast and jams to share. Still no pineapple jam, and only one sachet of Nutella this morning, so I let Syd have it. Syd had the same omelette again today, but she thinks there was a different chef as this one wasn't as good, it did look visibly watery. I went for thick rice noodles and chicken. I had also ordered some rice and a fried egg to go on top, but instead, two fried eggs turned up and no rice. I didn't say anything as we had enough anyway.

Syd had two glasses of apple juice this morning, I had a glass of apple juice and a glass of orange juice. Even though it had been raining during the night the sea was very calm, but it was still a little misty. The mountains over on Phuket were slightly hazy from the mist.

There were a few boats out on the water - they were kicking up a lot of black smoke. We had no idea what they were doing. Syd thought they were looking for oil... It was a shame we didn't have any binoculars with us. I remembered I could use my camera to zoom in so I ran back to the room before our food arrived and picked up the camera. It turned out they were just fishing boats.

No idea why so much black smoke was being produced from them though. Probably just very old.

The stray doggo came up to us again, I gave him a cautious scratch on the head, and gave him the compulsory "good boy" speech. The waitress later came out and moved him on again. I think we're going to try to sneak out a sausage or two tomorrow to feed him. As we were eating Syd noticed a gecko walking up a tree, proclaiming that she is yet again David Attenborough.

Back in our room, we cooled off for a bit. With no real plans for the day. We had intended to go find somewhere to do the laundry, but the hotel offered 80 THB per kg service. That is on the higher end of the scale. But there really isn't much option on the island, so I can't complain.

I dropped off our bag, weighing it with our suitcase scales first to ensure they didn't try to over-charge me. I showed the receptionist the weight and she took a picture too. I think they probably just subcontract it out to someone on the street anyways. She said it would be done by tomorrow morning, maybe later this evening. She'd phone our room when it was ready to collect anyway. Thinking about it, I probably could have paid upfront and then have them drop it off at my room with the cleaners. Oh well.

After getting ready, I sat on the balcony cutting my toenails, it was long overdue. After this, we still didn't really know what we wanted to do today. We decided to just chill by the pool. Again no one was about. It's quite eerie really. Syd finished her second book while we were there.

The resort is very nice, right on the beach, with very well looked after grounds. There are lots of plots of land on this island with for-sale signs on them. It does tempt me to buy one up and hold it to build a hotel on it one day, once this island becomes well known because I'm sure it will. I might give them a call anyways to see what sort of price they are asking.

While we were sitting at the pool, the doggo came out from somewhere. I popped into our room to grab us a drink, and a bowl, to pour some water out for the dog too. But by the time I got back, it had gone. Syd said she tried to whistle it back, but it didn't do anything with the noise. I suppose if it's a stray it might not know the whistle command. She said it went towards the beach, but I couldn't see him there anywhere. Either way, I kept the water and bowl out in case it returned.

Speaking of animals. There was another frog sitting at the top of our umbrella. No idea how it got there. May have been the same one from the other day! It looked fairly comfy up there though. We spent a few hours by the side of the pool, during this time, I walked down to the swing on the beach, where the dog was having a rest. I gave it another head scratch and tried to call it back up to the pool for some water. It didn't understand, although two other dogs appeared from my whistling, a brown and another white one.

The brown one had some water to drink, the other white one just lay in the shade on the other side of the pool. I went in the pool, but Syd didn't fancy it today, the brown dog stayed lying by Syd's feet at the bottom of the lounger.

We started to get a little hungry, so decided to go to the southernmost part of the island, taking the ped. The road turned into a rubble road, which then turned into a dirt track. Unfortunately, there wasn't anything to eat, but at the end of the track, there were two men making a long-tail boat. They were friendly and let me take some photos of them working. We turned the bike around and started heading back toward civilization.

It was already about 16:00 at this point, so I said to Syd why don't we go to see the tip of the island (The Point) up north. We had planned on doing that tomorrow, but I thought if we did it today, we could hand the bike back today and have a day by the pool or just chill tomorrow instead. We thought it best to add another bottle of petrol, initially, the shop quoted 48, but I said would they do 45, which they did. The visibility was really good today, we stopped to take a few pictures every now and then.

On the way, we were looking for a drink stand that would do bubble tea. We saw a few stands, but unfortunately, none of them did bubble tea. We saw one about halfway through which had bubble tea in their advertisement banners outside, but they were closed. Luckily just about a mile from The Point, there was a stand that did some! Yay! I had a browned sugar and caramel one. Syd didn't actually want a bubble drink as she thinks they are a bit slimy. She had a chocolate milkshake instead. It tasted just like Nesquik.

We took these drinks with us to The Point. Again, the road ended up becoming just a sand pit. Syd had to get off at one point as we'd got stuck. I revved it up and got unstuck, sliding all over the place. But I was used to that from gravel biking with Ed back in England on his "Mystical Tours", so I was able to move my body around to get it under control.

On the beach, it was very similar to the Maldives (not that I've ever been, but from the photos). It was beautiful to see the waves coming over the sand from both directions. And with the mountains of Phuket on one side and Krabi on the other side. It is paradise.

There were a few beached jellyfish on the sand. I helped the biggest one back in the water, and Syd also did the same with another one. The bigger one then beached itself again, Syd pushed it out further as she had sandals on so she could get her feet wet. Syd drew on the sand a "J" and an "S" with a heart in the middle, while I was taking some more pictures of the utopia around us.

We then made our way to the busy restaurant next to the 7-11. Leaving the beach, once again, Syd had to get off the bike so I could get through the deep sand parts. Syd is singing for our entertainment on the ride out of there. After all the sugar from the drinks earlier, she was singing "Bubble Butt" mainly on repeat, because I had bubbles in my drink. "Hey chick chick chicken, lay a little egg for me" also featured a few times! Basically, every time she saw a chicken on the side of the road, which was a lot.

Once we got to the restaurant, it wasn't as busy as usual, which was good because we wanted to get a table. We ordered quite a bit (as is the theme), even though there weren't any prices on the menu here either. It's a risk but it's never going to be that expensive, and with the place being usually fully packed, it won't be silly prices anyway.

Syd had a chicken noodle soup, with some fish dumplings (she wasn't a fan of the dumplings, so I had them). We shared some chicken tendons, which we ordered to see if the first place we had them on Phi Phi Dom was a one-off. But these two were gristly too, they weren't as bad as they had been fried for longer, so I finished them as the batter had a nice taste. We also shared a bowl of chicken tom yum.

I had some crispy fried breaded chicken stir fry, with a side of rice. I had also popped over to the 7-11 to get us a drink. But their drink machine was empty. Instead, I got us a bottle of strawberry milk. The food was really tasty, the tom yum was a bit spicy though. We also ordered a cheese roti to share, it was very tasty, and sweet. The flavours and textures worked well together. This all came to 325 THB (£8 ish). Which is a lot cheaper than yesterday, and it arrived quicker too!

We finally dropped the bike back off. With more fuel in it than it had when we picked it up! This was fair as we had dropped it off at 19:00 which is about two hours later than it should have been. The lady didn't say anything though. We were going to go there for dinner tomorrow too, so I didn't feel too bad about it.

I stopped off at reception to pick up our washing. I tried asking the guy about booking a taxi for when we check out back to the pier in a few days. He didn't seem to know what was going on. It was the night staff so, as usual, they're not much help really. I'll just head back in tomorrow morning to ask the normal lady.

Back in our room, Syd went to shower her feet by the pool, as they still had a bit of sand on them from earlier. By the time she got back, the brown dog was at the bottom of our steps! He started walking up them too! We said goodnight to him, and we went in. We spent the rest of the evening watching some more of the third Pirates of the Caribbean movie. Syd was drifting off to sleep, so I turned it off, before going to sleep myself.

HOWLING DOGS AND PIRATES

KRABI | DAY 8

9th May 2022

https://twobritsinasia.com/howling-dogs-and-pirates/

I was woken up by Syd at about 4 am, this morning. She had heard a weird noise and wanted me to see what it was … it sounded like a faint mooing but was regular, every 2-3 seconds or so. I then thought it might have been our air-con arm swinging and rubbing against something inside itself. But it wasn't swinging.

I tried to ignore it, but it was keeping me awake now. I got out of bed and looked out the windows. All three dogs had put themselves on our balcony, sleeping. So, I'm going to assume it was one of them snoring. About 10 minutes later it stopped but then started again. Not for long this time, we could drift back off to sleep.

Until 5 when we could hear the prayers in the distance, and so did the dogs. They started howling!! Bloomin' heck! Thankfully it didn't go on for long and we went back to sleep. Then for some reason, my phone alarm went off at 5:30... Great...

After turning that off we were zonked out again till gone 9. Once we had awoken properly, we walked over to breakfast. Followed by the first white dog. It was still raining this morning, so we sat in our usual spot under the shelter. Syd had the same as she usually has. This time with some ham and sausages, she kept the sausages to feed to the dogs later.

I had yoghurt, toast, pad Thai, fried rice, and two fried eggs. I really liked the spoon which we had the yoghurt with. It may have fallen into my pocket... Oops.

Since it was still raining, we went back to our room. Thankful that we dropped the bike off yesterday as it would have been a waste of money today in this weather. We decided to have a movie day until it cleared up (if it ever does). It never did... so we had the whole day watching the rest of Pirates 3 and all of 4.

We had a slight break in-between the two, during which, we popped down to reception to ask about the taxi tomorrow. It was booked for 13:40 and since there wasn't anyone else at the resort (literally I asked the receptionist, Syd and I are the only guests now) we could have access to the room until the taxi arrived. It was strange that we were the only ones here; I had thought it was eerily quiet. They still had at least 20 staff about doing the gardening, cleaning, chefs, waitresses, and of course the receptionist.

On the way back to our room we found the dogs and gave them the sausages. The second white dog seems most skittish, as we threw it the sausage and it ran away scared of it. Before coming back and eating it. I'm not sure if the brown dog ate his or if the first white dog managed to eat his too.

After a hard day finishing off The Pirates of the Caribbean 4, we started to get hungry. The rain had stopped a bit, so we walked down to the beach, and the brown dog followed us. We walked along the beach and watched the sunset from a viewing platform. A green bug landed on my shoulder as go to the bottom of the steps, I think it may have bitten me as I started to bleed from where it had landed. It didn't hurt, but Syd was quite worried about it.

The other dogs joined us, walking back to our room to look at my shoulder. All three of them were playing together, one put the other's whole head in its mouth. It was funny to watch. My shoulder was fine, Syd just cleaned it up and put some Anthisan cream on it. We then headed out for dinner.

Again, the dogs were padding along with us. They followed us the whole way down the street. It must have been quite a sight. After walking to the end of the village and seeing that the usual restaurants were closed we realised that it was a Monday, so we started walking back to the hotel, aiming to have some food at the restaurant there. Even though we were the only guests staying we had seen earlier that some people were sitting there, they were most probably the worker's families.

Either way, on our walk back, the first place we had dined at, and where I had hired the bike from, had put its lights on. So, we went in here. We did order quite a feast as we were hungry as we'd only had Pringles for lunch while watching Pirates 4.

We ordered a plate of vegetable fried rice, some chicken thick noodles, battered fried prawns, crispy beef, sticky rice, and mango (finally found somewhere that had it in stock)! I also had a lemon smoothie and Syd had a Watermelon fizzy drink. It was all very tasty. It came to 820 THB, but I gave them a bit extra as I had dropped the bike off late yesterday.

Back in our room, we got ready for bed and watched the last Pirates of the Caribbean movie before falling asleep.

FLYING SNAKE

SURIN ISLANDS | DAY 1

10th May 2022

https://twobritsinasia.com/flying-snake/

We woke up naturally this morning without any alarms. At about the same time the alarms would have gone off funnily enough. There was a massive moth on our balcony, but it was dead with lots of ants feasting on it. We walked down to breakfast, with the white dog in toe, he had slept on our balcony last night again. On the way to breakfast, we saw a Golden Tree Snake, also known as a Flying Snake. It certainly was very quick and made its way very fast across the grass and up a tree.

Since it was our last breakfast here, we had a bit of a feast. We both had the usual yoghurt and the toast basket. This time it had pineapple jam in it! Finally on the last meal here! It was very tasty, Syd said it was like marmalade, which I could kinda see. We had large glasses of juice today, Syd with apple and me with orange again. We also had fried rice each, and I had a thick noodle chicken dish too.

We both ordered sausages and ham for the doggos later. Syd also ordered some grilled tomatoes, not for the dogs, for herself, but she only ended up eating one. I think she was full of everything else! We made our way back to our room, the white dog got up when we left but didn't follow us back. The snake was gone too by the time we walked past where it had put itself in the tree.

Back at the room, we just chilled for a bit, it was quite a hot day today, so we didn't fancy getting burnt before our snorkelling trip. About an hour before pickup, we started to get ready and pack our suitcases. I called reception for them to pick up our luggage, while we walked down the beach to try to find the dogs to feed.

We could only see the brown one first, which was being stroked by another guest (I assume) who had arrived earlier in the day. I thought I saw the first white dog again but turned out it was just a bit of driftwood. We did see the second white dog, but he was nervous. Syd threw a sausage in his direction, but he ran off. We gave the rest to the brown dog; he had a feast!

I settled our bill at reception, and we got into our taxi to take us to the pier for our transfer back over to Phuket. He was a slow driver; I could have made it quicker on the ped! We stopped off at the drink shack, I had the same as yesterday, which the lady had already made for herself, so she gave me that one (it was just made and not drunk yet). Syd has the same but without the balls in it.

The driver didn't seem to know what pier he was going to, as when we stopped for the drinks, he was facing the way to the other pier. I let him know and he turned the car around towards the right pier. We arrived early still so it was all ok. We checked in for the ferry and sat enjoying our drinks. Syd had started reading her third book this trip. While we were waiting, we noticed a bird feeding on some food that had been left out for it, and a cat taking a nap in the shade from the pier construction.

Once on the boat, we were able to sit right at the back. The boat did pull around to the other pier anyways, but no one got on. They only brought on some boxes of cargo. The ride was only about half an hour back to Phuket. I text our taxi lady to meet us there. During the ride, we were taken to other stops before ours. It was beautiful seeing the mangrove trees growing in and along the water's edge.

Strangely when we arrived, there was a man from our hotel (Panphueree Residanf) holding a sign with my name on it. Oh dear... We went with our lady as she was there too. At the hotel, after a discussion, the receptionist took the price of the taxi off our room as we didn't use it. I felt kind of bad as I had forgotten that there was going to be a taxi transfer. It was nice to see our taxi lady again though.

Up in our room, we just dropped off the bags and went to see the pool. It's a nice pool and we had planned on using it once back from our snorkelling trip... The breakfast bar looked to be newly updated too, which we will be using once we are back. There was also a private residence, where locals were staying on the sixth floor. Outside the window of our room, we could see they were using the space for airport storage, things such as airport shuttle buses, the stairs to the planes and random bits of other pipework. It was interesting to see.

We went back down to our room and picked up my bag and the camera. Making the walk across to Mai Khoa Beach (the aeroplane beach), where the planes fly only meters away from the sand. This is because the beach turns into the runway. When we arrived on our plane here a few weeks earlier, Syd thought we were going to crash into the beach it was that close!

Initially, we walked towards the airport, but after speaking with a worker and a guard, we realised we'd have to walk out and around to get access to the beach. This was because the airport was fenced off all around, obviously. I had hoped there would have been a path we could walk to get to the beach. Not the case, not to worry, it was a nice walk along the sand.

At one point on the beach, the waves were so rough that they covered a whole stretch of sand. So, we had to time it in between the waves to run across this section. We slightly miss-timed it, well I managed to get across dry, but Syd got wet... She wasn't best pleased. She took her shoes off (they were on, like mine, because there was a bit of rubbish on the beach). Thankfully they were only her sliders, and I carried them for her anyways.

Once we got to the spot, we found a large driftwood log to sit on and watch the planes. Today they were taking off over the beach, and landing from the opposite side. Which is a shame as when they come to land on the beach side they are closer to the ground. Not to worry maybe we will get a bit of time to come back in the morning on the day we leave.

We sat here for about 40 minutes watching a few take-offs, and a few landings from the other side. It was quite something seeing them come directly towards us and stopping just in time! We started walking back, and thankfully on the way back, we timed the rough wave section perfectly. A bit further round the beach, near to where we got onto the beach, there were some kids playing in the water. It was a bit rough for my liking, but they looked like locals so probably used to it.

Getting hungry, we walked along back towards the hotel, as we had seen a few eateries on the way to the beach. We stopped at 7-11 to pick up a drink, encase where we ended up going didn't have a great drink selection. Ironically there wasn't the usual 7-11 selection at this one, but they did have 4 other flavours, we tried them and picked the one we liked the most. I think it was caramel, but who's to know really...

A bit further up the road, we found a spot that was the busiest restaurant that we had seen on this strip. We looked at the menu and the pad Thai price was 60 THB, which is a great price for Phuket. It had a kitchen at the front and seating at the back in an air-conned room. We went in and sat down. Again, we did order quite a feast... It seems to be the norm...

We shared a large bottle of water, chicken Thai green curry, prawn cakes (these ones were massive), minced pork with basil and chillies, fried chicken wings, and fried pork. I had a portion of sticky rice, and Syd had normal jasmine rice. I had ordered two portions of sticky rice, but she bought over two of the steamed jasmine rice. I explained again I wanted the sticky rice (there was a poster next to us with the sticky rice and mango, so I pointed to that and covered the mango part with my hand). The waitress only took my rice back and came back with one sticky rice. Syd wasn't too bothered about it though, so we just carried on.

Either way, we couldn't finish everything we ordered, which was a shame. It was tasty. The lady asked if we wanted to take it away with us, but since we are off early tomorrow morning for the snorkelling trip, we'd have no way of heating and eating it in time. I paid up, the lady had handed Syd the bill, ha an unlikely story! We both laughed and then walked back to the hotel around the corner.

We packed just my mini suitcase for this next sub-trip, as no point lugging all the suitcases. I've booked this room for the whole time we are away on the trip anyway. One to keep our luggage safe, and two in case the weather wasn't good we'd have a backup place to stay instead of going on the trip. With hotels so cheap here, it's really no difference, probably something like £20-30. In fact, after factoring in luggage storage costs at the airport, it would have been probably less than what it costs me to run our hot tub at home for a day...

Anyways, once we were all packed and sorted, we got into bed for an early night, ready for our early start in the morning. The plan is for the driver to pick us up at 6:30 am. I had phoned them earlier in the day to confirm, it was a bit of a painful conversation.

But we got there in the end. Let's see what happens in the morning ey!

TO TENT OR NOT TO TENT, THAT IS THE QUESTION...

SURIN ISLANDS | DAY 2

11th May 2022

https://twobritsinasia.com/to-tent-or-not-to-tent-that-is-the-question/

Unfortunately, I was unable to sleep very well last night. I assume the drink we had from 7-11 must have had caffeine in it. It was a big drink too. Oh well, I finally managed to get to sleep at about 1:30 / 2-ish. Syd was able to sleep through the whole night.

We woke up early at 5:30, not feeling completely rested, but still functioning. We got up and ready and made our way downstairs. We just had my smaller suitcase which we had packed up the night before ready for the trip ahead. Once we were downstairs the receptionist thought we were checking out. Syd told him no and explained that we were just off out for a trip but will be back in a few days.

We walked outside to find the taxi. Our driver arrived, walking towards us, at exactly the same time that we walked down the outside stairs - great timing. There were already a few other people in the van. We were the last pickup. I asked the driver if we could pop into 7-11, as I needed to top up my phone balance to allow me to purchase a new phone service. I had to do it this way around as I don't have a Thai bank account, Thai ID, or a Yellow House Card. But I can use phone credit instead to modify my plan. I can add extra credit to my phone with cash at the 7-11 registers. The driver also bought a few things for himself while we were there.

I used the pin code machine (card terminal) to enter my phone number, and then the amount I wanted. I only chucked 100 THB in. I gave the cashier my money and then walked back to the bus. Once I sat back down on the bus, I checked the online portal, and the credit was already on my account. From here I was able to then purchase the plan I wanted.

After some deliberation, I decided to get the data-only plan, 15MB speed but unlimited. There was a deal for 120 hours for 75 THB. 5 days of unlimited data for less than £2, can't go wrong. There were other data packages, like unlimited speed but it was capped at 30GB of data. This was about 300 THB for a week. I didn't need a week, but also, I didn't know if I would use more than 30GB, as I was using my laptop and Syd was using her phone off my phone's hotspot too. (The 15MB speed ended up being plenty, sometimes it was slow but overall fine).

It was a long drive to the pier, Namkhem Marina. The tour company we used was Sea Star Andaman, this was their own private pier. They are a fairly big tour company in and around Phuket. This pier itself wasn't in Phuket but in the next province directly north. The ride took about 2 hours, and we both snoozed for most of it.

When we arrived at the pier, there were lots of people already there. They were mostly Thai and surprisingly a lot of older people too, most actually. Syd and I both wondered how they would be snorkelling.

We proceeded to the check-in desks and were given two separate bands each. One blue one and a purple one. The blue represented the day tour on the Surin Island boat, and the purple was for those staying on the island. We also went to the equipment pickup station. Trying out flippers for us to use.

The lady at the flipper station took our suitcase to be placed on the boat. She let us take what we needed out of it first. As she said we wouldn't be able to get at it again till after lunch. So, we changed into our swimming stuff and packed away our other clothes.

While Syd was getting changed in the toilets, I noticed some beach shoes. I tried some on, there was a cheap pair for 200 THB, these were too flimsy though. The other type they had was 400 THB and had a more solid sole. I asked the lady to put these to the side as I would come back in with Syd to get her a pair too.

After trying a lot of different sizes on, Syd finally found a pair she liked the feel of. I tried to get a discount for buying two pairs at the same time. But the lady wasn't having any of it. Fair enough they were a good price anyway, I thought.

They had supplied us with toast and cakes for breakfast, along with some biscuits and juices. I had some jam on my toast too, but it was more jelly-like than jam. We had a bit of lemon cake and a chocolate brownie each. The lemon cake was about an inch cube with the brownie being an inch square but about half an inch deep. Tasty but scarcely a feast.

After we had eaten, the main tour lady started speaking in Thai to the group. Thankfully shortly after another lady tour guide said for those who need English come this way. So, we followed her. She explained some history about the islands and the boat gipsies that live there. She also explained what stops we would be making in the morning part of the trip.

After the introduction, we were then called back to the main day-tour group. We were shown onto the larger boat, there were a lot of boats that were there that day. We had our photo taken before we got onboard, they said it was for insurance purposes, but also mentioned we could buy them at the end of our trip. It could be needed for both, but I suspect it is really to try to get us to buy them later.

We sat right up at the front of the boat. The main tour guide, Latte, apologised to us that most of the tour will be delivered in Thai. But she would speak to us first in English before addressing the group, as Syd and I were the only English-speaking onboard. Latte joked with us about how the average age group today was mostly over 75!

It was about an hour and a half ride to our first stop. It was very windy being right at the front, but it was nice and soothing on our faces. We both had another nap, along with most others too! We were handed mouthpieces, snorkels, and towels. These snorkels were really good quality, better than the Phi Phi Island tour (which were fine too, but these were clearly higher quality), and much better than the ones we bought that we later had to return.

The tour guide spoke to us first then let us jump in while speaking to the rest of the group about where the best places were to snorkel at this stop. Syd had put on a life jacket again, as she had on the Phi Phi tour, to help her float. She didn't feel brave enough to try the flippers just yet. I put mine on and flopped straight in. The water was so clear. And warm! There were so many, many things to see, lots of different tropical fish and coral. So many colours, vibrant blues, and purples!

We saw lots of fish that looked like an electric rainbow of colours. Hard to describe, almost a metallic shine. We also saw an enormous purple starfish with big spikes on its arms. It was about the same size as my torso! We saw lots of sea urchins too. I enjoyed diving down with my flippers on to take a closer look. I was able to go down further as it was quicker with the help of the flippers on my feet.

It was amazing to see the different things attached to the coral, it was truly alive! We saw lots of clown fish too, hiding in their well-known home. As depicted in the children's movie Finding Nemo.

Syd decided to head back on the boat as she was getting thirsty. I joined shortly after for a wee stop. The onboard toilet was a big room but the toilet itself was tiny, about the size of a kid's potty. I had to almost lie down using the walls around me for leaning support to go. It was too low down for me to sit on, I think I'd have fallen over backwards!

We stood at the front of the boat for a bit, I had thought the guide said to be back on the boat by 11:20. But it was already 11:25, so I asked Latte what time we were going, and she said 11:40 now. So, I got back in the water, she said to me not to worry about how long I take as she could see I was a strong swimmer and could easily get back to the boat at a moment's notice. Syd stayed on the boat having some more to drink and took some photos of me. The water was so blue!

We noticed that the older people were getting dragged around with large floats, so that answered the question of how they would be able to snorkel. Latte called us back, so we all got on the boat ready for our next stop. It was only down the island slightly, on the way there our tour guide pointed out which the north and south islands were.

There were already two other boats at this next stop. They were all lined up and tied together. It made sense as it meant they could all be at this good spot without bumping into each other. They were all part of the same tour company we were with anyway.

There were even more breathtaking things to see here. Syd was in the water for quite some time at this stop. She had put her flippers on to help her move faster and in turn, see more. We were at this spot for a good 40 minutes. Syd was still using a life jacket to help her float, which caused her backside to rise above the water. Her bum was getting almost as red as her bikini! I said "Let's head in for some shade". We sat in front of the boat again, while we were drying off. We could see the fishes and corral from up there too.

Once everyone else was onboard, we stayed at the front, even while it was moving. The crew and tour guide didn't mind. They didn't even ask us to put our life jackets on this time, which they had asked everyone to do while the boat was moving before. This was freeing as they were hot and sweaty in this heat. We only went about five minutes, and then hopped off the speedboat to the line of six or so traditional Thai long-tail boats in the water. These long-tail boats then took us to the island, as the speedboats weren't allowed on the shoreline to protect the corral.

There were loads of people eating here, there was covered and outside seating. It was a buffet lunch and drinks, having to wear a plastic glove they gave us while dishing up. We got ourselves a plate of rice, fried chicken wings, and a bowl of chicken green Thai curry. I also had a bit of the mixed prawn and crab dish; Syd wasn't a big fan of this.

Before eating we dropped our bags off. Meeting our personal tour guide Anda, which was short for Andaman, the name of the sea we were in. After lunch, we took the bags to our tent. It was right on the shoreline, with a beautiful view out of the door. But Syd was not best pleased as there wasn't much of a bed... Well in truth it was just a folded-up bit of foam... And of course, it was hot in there since there was no air-conditioning. There were a lot of critters on the island, and the tent wasn't doing a very good job of preventing them from coming in.

I Asked Anda if a bungalow/lodge was available. He said he would go have an ask around and see. We met back up with him about half an hour later, he had good news that a bungalow was available. It had amazing views too, and air-con! We didn't move our stuff just yet as we were heading out for another snorkelling session. This time on the long tail boat, with only three others who were also staying on the island.

At the first spot Anda wanted to take us, the tide was too high to be able to see anything good enough. He didn't even want us to get in the water, as he wanted to wait for tomorrow to show us at low tide then, this way the corral would be closer and we could see them easier.

We then went to another spot. This was the best I'd ever seen. Anda then got out a big float for me and Syd and dragged us around. We were in the water for quite a while again. Anda and I kept diving down to get closer to the coral. Syd's bum was really very red now. The current was fairly strong, so we let it take us while looking at the coral and fish. The boat then went ahead and met us lower down where the tide took us. This saved us from having to swim back to the boat against the current.

Our next stop was the gipsy village. There were settlers who usually spend most of the year on the water in their boats. Then during monsoon season, come on land to their huts. They had a school, a market, and village huts where they lived while on the island. We weren't allowed where the living huts were due to Covid concerns. The young children had no nappies or any clothes on, it was interesting to see the cultural differences. There was a very old lady, she looked at least 100! She stood behind one of the stalls selling bracelets and necklaces, which they had made from the shells and dead corral.

We noticed that their teeth were very yellow, black, and rotten. I guess they don't have any toothpaste on the island, and I didn't see any cows so they can't be having much calcium in their diet. It was like we had gone back in time a few centuries! It was beautiful there though, with the rainforest in the background, in the mountains behind.

The guide took some photos of us, making it look like we were moving into the village. We saw a tiny kitten in one of the village huts. Anda then went searching in what looked to be a tip. It was well organised; I wonder how often it gets removed from the island. He came back with a nice-looking, black marble-style, buoy float. There was also lots of chicken walking around this island. And tons of ants!

We got back on the boat, the water was actually hot to stand in, hotter than a bath, it was very strange! They said that was normal here in this village because of how the cove traps the heat. When we got back to the main island, we moved our stuff into the bungalow.

The island doesn't have any mains electricity and only gets its power from petrol-powered generators. They only turned the generators on at 18:00 and turned them off the next morning at 8:00, the air-con was turned off two hours earlier though at 6 am.

When it hit 18:00 the air-con started working, which was much needed! However, the lights weren't working. Oh well, we were just happy to be in a cooler place with an actual bed, rather than in that tent/sauna. It wasn't that cold in the room, even with the air-con on, and the beds were hard. But it was masses above the alternative.

We had to use our phone torches to go to the loo. Putting one on the sink next to the toilet and hanging the second up on a rail. It worked all right, and we could make do for these two nights.

We cooled off as much as we could, before heading down for dinner. This wasn't a buffet like it had been earlier for lunch. Instead, Andaman brought us out a selection of plates he had chosen for us. We had a big bowl of steamed rice to share. A plate of thick cabbage leaves, with small fried shrimp in. A chilli octopus and squid spicy salad. Some sort of fish with red onion, ginger, and chilli reduction sauce on top. And a bowl of what I think was tuna soup. It was mostly nice; Syd wasn't the biggest fan of the cabbage or soup dishes though.

We both had a Lipton lemon iced tea and water each to drink. There was a lot of this iced tea and Pepsi on this tour, I think they said they are sponsored by Pepsi Co which makes sense to have all these drinks. While we were eating, the guide asked about what breakfast time and choices we wanted tomorrow. I went with the local choice of fried rice and fish. Syd asked for the American breakfast. We said we would be down for 8.

Back in the bungalow, since it was fully dark now, we couldn't do much. I replied to a few messages, I was speaking with Lawrence about the Crypto crash that was going on. (It became one of the worst crashes in crypto history to date).

WLUNA, in the top 5, possibly top 3 crypto coins, lost 80% value in a matter of hours (dropped 99.99 total in the space of the following week). And with the stablecoin UST being de-pegged from the dollar, things were really bad. After speaking with Lawrence, and licking our heavy loss wounds, I went to bed. Syd had already fallen asleep.

MONSOON SEASON

SURIN ISLANDS | DAY 3

12th May 2022

https://twobritsinasia.com/monsoon-season/

I struggled to fall asleep again last night. Maybe it was thanks to all the lemon-sugar drinks yesterday. There was a cockroach in our toilet at 1 am this morning, I didn't fancy trying to move it with no lights working. It was gone in the morning though.

Once we both woke up at around 7:30, it was raining outside. But hot in the bungalow. The air-con had turned itself off, so I switched the breaker, as there was a poster that said when it was morning it needs to be on the other setting. The lights turned on, and the fan above our head turned on too. But no air-con. Well, at least we could see now... It was boiling in the room; I'd hate to think how hot it would have been in that tent.

We could see out our balcony window that a few tents had blown down in the storm last night. The one we were going to be in was still standing. But we were glad to be in the bungalow. The mobile service was non-existent this morning, which I think was due to bad weather conditions.

Down at breakfast, we had the meals that we had ordered last night. Syd's American breakfast had two chicken sausages, a slice of ham, a poached egg, and three slices of bread (which Syd toasted on the BBQ provided). Making herself a club sandwich with everything she had. She also had a few slices of tomato which went in. These were placed on some marijuana-looking leaves. She didn't have those as we weren't sure if they were just rocket or otherwise...

I had fried rice, which was a massive portion, with a fried egg on top. The meat of choice was fish, which was the first time I'd had fish fried rice. It was very tasty, and the fish was clearly very fresh. Very meaty and moist.

Halfway through eating breakfast, the lights turned off. So, it looks as if even the restaurant is on the same power generator. The rain had eased slightly while we were eating, so we decided to go for a walk along the beach to see the other tents. It only seems a few had blown over, and they all looked empty. Which is a relief.

We then saw a sign for a tsunami escape point, and following it, we walked up the side of the mountain (well, a hill) to see where it led. It just seemed to be some more bungalows higher up. The guide had said to be back down for 9:20 ready to go snorkelling. But once we were back in our room, the heavens opened again.

At 9:20 we walked down to the meeting point. Our guide wasn't there yet but we just sat and waited. There hadn't been any phone signal since about 7:15 this morning, or at least that's when my notifications stopped. I tried turning my phone off and on and flicking airplane mode on and off too. But no luck. I tried to use Syd's new gold earring to pop the SIM card, but it felt as if the gold would bend as it's quite a soft metal. I also tried the clasp from one of her bracelets, but that was too big.

I asked the shop if they had any paper clips, but they didn't seem to know what I meant. One worker thought I meant a mushroom...? We managed to understand each other, and they gave me a crocodile clip, which I took one of the arms off to see if that would fit. Unfortunately, that was too big too! I gave the clip back to the shop; they must have seen what I was trying to do as they had straightened out a stapler staple for me. That worked perfectly! I kept this in the back of my phone case for future use!

Unfortunately, even after taking my SIM card out, blowing down the hole, and cleaning the card. Still no signal. At this point

Anda had turned up, apologising for the delay but he was trying to find the other three people. The two girls had not come down to breakfast, as they were sleeping. He said he was told they'd meet us here and go without food. But they didn't turn up.

Just as we were leaving, he spotted the group, running over to them. He returned empty-handed, saying the girls decided they didn't want to go out in the rain. Which is fair enough. So off we went, alone. The first part of the ride was smooth, wet, but smooth. However, once we'd left the protection of the island, the next bit of land was over 2,000 km away, India. The sea was rather choppy, as there was no land around us to break the waves, especially in a little long-tail boat.

Once we got to the snorkelling spot the rain had eased up a little. No sun and there was mist over the trees on the shoreline. But the water was still clear enough. We got our flippers on, cleaned our goggles with some shampoo, and then jumped in. The reason for using shampoo is to reduce the goggles from steaming up. At first, Syd was a bit spooked as it was rougher than the other days. But once I'd calmed her down, she was enjoying it.

The tour guide jumped in; he didn't have the large floaty today to drag us along though. I went solo and he used another life jacket (as well as the one Syd was wearing again) as a float to pull her along. The water was very clear, even though the corral was a good 5-10 meters below us. Anda and I kept diving down and taking a closer look, Syd was too worried to try that.

There were lots of different shades of blue coral here, it was very pretty. There was also a massive table coral, which this part of the bay is well known for. I even spotted a white/grey-ish octopus hiding out in a cave under one of the table corals. It was quite large; I called the tour guide over and he looked too. He said, "Great spot."

The rain had picked up a bit again, so we decided to make our way back to the boat. On the way back it really hammered it down. It's funny as it was so much warmer in the sea than out of it. And even stranger, the further down, and closer to the coral I got, the warmer it was. I suppose it trapped the heat and was radiating it off. Syd found it funny feeling the raindrops on her bum as she was swimming along.

Back on the boat, we wrapped ourselves up in the towels to dry off, but mainly to keep warm. We also had some water again, they were in cups with a plastic cover over the top, but there were no straws. The guide showed us a cool trick on how to open them. You need to slightly squeeze the cup, and then slap the top film lid quickly. Doing this cause a shockwave in the cup and the pressure pushes back on the underside of the lid and opens it up for you.

The captain pulled up to our beach, instead of making us walk the long way around from the main landing zone. Which was nice of him. Anda gave me his phone number to call him later if we wanted to head back out. We then walked up the beach, where thousands of large mosquitos were swarming, because this weather brings them out. We walked briskly to our room, one to get out of the rain, and two, so we didn't get bitten to death by the swarms. I think we made it out all right with only a few bites.

We chilled in the room for a bit. I had opened the balcony doors and put across the mozzy door sliders, to let the air in, but keep the critters out. At this point, all-electric was off. No air-con or even fan! We both ended up having a bit of an unexpected nap.

By the time we woke up, the phone service was working again. After replying to messages, and checking the more crypto crash damage, we walked down for some lunch.

The day groupers were already there, they had some music playing that I heard from the room, but it was turned off by the time we got there. It was a buffet lunch again. Everything is the same as yesterday, other than the curry dish. Today it was a take on Massaman, with peanuts in. It was very nice.

It was still raining, and the undercover part was full of the day tourers. Our guide took us to a separate part which was right next to the sea. There were information cards on the different sea life and corral around the room which we read. We had seen most of the things depicted on the poster while we had been out there the last couple of days.

Back at the room, we rested a bit more, no nap this time but just relaxing as it was too rainy for anything else. A little later it had calmed down, so we walked down to try to find Anda and head out again. I had tried calling him but unfortunately, the package I've bought for this final week seems to only allow data, no calls.

When we got down to the main area, it seemed he had already gone out with the other three somewhere, as all the boats were gone. Not to worry we went snorkelling off the beach instead. The whole island was basically empty. It was quite strange. Like back in Koh Yao Yai.

There was a lifeguard shack, with a lifeguard, but he was sleeping in his hammock. There was a life jacket under the hut which

I washed off for Syd. I'm glad I did as the undercurrent here was actually quite strong. The flippers helped combat it though!

Unfortunately, there wasn't much to see here. Other than a few fish that were guarding different holes on the floor. I watched them for a bit, in the holes were little rainbow lobsters. It was a great bit of teamwork. Seemed the fish kept a lookout, as when I got closer, they would put themselves in the hole to stop the baby lobster from coming out. And the baby lobster was digging them a home. I saw one about three inches and it had two fish guarding the hole. The others were all about an inch and only one guard.

It had started raining again so we made our way back to our room. Again, more chilling, but it has started to get dark, so we played a few quizzes on my phone until dinner. Before we headed down the electricity came on, so the room started to cool down with the air-con. But saying that, the room had been a lot cooler today thanks to having the balcony doors open with the mesh slider across.

The rain was the heaviest we had seen as we made our way across to dinner. Syd was even worried to be walking in it as the drops were so big! We made it across without an issue though. There wasn't any sign of our tour guide, nor the three others. But a few more groups had turned up today and were sitting eating.

For dinner, we had large, steamed rice to share again, a fish omelette, some type of grilled fish, a fish curry, and a prawn and octopus salad. There really is a lot of seafood on these smaller islands, as it's all self-sourced. We also had a big portion of water-melon between us.

Once we had finished and the rain died down, we made our way back to our room. We noticed every other bungalow had its lights on. Strange, so it wasn't just a morning thing... I switched around the switch to the morning position (which the lights worked for this morning) but nothing. I then put it in the night position. The fan started to spin briefly. I pulled down harder on the breaker and then the lights turned on! The breaker must just be old and needed more oomph.

I couldn't believe it! We'd spent yesterday in the dark!! Oh well, at least we had some lights now! We lay down in bed; I was going through messages and Syd was scrolling through Instagram reels. Once we were finished with that we decided to head to sleep. Looking forward to a hot powerful shower tomorrow at our hotel in Phuket!

SLIP 'N' SICK, FRIDAY 13TH AND BROKEN BONES?!

SURIN ISLANDS | DAY 4

13th May 2022

https://twobritsinasia.com/slip-n-sick-friday-13th-and-broken-bones/

I woke up fair early this morning, not feeling great at all. I went for my morning wee but really things were not good. I got back in bed but had to get up again up shortly after to go for something more serious. Once I was finished, I got back in bed and tried to sleep a bit more. The air-con was off, so I turned on the big fan.

A few hours later things weren't getting any better. I sat up, saying "not good" and then went back to the toilet to be sick. I'm very rarely sick, I think Syd said this is only the 3rd time she's ever seen me sick. To be honest, I'm surprised it's that many.

I got back in bed, but I was still feeling rough. Not sure why, it might be to do with all the fish and the questionable cooking and storing methods. As this food isn't piping hot when it's served. But we don't have much choice but to eat it. As there is nothing else on the island.

We decided not to go down for breakfast as I couldn't really move. As any movement made me want to be sick again. I took small sips of my water and drifted in and out of sleep as much as I could to reduce the sick feeling. Syd packed up the room for me and then we made it downstairs.

Our guide was waiting for us, he had kept our breakfast out, but we said we didn't want it. We sat and waited for our boat which left about an hour later. We could have waited on the island for the larger boat to take us back, but they would have stopped off on snorkelling spots, which I wasn't feeling up to. Neither was Syd really. While we were sat down there I distracted myself by playing with Pinarello My Way customization colours. This Dogma F is my dream bike and I really want to get one. But they are just so expensive, around the same price as Syd's car!

I had to pay an extra 4,000 for the bungalow which I didn't know about, but either way, it was worth every bit of that. I would have hated to be in the tent during the storm and feeling so rough today. Unfortunately, it was cash only on the island, and I didn't have enough cash on me. They let me pay when we got to the other side with the card machine though.

I decided to take a sea sickness pill before getting on the boat back. Syd had a bit of food before boarding, just some rice. Before getting on the long tail boat to take us to our speed boat, I gave our guide a 500 THB tip for being so helpful. He was shocked and said he would find me some change. I said that won't be necessary. He threw his hands in the air and said a big thank you to the sky!

The speedboat ride back was choppy, we were sailing through the storm. It was only us and the other three who stayed on the island over the same period as us. I slept basically the whole way back. Syd had a bit of a snooze too. One of the girls in the three-person group was sick a few times on the boat. I didn't see it the first time as I was sleeping, but Syd said the crew were holding her up.

Back on the mainland, we bought the two photos they had taken of us before getting on the boat a few days ago. They were framed nicely. We will give one as a gift to my Nan and keep the other. The rain had died off a little thankfully.

Since I hadn't eaten anything all day, I was a little hungry. I got myself a plate of snacks and some orange juice for us both. Once I finished my first plate I headed back for some more. The lady said they had noodles too, so I got some of those, they were served on small plates, so I got two. She also gave me some fresh fried battered chicken wings, which were nice and hot.

I ate these up, she also brought over some BBQ chicken skewers, I wasn't a big fan of these though. They had a weird surface texture to them. After eating I had another lie-down and snooze, while we waited for the other boats to bring those who had been snorkelling, as we had a shared taxi with them. I had tried looking at Grab, to see how much a private taxi would cost back to Phuket, but they didn't have Grab in this area.

The boats started to arrive back. It was very wet now. We were only a few meters from the sea, but you couldn't see it through the rain curtain! It was quite something honestly. I'm glad we got the earlier boat back, as it was much rougher now than when we left, and even that had been rough enough.

Syd decided to get some food now too, she had some noodles and chicken wings. She also had a plate of papaya salad, thinking they were other types of noodles. She didn't fancy them, so she went and got ice cream instead, which she'd been seeing people with. She's wanted ice cream for a few days now but couldn't figure out where they were getting them from. She was able to find them on this pier. She enjoyed it, even though it was coconut, which she wasn't a fan of when we were seeing the White Temple. A cat jumped up onto the table once Syd had finished eating, looking for the scraps.

We were both in and out of sleep on the taxi ride home. By the time we got back, we didn't feel like going out to eat, so we were going to have showers before ordering some grab food.

Syd washed off her feet in the shower with the jet gun, not drying her feet properly... With her wet feet, still feeling like she was on the boat, tiredness, and the step outside to get out of the toilet was all too much for her...

She hit the deck. I rushed over, instantly seeing she was in a lot of pain. She was grabbing onto her arm, trying to fight back the tears. She was drifting in and out of conciseness while I was keeping her sitting up. I eventually managed to get her over to the bed to lie her down. The pain wasn't easing, I told her to take off her rings and bracelets in case her arm and fingers started to swell, so she did.

I looked online to see the closest private hospital. Bangkok Hospital Phuket wasn't the closest, but it was the best-rated, and only about half an hour away. Syd started getting a little teary now with the initial adrenaline wearing off. I tried calling them from my phone, but I remembered I've only got data on my phone now, not calls. I tried using the room phone, but it wouldn't let me call externally. It just put me through to reception. The receptionist didn't seem to know what I was asking, it was the night staff... She was thinking I was talking about Wi-Fi problems or something...?

I rushed downstairs to ask if I could use the reception phone. That phone can't call externally either. So, the lady phoned her boss to help try to translate. The lady at reception then came up to the room with me. Phoning Bangkok Hospital Phuket on the way up. She spoke with them on the phone first, then handed the phone over to me.

I explained to them what had happened, they said if she can walk to get a taxi as the ambulance would cost me a lot of money and take longer. It would have been about £80 which isn't masses, but a taxi there would cost about £3. I got the lady to phone a taxi for us. I had texted our taxi lady, but she was 50 minutes away. The taxi that the hotel had arranged arrived within minutes.

Halfway through the drive, he stopped off at a petrol station, where a worker tended to him. Quite interesting, it would be cool to have that back in England, to save us from getting out of the car. Anyways, back on with the drive. We arrived at the hospital, met at the door by a porter who asked what had happened, so I explained.

Then to check-in. I had picked up our passports before leaving as I thought they might ask for them, which they did. This check-in lady then asked again what had happened, so I explained. She asked if we had international insurance, which we did. She asked if I had a claim code, I said it only just happened, so I haven't even contacted them yet.

We were shown to some seats, where I filled out a form with Syd's details. Another lady came over who was from the international team. Also asking about what had happened and insurance. I explained again. She asked if I could send her the insurance policy, which I did.

Next, we went into the triage room. Yet again explaining what had happened. She then showed us to a doctor's room. Which, yes you guessed it, having to explain again. The doc then examined Syd, but this caused Syd to have a few tears as it was hurting her.

The doc ordered an X-ray for Syd. We were shown to the imaging department. The staff here took Syd into the X-ray room while I had to wait outside. The international team's lady found me again. She said the email didn't turn up, so she took photos of it off my phone instead.

Once Syd was done with the X-ray, we went back to the main area waiting to see the results. When we walked into the doc's room again, I could see the scans on the screen. I was relieved to see no easily visible breaks. And the doc confirmed this with her saying there were no breaks at all. Meaning it was either muscle, ligament, or something less serious.

While we sat waiting again for the next doctor, the first doc came over and said she thinks she might have seen a break on the elbow. This made Syd start to cry again. I couldn't see anything on the scan, but we were going to wait for the specialist anyways. The doc had asked if they could put Syd on injected painkillers to help ease the pain instantly, but Syd was scared and decided against that.

Syd later told me she worried about the cleanliness of the needles, as she had heard bad things about hospitals abroad before. This wasn't the case for this hospital, it was a very well-regarded private hospital, very clean, and very well-organized. We never had to be sat around waiting for any more than a few minutes at a time. Syd also mentioned she was worried about how much it would all cost, and with already seeing multiple doctors and having the X-ray imaging she felt bad about how much it would be. I don't know why she was feeling that money is never an issue when it comes to health or well-being. She agreed she knew this but was just worried in the moment with everything going on.

Anyway, once they had brought over the specialist, he looked at Syd and the scan. Confirming there wasn't a break. Which was great news. Asking for the final time what had happened again.

He was able to examine Syd's movement more than the first doc. I think Syd was more comfortable moving her arm now she knew it wasn't broken.

He dressed Syd's arm up with a temporary half-cast, which will last a week. It did go hard so it kept Syd's arm in the right position. They also gave her a sling too. The doc proscribed some medication which we picked up after paying. Syd was still worried about how much it would cost. Causing her to tear up again.

The international lady had said that since we weren't able to get hold of our insurance that I can pay and then get it claimed back after. I had tried to get on our insurance's web chat, but it was travel related only. The international lady had also said we could wait to hear back from them to cover it, but that can either be a few hours or in some cases a few weeks. I wasn't going to wait here for a few weeks! That's ridiculous.

It was 16,000 THB so about £400. Which was a lot less than I'd thought it would be. So, depending on what the insurance excess is, I might just take the hit. We got a CD with contained the X-ray scans. I looked forward to loading those up later to look at when we got back home! Battle trophy!

I had been in contact with our taxi lady all evening. She drove us back to our hotel, arriving just before midnight. She said she thought we'd already left. We said our goodbyes and headed up to our room.

I had a shower, showing Syd how to safely exit the bathroom. A bit of a cruel joke, but it made her smirk. I helped her undress, and we went to bed.

THE NAMES BOND, JAMES BOND

SURIN ISLANDS | DAY 5

14th May 2022

https://twobritsinasia.com/the-names-bond-james-bond/

We woke early to our alarms this morning. Syd was in a little bit of pain so we headed upstairs for breakfast so that she could take some of her tablets with food. We took our bag up to breakfast with us so we could head straight down to the lobby after, ready for our taxi.

Breakfast was 150 THB each, I had some fried rice and some noodles. I also had this strange purple drink. It was refreshing but I'm not sure if I liked the taste. Syd had some toast but could only manage one slice. She had her tablets though which was the main thing, she didn't risk any of the purple drink, she just stuck with water.

After breakfast, we made our way downstairs to the hotel lobby, noticing the cool design of the interior blinds. They were like traditional Venetian shutters you would see lining the streets of Italy. The taxi arrived shortly after. Again, there were already others in it and three others, who were in the hotel lobby, joined us too. It was only about half an hour's drive to the Royal Marina, but I slept most of it as it was a late night last night with the early start today. Syd said she stayed awake on the drive-over.

At the pier, they did not have any breakfast available. Not to worry, we got some orange juice, and I went to the loo again, still not feeling 100% and unfortunately still not solid yet... It looked to be a sunny day today, which is good timing as the last week has been quite stormy.

We were given the introductory talk, by our guide Coco. He was very funny. We then waited about 15 minutes before boarding the boat. While waiting Coco came over and asked how many kayaks we wanted. I said one as then Syd could just sit behind me while I row. There are jet skis later today too which I had wanted to do with Syd. But after last night's debacle, this didn't seem likely. Not to worry.

On the boat, we sat at the back to reduce any movements, so it was not as sharp for Syd. It was a full boat, so it weighted the boat down, this with the smooth water conditions made for a nice ride. Which was convenient.

The first stop was passing along the cliffs of Phang Nga. The boat didn't stop, but the captain went really slowly. The crew dotted around the boat, to take pictures of the beautiful cliff background for us. We had some photos of us at the back and front of the boat.

Unfortunately, we had some right tools onboard. Not listening to the crew, talking over them, and not putting out their cigarettes when asked. Everyone else on the boat was getting quite tired of them, t we just tried to ignore them. Annoyingly one of them was sitting right next to me.

Next, we continued up the Strait of Malacca, where we stopped off at a cluster of islands (mainly known as Hong Island, which was part of this collection). Here the boat stopped, and we got on an inflatable kayak. There was a guy at the back that was paddling for us, which I'm glad about! He took us around the islands, showing us different sights.

Syd spotted two tiny blue eel-looking things. I didn't see it originally but saw the second one she spotted. We also saw a mushroom-looking jellyfish. The guide pointed out things in the rocks that looked like all sorts of things. Such as a massive turtle, a Buddha, heart shapes, and a Scooby Doo (which looked as if it was placed there, to be honest).

I had taken my top off and put it over Syd's shoulders to save her from burning, as we had forgotten to put our sun cream on this morning. The boat staff were helpful in getting Syd on and off the boat, being careful of her arm. One crew member wasn't too careful, he was trying but was holding Syd's bad arm.

Back on the boat we then made it to the all-so-famous James Bond Island. Or known by the locals as Khao Tapu. No one can actually get onto James Bond Island itself, you land on Ko Tapu, which is where the famous photos are taken. The James Bond film, The Man with The Golden Gun, had parts filmed here. Hence the name.

Once we arrived on the island, the crew had golden gun props and took many different photos of us with them. There were a few different photo spots, which we took advantage of. There were also stalls along the beach selling all sorts of items. A lot of pearls, and relatively cheap too, I'm not sure if they were real or not. They did put fire to it, and it didn't make a mark, but I have no idea if that actually means anything.

Further around the island, we saw a stall selling a fishbone necklace. It was in the shape of a massive tooth with a tiger sitting on the top. The lady seller originally said 850 THB, but I managed to get her down to 100. That's my biggest reduction yet! I put it on, after watching so many of the Pirates of The Caribbean movies recently, I pretended to be Captain Jack Sparrow. It made Syd laugh.

We got an ice cream each and sat in some shade enjoying them. After resting up here sat looking at the rock, we made our way back to the boat. Both of us lost a flip-flop when getting on the boat. Thankfully one of the crew members jumped off and picked them up for us. They were the hotel flip-flops so I'm glad we didn't lose them.

From here we headed to the floating island. 100% of the residents here are Muslim. They originally came from Indonesia. There is electricity on the island, however, they are unable to make fresh water for some reason. They did have a floating football pitch, as well as a school and mosque. Before we arrived, we did a circuit around the island, stopping at a cave with what looked like to have cave-man drawings within.

We docked at a restaurant called Sunny Seafood Restaurant. They had a buffet laid out ready for us, it had a fire under the trays to keep them hot, so I was happy with eating there. We both had some vegetable fried rice, pad Thai (which was made with linguine pasta), it was also meat free which is different, and a side of fried onion rings. I also had a sweet and sour dish which had some sort of sausage in it, some prawn balls, and a chicken drumstick and thigh. A strange collection.

Back at the table, we sat with three others, a couple, and their adult son. They were from Hungry I think, based on what little I could pick up. But I am probably miles off. They were friendly though. While eating we could see the other boats go past, some had a really high slash-back. It was beautiful with the mangrove forest behind the water, and behind that more limestone sheer-drop mountains with trees on. Truly an idyllic paradise.

Once we finished our lunch, we had about an hour of exploring the village. We made our way to the floating football pitch, where a game was just coming to an end. There were young girls selling stuff in their baskets. It seemed most of the island was tourist shops, with housing behind and above the shops. We could see right through some of the houses, they were quite big and had amazing views. I'm not sure I'd like to live here though, as I could imagine it getting fairly boring quite quickly.

Syd had noticed that no one had any sofas in the houses. I did see some wooden benches and a house with a TV. They were watching cartoons. Once back at the boat, we had some more water and sat at the front, waiting for the others to get on.

We then made our way to Khai Nai Island, which was opposite the GLOW Elixir Resort we stayed in on Koh Yao Yai island just under a week prior. On the way there after a big lunch, and not much sleep from last night's hospital antics, I had a bit of a snooze. It was about an hour to the island so I thought it best to use the time wisely while I could.

We were on this island for about two hours. The tour company had a stand here which had free drinks, snacks, and fruit. From here we found two lounge chairs, which cost 150 THB. I thought it a little cheeky as there was nowhere else to sit other than the sand and we didn't have towels.

Oh well, it's not a lot of money really, and it gave us shade. We had to keep moving the chairs though as the sun was going down. There were people snorkelling. I didn't fancy it since we would be off tomorrow morning to fly to Singapore and would have had to deal with packing wet trunks. Also, the tide was quite far out so the corral was at hip height, and I didn't want a sea urchin sticking its thorns in me.

Syd just sat on the lounge chair reading her book, while I kept going to and from the drinks stand to keep us hydrated. I also took some photos of around the island; it was only small so didn't take long. We saw a shell crab walking along the beach which I also took some photos of it looked quite cute.

By the time it reached 17:00, there were a lot of speed boats on the island. We left back to our pier in Phuket. The ride back was only short, about 20 minutes. On the way, the captain made a sharp turn, and we all wondered why as the pier was dead ahead. We then saw a jet-ski had been moored up out in the bay, but no driver could be seen. The captain was looking to see if the driver had been thrown off, but thankfully no one was in the water, and we carried on back to the pier.

Our taxi was waiting for us right at the entrance of the pier. We got on and waited for a few others to finish their tours. We weren't waiting long, maybe 10 minutes. The ride back to our hotel felt longer than the ride this morning, but then again, I was asleep during the ride this morning so I can't really judge.

Once back at the hotel, we asked reception if they had any bin liners and tape. We wanted to wrap up Syd's arm to save it from getting wet in the shower. They found some for us, and we went up to our room. I put them on Syd, testing the tape on my skin first to make sure it wasn't painful once it was to be taken off, it wasn't.

I gave Syd a shower, washed her hair too, and shaved her armpits. She got out and then I washed myself. Thankfully the plastic bags did their job, and Syd's arm was all nice and dry. Syd felt better now she was clean. She smelt better too... I then did the monthly accounts. Not good. With most of the stock market having a hissy fit, crypto markets having one of the biggest crashes to date and spending 5 figures on this trip. Oh well, I can always make more.

I ordered us some grab food. It didn't take long to arrive and was under a fiver for what would be considered a large takeaway at home, costing probably £40-50. We had a portion of minced chili pork with Thai basil, which came with steamed rice and a fried egg. Some fried, what I think was pork, it was tasty and came with some steamed rice. A portion of chicken and prawn pad Thai, with thick noodles and pork crackling. There was also another pot of steamed rice and a pot of chili sauce. It was all very tasty and had a good spice level too.

We then lay in bed for a bit, before heading to sleep.

COUNTRY HOPPING

SINGAPORE | DAY 1

15th May 2022

https://twobritsinasia.com/country-hopping/

We woke up at about 8 am in Thailand, well Syd had a bit of a lie-in while I got up and ready. Her arm was less painful today and had more movement in her fingers. I still wasn't feeling great though. I packed up for us both as Syd couldn't do anything.

Syd didn't fancy breakfast at the hotel, so I thought we could have it at the airport. This way it would pass the time while we were waiting for take-off. After packing, we walked down to reception, I managed to take all four suitcases myself. We sat in the lobby waiting for our taxi to arrive to take us to the airport.

At the airport, I grabbed a suitcase trolly to help me move all the cases about. We eventually found our check-in desk; it wasn't very well signposted for any flight provider. Chatting to an older couple behind us, who were heading back to their home in New Zealand, using Singapore as a stop-over. I dropped the two large bags off on the conveyor belt. Slightly worried they might be over the limit as they were both close to the 20kg limit when I weighed them myself this morning. Thankfully they were both under.

The rest of the process was quick. The security even let us take a bottle of water through bag check as they could see Syd needed it for her medication. That was nice of them and saved us from having to pay stupid prices for a bottled drink either at the airport or on the plane.

We first walked around downstairs to look for some food, but they were all quite expensive. Even for UK prices. Next, we ventured upstairs where the sign for food was, however, all the vendors were closed! There were two lounges up there though. The first was for Singapore airlines only and the other was a pay-to-use. It was 2,000 THB for the both of us, I checked to see what food they had. It was only standard fried rice which I thought was a bit cheeky for the price, as the seats weren't much better either.

After deciding to go back downstairs, we walked along a bit more and found a Subway. We carried on looking to see if there was anything else, but nothing took our fancy. So, we walked back to Subway. I had a spicy Italian with chicken and extra cheese. Syd had smoked chicken. We shared a cup of 7-up.

It's funny after about 6 weeks in Thailand we haven't had any food we could have easily had in England. And now within the final hours, here we are... it was quite expensive though, at 907 THB (about £20), it wouldn't be that much even in England! Oh well, we enjoyed it, and I had some leftover cash so basically a free meal anyway as I wouldn't have bothered to exchange that small amount of cash back for GBP in England. I might not have even been able to.

I unwrapped Syd's sub for her and then squashed it, so it was easier for her to pick it up with one hand. She was able to eat it without any help. We both enjoyed our meals, Syd said hers wasn't very smoky though. Over near a pillar, I found a plug socket, so I decided to charge my phone. Syd had some more of her tablets while I went to the loo.

We stood watching the planes come in and out while watching the suitcases getting loaded onto our plane. We saw our pink one making its way up the ramp, but not the red one. Oh no... Maybe there was another trolly. Either way, we showed the boarding lady our pass, and she said oh you need to come with me. Brilliant...

We followed her down past everyone else waiting in line, through the security doors, and down the hallway. Only one of us could go through the second set of security doors, and since Syd was less than fully operational, I followed the lady down through them. I could see my red suitcase on the side next to the plane with four security guards around it. Ooopsie. They asked me to open it, which I did...

They didn't seem mad, so I wasn't too worried. They pointed out my power banks and said I needed to take them on board with me. They handed me a piece of paper and that was that. I apologised and went back upstairs to Syd. The couple from earlier asked if I got told off, I laughed and said no, and explained what had happened.

We then got on the plane and got ready for take-off. Yet again we had a screaming child sitting right behind us. The plane took off basically on time, even with my delays... Thankfully the crying kid stopped once we were in the air. Syd had a little snooze on the ride over too. I pretended to sleep next to her and take a photo of us both "sleeping".

As we were coming into land, we could see loads of cargo boats in the sea. There must have been over a hundred total, which is quite something as they're huge! We could also see the other runway, only about 500 meters parallel to the one we were landing on. It was strange seeing it; made us think the pilot had miss-aligned the landing.

Saying this, I do think he had come into landing a little late, as we were still quite high up when our actual runway started. And once we landed the engines were really really loud, I'm assuming put into reverse or something to help slow us down. It was sharp braking we were pulled forwards in our seats. You could see everyone jammed their legs out in front of them to hold themselves up.

We then taxied to the gate and then got off the plane. They didn't do it row by row like they had done when we travelled around Thailand. I quite liked the row-by-row system, it emptied the plane quicker, as people weren't rushing and pushing about. There's a lesson to be learned there somewhere...

The border security didn't have much of a line, but we did have to go one by one to the booths. So Syd and I ended up at different booths at the same time. A bit silly as she couldn't really hold her passport as her hands were full of her hat and water bottle. I placed it in between her fingers and thumb on her bad arm. They needed finger scans, but Syd was only able to do one hand as she couldn't get her arm high enough. From Syd's account, the border security was okay with this though and was helpful and understanding.

On the way walking to pick up our bags, I connected to the airport Wi-Fi and tried ordering a Grab. Since my Thai SIM card didn't work here, I had to keep within the building to keep the internet, but it was hard for the GPS to know exactly what part of the building we were in. This made it difficult to give a pickup location for the driver to meet us.

It was initially confusing about where to meet the drivers. There were signs for taxi pickup, guest pickup, or car service pickup (which Grab falls under). They all went down different stairs and escalators. But all ended up in the same place. We got a bit frustrated trying to find where we needed to be.

Once I got the hang of it, it was okay. And, once I had cooled down from my huff, I realized the airport was beautiful. It was basically like a mall, with an airport as a feature in it. There were amazing gardens with awesome plant arrangements, and of course, the famous massive circular inward waterfall, which was stunning.

The first driver cancelled for some reason, and the second driver also cancelled, but I got charged the second time. I'm not sure why. The third time lucky, we got in the car, and he drove us to our hotel, Naumi, which is right in the city centre.

Once we arrived and checked in, we went up to our room. I got the wrong room originally, and when I tried the door, it did open, but someone was already lying on the bed. I apologised and closed the door. Realising that was the room next to ours. I'm not sure how the door opened, so I tried the door opposite ours without using my card. That door opened too! I didn't open it all the way just a little to test. Strange... I tried our door before unlocking it and it was locked.

In the room, I made sure we kept our deadbolt across like I usually do anyway. We rested for a bit. I saw some snacks and drinks around the room. But no price charts anywhere, so I called reception to ask as I didn't want to get stung, they said they were free which is great. We had a drink then headed out to try and find me a SIM card.

We walked down the road looking for the 7-11 the receptionist told us about. We couldn't see it, so I popped into another shop to ask for directions. They pointed us down the road, so we kept walking. It was about a two-minute walk and then we spotted it on the corner.

Inside we found that they did have a SIM card, but the worker didn't seem to know what it offered. So, I decided to go to the mall to find a shop specializing in SIM cards. We searched around the mall for a while, before finding one near the entrance where we came in. Only a different direction from where we had gone. Oh well.

The lady at the shop door said I needed my passport to buy one, so we made our way back to our hotel to pick up my passport. By the time we got back to the shop after picking up my passport, it was getting close to dinner time. After buying the SIM card, we made our way upstairs where we had spotted some restaurants earlier.

Most of them were cook-it-yourself type. We do want to try these, but with still not feeling 100%, I didn't want to spend all that money now and not be able to enjoy it. There were a few places up there that offered off-the-menu items, but these eateries were full and had long waiting times.

We left the mall to walk along the street to see what else was available outside. Again, most of them were cook it yourself. We walked past our hotel as there were a few places on the same street. But these all seemed to be mainly up-scale cocktail bars, with very few actual food options. They looked very fancy, but just not what we were after.

Back at the mall, we saw a ramen bar. We decided to go here. On their menu, you could order just the ramen for one price, or buy it as part of a meal deal. A bowl of ramen, a drink, and a side depending on what ramen bowl you had depended on the price. It wasn't too expensive relative to Singapore prices, but it was a shock to the system after the cheapness of Thailand!

Syd had a bowl with pork slices in it, and I had a bowl with a bit of roast pork, some thinner shredded pork, and the same type of pork slices as Syd. Both our bowls came with a boiled egg. We shared the sides; they were a fried breaded chicken cutlet and some crispy gyozas.

For drinks, I had a cold green tea and Syd had a cold lemon tea. All together including tip and tax, it was about S$40 (£22 ish or 900 THB which would have been an expensive meal in Thailand). Realistically though, for £20 odd quid, two mains, two sides, and two drinks in a city like Singapore, this is a brilliant price. Even at home that would only get you one main, a drink, and maybe one of the cheaper sides at Wagamama's.

We made our way back to the hotel. We popped into a 7-11 that was right on the corner of our hotel's street. This was the one the receptionist must have meant, but we had missed it earlier. We wanted to pick up some breakfast items, but they were quite expensive, so we decided we'd find a bakery or something to-morrow for breakfast. We really wanted to pick up some of the juice we had in the room too, but we couldn't find it.

Back in our room, we got ready for bed. The shower was really nice. I'd actually say it was probably the best shower I've ever had. We then unpacked; Syd was able to do a little bit but didn't want to strain herself too much. We got into bed, with no real plans for tomorrow other than finding a superstore to find some breakfast items for the next few days and that juice!

BROKE AT THE FOUNTAIN OF WEALTH

SINGAPORE | DAY 2

16th May 2022

https://twobritsinasia.com/broke-at-the-fountain-of-wealth/

We woke up late this morning, both feeling hungry. As I was going for my morning wee, the cleaning lady tried to come in. Thankfully the deadlock stopped the door from opening. Once I had finished, I opened the door and said to her we were still in bed. It wasn't too late, it was about 9:30. Which seemed a bit early for a room clean. But maybe this hotel is used a lot for business travelling and most rooms would be empty at this time as it was a Monday.

By the time we got up and ready, it was about 11. Syd tried to dress herself this morning, but she got stuck so I had to help her out. We walked back to the mall down the street as we had seen a bubble tea stand last night. It was closed last night so wanted to see if it was open this morning. It looked as if they had some really nice flavours, with lots of balls! Once we got there, unfortunately, they were still closed, so maybe they've gone out of business, which is a shame.

We got an escalator down to the bottom floor of the mall, where there was a food court. There were all sorts of different food options here. From fresh pasta to curries, sushi, noodles, baguettes, and cakes, the list goes on! One stand stood out which had massive plates, called monster curry. The plates were huge! We didn't go in but will be back at some point in the week I'm sure!

After doing a few laps we settled on a different curry spot, with smaller bowls but a cheap price point. This was because we only really wanted something small to tide us over till our actual lunch. I went to order Syd a chicken cutlet, and I was going to have the pork one. They both came with rice, a fried egg, and some curry sauce. But unfortunately, they didn't accept card payments, and I didn't have any Singapore Dollar cash on me. So, we moved on.

Most of the food options seem to be Japanese, well behind Malaysian and Singaporean. They did also have a French scene here, with different types of bread, baguettes, and other patisseries. We decided to go to one that accepted Mastercard, I say decided, we didn't have much choice... Syd went for a cheese twist stick, and I had a fluffy pork bun, which was basically a milk bread bun with some sort of fluffy pork-flavoured topping.

They were both very tasty, and fresh too. We found some tables round the corner and sat and ate our brunch at them. Mine also had an offer of a chocolate latte for only about a dollar extra, so we shared that too. After having this we decided we wanted to try and find some bubble tea. I looked online and found a place called Koi The Singapore, which was the highest-rated in the area.

We made our way across the bridge over the road and walked to Koi. When we got there, there was a machine outside where we could order our drinks. It was fully customisable, including how much ice you wanted, the amount of sweetness, and different toppings (ice cream, various types of balls etc). We made our drinks up and went to pay, unfortunately, they didn't accept Mastercard payments.

I went to the actual counter to ask if they accepted it there instead, but unfortunately not. So, we walked into the other mall to find a bank, ATM, or currency exchange desk. Once in the mall, we used the information directory system to search for the services. It recommended a spot upstairs with three different bank ATMs.

We went up, and the first ATM with OCBC bank tried to charge $8 for withdrawals. Not having that. I tried the one next to it with UOB (United Overseas Bank), and they didn't charge any fee! Perfect. I got $200 out and used Mastercard's exchange rate through Starling, it was about £118.14 (0.6929 was the rate), which isn't far off Google's "official" rate.

With our newly converted cash, we went back to Koi, first stopping at a shop which sold cartoon statues, I thought they looked cool. At Koi, I had taken a picture of our order on the kiosk earlier and showed the server. He put the order through, but a couple of minutes later he called us back and said he had run out of the Koi Cafe type (which I had chosen a caramel flavour). Not to worry I picked a caramel milk tea instead, which they did have. It was 90 cents more, I thought since it was his mistake, and it wasn't really the one I wanted, he would have waved the difference, but he didn't. Oh well.

Syd ordered a hazelnut milk tea, 50% sugar, with some ice cream, no bubbles. I had mine at 120% sugar, with coffee and gold balls. Both of us went for less than normal ice, to have more liquid to drink. Unfortunately, there weren't any golden balls in mine. Humph, not too successful. Either way, they were both tasty. We walked to The Fountain of Wealth, which was about 10 minutes away.

We crossed over another bridge, this time out in the open, across the main road which was heading towards the skyscrapers. I took some photos, it made for some cool pictures. There was also some construction work going on down below. This made for a good juxtaposition of the modern skyscrapers in the distance, with the workers building the next load of them as we stand there, out of the "wasteland" that was there currently.

Once we got to the Fountain of Wealth, we ran across the three lanes of traffic to the island in the middle, where the fountain was. It was impressive to see all the different water features, and also being towered around us by 5 skyscrapers. Quite ironic that we were here, as after all these trips I was as broke as I had been for a few years...

From here we walked down into Suntec City, which surrounded the fountain underneath. There were three different atriums, West, North, and East. Each atrium was very grand and had about four or five floors! There is so much to see here. We first went into an atrium which was full of a pink Disney display. There were also a lot of carnivals and arcade games here too.

The fountain acted as a middle point with these three atriums jutting off to the sides, each atrium was like a huge mall in itself. They all connected around this fountain. Very impressive architecture.

We walked around next to the floor of the fountain, separated by thick high floor-to-ceiling glass. It must have been at least three stories high. We passed all sorts of different shops. From jewellery to toy shops, clothes, food, supermarkets, and well basically anything you could think of.

Syd saw a pet shop, and obviously, she wanted to go in. It had some rabbits and other smaller pets, which we looked at. I also spotted a bush that we could stick onto a corner within our house, for our cut to rub itself against. We've been looking for one for a while but couldn't see any in the UK. I bought this to take home to Buttons.

We carried on walking around the different atriums, changing levels every now and then. Almost getting lost, multiple times. We saw a shop selling Monopoly, I couldn't resist a look. They were expensive though, so we left quickly before I got tempted. After some more exploring, we found a rooftop garden. It was empty up here which was nice as Singapore seemed much busier than Thailand was. I took some pictures of the fountain from up above, and the skyscrapers in the distance. It was nice to have the masks off for a bit, to give us some fresh oxygen.

Syd started to get a little thirsty for some water, so we went back down on an adventure to find some. On the way we saw a cookery class under-way, it looked as if they were making a cake of some sort. We then saw a conference centre which was massive! We walked around there for a bit, before heading back down into the main area.

We saw a Godiva shop, which is one of Mum's favourite chocolates. They've very expensive so we only tried one little bit each, and that still set me back just under $10! Either way, it was tasty and a nice experience, it was Syd's first time trying them.

Next, we saw a Japanese supermarket called "Don Don Donki". Which I said in a Shrek voice to Syd, it made her chuckle. We went in and it was mental. The isles didn't make any sense and there was nothing short of a million signs per product! So many graphics! There was so much for sale in here too! Different types of high-quality sushi, and wagyu steaks. We eventually found some water, but it was quite expensive for the small bottle it was. We decided to carry on looking elsewhere.

In our continued search for water, we saw strange names for things. One establishment was called "Ho Fook He" which sounds like "Hoe F*** Him" when said with an accent. Read into that as you will... But it was a soy sauce chicken shop, of all things...

Another place served a drink called "Duck Shit Tea"; I don't think I'm brave enough to try it. Maybe I will another day.

We found the doorway to go out to the fountain and be right in the centre of it. We could walk around and put our hands in the water. I did it for both of us, and Syd touched me while I touched the water to still be connected. She didn't want to risk touching the water in case she got her cast wet. The idea was to walk around the central part with your hand in the water and make a wish. Guessing from its name, most people wish for the same thing.

There was a McDonalds upstairs in the East atrium, so we popped in there. I asked for a cup of tap water, but they only gave us a little 150ml one. I asked if we could have had a bigger one, but the server said they don't do that here. Fair enough as it was free.

While we were up there, we saw some girls trying to win a big Winnie the Pooh teddy bear on a large grabber machine. They must have spent at least $50 on it, had and amassed a crowd. They had a few close attempts, but in the end, admitted defeat. We went downstairs to search for some water in another super-market.

Unable to see any cold water, we looked at the water in the aisles. We found one for 50 odd cents which was a good price. But we also saw a calamansi drink, which is a mix between a lime and an orange. This was cold, so we got this instead. We also picked up a packet of a Mala Hot Pot flavoured potato chips.

We ate these back outside by the fountain. However, we started to see dark-looking clouds coming over. So, we decided to go back to the sky garden and sit under the cover there. The rain started, and at first, it was okay, but then it got heavier, and the wind blew it under the cover. So, we decided to go back to the mall.

There weren't many seats, and anytime one becomes available, someone else takes the spot within seconds. So, I had to go into full ninja-mode to try and get me and Syd a seat. Thankfully the years of training I have had from running on trains to get our family a table seat paid off! Once at these seats, I noticed they had USB charging points on the tables there too, unfortunately, I didn't have my charger cable with me though.

We walked around for a bit more, before making our way to the large plate place, Monster Curry. I had thought about coming back here later in the week, but we decided we might as well try it now. We ordered a curry katsu chicken (sorry Lawrence), with extra rice and a side of battered fried prawns. This was only meant for one person, but we shared it between us, and it was plenty. We had a glass of ice water each, which was 50 cents, I thought that was cheeky as it was only water from their tap.

After dinner, we made it back to the Fountain of Wealth and watched the water dance around with the lights on. We then went back into the mall and bought some cereal and milk, along with some cheap bowls and spoons to eat with. We then made it back upstairs to cross the bridge back towards our hotel.

Once back at the reception, we asked for a plastic bag to cover Syd's arm up with. The receptionist wasn't able to find one originally but brought one up to our room a few minutes later, which was nice of her.

I had a sad phone call from Shez, a good mate and someone I used to work with at JP. Our boss, Kieron Johnson, has, unfortunately, suddenly, passed away this morning. He was on a call earlier in the morning all fine but didn't make it into the office. I was only messaging Kieron yesterday about the Pinarello My Way bike I had designed. He was a top bloke and acted like a second father figure to me, even more so when my Dad passed away. He did a lot for me, I feel terrible for his young son Alexandra, and his wife Jo. Rest in peace, my friend.

After the news, we didn't really feel like doing anything else. Syd wasn't feeling too great either, she spent most of the evening on the toilet, while I was messaging my old team, making sure they were all ok after this shock.

EXPENSIVE BURGERS

SINGAPORE | DAY 3

17th May 2022

https://twobritsinasia.com/expensive-burgers/

I woke up relatively early today but didn't get out of bed as Syd was still sleeping. She didn't get up for another couple of hours. We had our crunchy nut cornflakes for breakfast, Syd had two servings as she was hungry from losing everything last night on the loo...

Once we finished breakfast, we wrapped Syd's arm up in the plastic bag the reception had brought up last night. We didn't have any tape, so I folded it over on itself a few times and used a hair clip to keep it in place. I then showered her again, but since it was getting later in the morning now, the hot water was running out. By the time I had finished her hair, it was cold. I then had my shower, quickly, and then finished getting ready.

We first made our way to the Civilian War Memorial. I hadn't planned on stopping here this morning, as we were going to do it another day. But I noticed it across the street as we were making our way to St Andrew's Cathedral, so we stopped off here first. The memorial was peaceful, it had four large modern spikes coming out of the ground. It was an elegant design.

While we were here a man approached, complimenting my beard. He claimed to be a fortune teller. I sat with him while he was doing his show. He first handed me a bit of paper and asked me to write mine and Syd's names down. I used fake names, I wrote "Jamz" for me and "Jannet" for Syd.

He was fairly good, he predicted a number from 1-9 that I chose, I had picked three numbers, 8, 4 and 7. So the odds of him getting one of those three for his guess are fairly high (3/9, so 1/3). But he made it a good show. He said I'd have some good news on 7/7/2022 (I didn't), and have an opportunity presented to me in

2024 with something to do with Australia (at the time of writing this edit, this date hasn't passed yet, so fingers crossed...)

He also picked a colour I was thinking of, well I was thinking aqua, and he said blue. He was wearing an aqua shirt and using a blue pen, so that could have been why. He said he could do a full reading, but it was going to be between $70-120. I said no thank you and handed him a 20 THB I had left in my wallet for his first few tricks.

Syd had started to get a little thirsty, so on the search for some water again. We walked past the cathedral on the way. First popping into a 7-11 to see what they had, it smelt weird in there, almost sewage-like. They did have a bit of a selection of water though, they were all about $3 (just under £2). The same bottle was 14 THB (that's 30p) in Thailand.

So, we thought to try a McDonalds again. There was one within a mall next door, but they tried to charge me $2.90 for some tap water. I said no thank you, and we left. The mall itself was cool. It had a cycle lane through the middle of it! It was a great design in general actually, with interesting lights around the overhangs. The Razor gaming store had letter lights defusing through what looked like slate tiles.

We went back to the 7-11 to get their essential 1.5L bottle of water. Then headed back to the cathedral to take a closer look but unfortunately, since it was a Tuesday, it wasn't open to the public. We could only look from the outside. It is open tomorrow at 12:30, so if we are about maybe we might pop down again.

From here we walked along the park at city hall. There was a thin stairway leading down to what seemed to be an underground walkway. It was empty and was clearly under some construction or renovation work, so we left. We walked down Esplanade Drive and then over Esplanade Bridge.

On the bridge, we had an amazing view over the harbour to the Marina Bay Sands, where we will be staying this time next week. Along with Merlion Park and the "Business Corridor" in front of us. On the bridge, Syd spotted some turtles in the water below. There were some baby ones too, along with a fish! It was crazy how empty it was here.

Across the bridge, we went under it and sat on the wall for some shade. There was a 7-11 under the bridge, which must be up there for one of the coolest places they have a store.

After we had cooled down a bit, we walked up to Merlion Park. I took some photos while Syd found a tree to sit under. Once we were finished there, we walked towards a burger place called Meat Smiths. I had seen an Instagram story from Mike Majlak, where he shared a burger review, not from the same place, but got us in the mood for a burger nonetheless.

On the walk there we saw some workers ripping up and putting down a new road. We joked that in England it would have been a closed road for 12 weeks minimum. They had the rest of the road opened and traffic moving as if nothing was happening. I bet they had the whole road re-opened within a few hours!

It was cool walking under all the skyscrapers. We saw a lady walking with a JP bag, it made me miss the hustle a bustle a little bit - when I worked in different cities around the world. Although the sad news about Kieron, yesterday, reaffirms my gratitude to be out of that stressful environment.

We made our way into China Town, where Meat Smiths is located. We had missed the lunch rush, which was kind of a good thing really, as it meant the place was basically empty. There was only one other table of two lads still eating. The servers were all very friendly and gave us the menus.

There were three menus, one for food, which we needed to scan the QR code to see on my phone. The middle one was a wine list, this wasn't a QR code, but just a one-pager with the wines on, there wasn't anything under $100! Lastly, there was another drinks menu, this, like the food menu, was a QR code too.

We just had tap water and ordered three burgers to share, cutting each in half and a portion of their crinkle-cut fries. We started with their original Meat Smiths Cheeseburger. It was a good-tasting burger, at a good price point too. It was a little small, but for a lunch meal, it's fine. The second one we had was their fried chicken sandwich offering. It had a nice house mayo sauce on it.

Finally, we had their wagyu beef burger. This was expensive, as expected for wagyu, at $32 plus 10% service and 7% tax. All three were very tasty, my favourite was probably the original, although we were already full before starting the wagyu. So that might have had something to do with it, maybe if we had that first it would have hit differently.

Syd's favourite was the original too. She wasn't the biggest fan of the chicken one, she said it was a bit too tough for her with only one hand. She said the ones I make at home are better. I'd expect it's because I use free-range organic chicken, and I doubt that's what's being served in a burger joint.

It was a fancy place, they had good quality meat being hung at the back in a glass case which we could see. I got speaking to the manager, they have a few branches dotted around Asia. Two in Singapore. The guy that started it has a Michelin star, and I could believe that. Our water was constantly being topped up too, which was nice since, apparently, water is a hot commodity here in Singapore!

Once we had finished, we were both really full. Syd couldn't finish her half of the wagyu burger, so I had hers too. Neither of us could finish the fries though! I paid up, about $80, ouch, some expensive burgers. Syd started to feel a little queasy again, so we just walked back to our hotel.

She was almost sick right outside the door but managed to control herself. She didn't end up being sick at all thankfully after that expensive meal! We cooled off in the room, I think we both had a nap, I'm not sure if I did or not, which probably means I did...

We decided to go up to the pool for a bit. Syd wasn't going to go in, but she wanted to watch me. When we got up there, a group of people were taking some wedding photos. They all looked very nice, we just sat ourselves in the corner out of the way while they finished up.

The pool wasn't very big, but it had an amazing view of the business centre. I could also see the towers around the Fountain of Wealth from here too. This hotel is a great location, when we're back in Singapore I'll probably spend some time here again. I couldn't see any other rooftop pools around either. It was quiet up here too, well actually it was just us and the bar staff. As we were getting ready to head back to our room, a few others did come up to the pool, but they too were respectful of the noise level.

Syd still wasn't feeling 100%, I was feeling mostly back to normal now, just a slight underlying headache. We rested in bed for a bit and decided to order a takeaway, as Syd didn't feel up to going out and eating. We ordered Grab Food from Orh Kee Noodles, as Syd didn't want anything spicy while she was feeling sick.

I had premium minced mixed meat soup with mee pok noodles, with a chilli and vinegar sauce. Syd had traditional meatball soup with yellow (egg) noodles. It arrived fairly quickly; I went down to reception in my dressing gown to pick it up. The driver and I locked eyes, I shrugged, and we both giggled.

We ate our soups in bed watching part of the Jonny Depp and Amber Heard trial. Syd was eating her noodles with her hands as we didn't have a fork. The noodles were intentionally dry, as the soup was in a different compartment below. The packaging was a really good design actually. It saved the noodles from going soggy on the transit over here.

Syd only had her noodles to start with and then put her soup to the side, with the plan of eating it later. She didn't want to eat too much too fast and make herself sick again. We watched the rest of the trial segment we were watching. Before the end, Syd had some of her soup, but couldn't finish it. I did.

We then saw that today's trial was going on right now in the states, so we watched a bit of that live before drifting off to sleep.

WHAT'S THE DIFFERENCE BETWEEN LAMB AND MUTTON?

SINGAPORE | DAY 4

18th May 2022

https://twobritsinasia.com/whats-the-difference-between-lamb-and-mutton/

I originally woke up around 8ish, but lay in bed for a while, drifting in and out. A few hours later we had both woken up properly. I got our crunchy nut cornflakes again for breakfast. Syd felt a little better, so we walked to the Mustafa Center.

We noticed down in reception that they had some pictures which were moving images. One also had a built-in mini camera and a small screen built into the picture. It showed us in the painting. I really liked the concept. Once we were done admiring it, we made our way to Mustafa.

The walk was only about 25 minutes, although it did feel very hot today. Luckily, I had brought the two canned drinks from the hotel with us, so we shared these to keep us cool. We were also finding any shade we could to help combat the heat. It was interesting seeing the transition from business and touristy areas, into the locals and where the majority of the people actually live. Syd made the observation that we were the only white people here.

On our way, we walked past Koi The, where we got the bubble tea from the other day. We also walked through a little side street, which was undercover, and full of loads of different shops. Mainly food stalls and street clothes. It was basically once we had gone through this ally it was into the local area. Passing a bus station with lots of people waiting and just living their lives.

We saw lots of interesting buildings, from hospital skyscrapers with big chunks of it taken out, which was the design to a semi-circle high-rise which had a massive circular ledge coming out from the side of it. I'm not sure how it could hold itself up without any visible support columns. We also saw lots of older-style buildings, these were from two to about five stories high. They were a mix of designs between Chinese and Portuguese.

Continuing our walk towards the Center, we saw a really fierce-looking car. It was fully blacked out, with a silver snake on the front. It looked almost like a Ford Mustang hot rod type thing. I took some pictures of it, there was a wall covered with colourful pelican graffiti behind the car which made for a great contrast.

Once we got to the Mufasta Center, we realised it wasn't really a mall, but more just a bundle of shops all in the same building. There weren't any food outlets or anything but this was okay. It was interesting to see where the locals would shop. The outside of the building had a cool glass design, which looked like the waves on the ocean.

The entrance floor was full of different pharmacies, with all sorts of different smells here. We then went up a floor. The first half was full of loads of different gold jewellery. I saw a ring with a tiger on the front which I thought would be cool, as I am a Tiger in the Chinese calendar. Unfortunately, the ring didn't fit.

I saw another one I liked, which had an opal dollar symbol on the front, surrounded by mini coins which would spin. This did fit; however, it was about £600 and I didn't know if I was a huge fan of the dollar symbol. It felt a bit too arrogant, even for me!

The other half of this floor was different clothes, mostly for men. Mainly cotton or silk collared shirts. We then went all the way down to the bottom floor. This was the tech area with lots of TVs, laptops, fridges etc. it was like Curry's PC World back at home. I saw a router I had been trying to get my hands on in the UK, the ASUS RT-AC5300, it was a good price too ($459). It's impossible to get these in the UK, so I thought about buying them, but I was worried that they might get confiscated at customs. There must be a reason why it's not sold in the UK.

We carried on our exploring, going back up through all the floors this time, to the top floor. Passing a floor full of just shoes. The top was a supermarket. Lots of different spices for sale here. And water! It was much cheaper too! A 1.5L bottle we saw for 70 cents (just under 50p). Still not as cheap as Thailand, but cheaper than anywhere else we have seen in Singapore. We didn't get it as it wasn't cooled, and Syd said if we were to get water, she would want it to be cold.

Once we were finished looking, we walked out and crossed the street to the other side of the Center. Realising there was a bridge we could have gone across over the road connecting the two. Oh well. Once we were in the second one we realised that actually, we had been in there. We must have crossed the bridge without realising and then crossed it again back to the first side, before crossing the road.

Not to worry, we left and saw an eatery across the road, called Al Mubin. It looked like a lot of locals ate here. So, we took a seat. I went up to order, but they said they'd come over to us. The (what I assume was the manager or owner) took our order. He was very friendly and everyone else seemed to respect him as if he was the owner. He was asking Syd lots of questions about her arm, making sure she was okay.

I ordered minced mutton (kheema), a dhal and two chapatis, with a honey lemon drink. Syd went for a mutton kadai with garlic naan. She had wanted a mutton Rogan Josh, but they had run out. The fella said it was one of their hottest dishes, so we were excited to try it. Syd also ordered an Oreo milkshake for her drink. The guy said if her arm was broken drinking icy drinks wouldn't help, we let him know that thankfully it wasn't broken.

I'm not sure if his comment was accurate either way though. I've never heard anything like that.

We also shared a portion of chicken bites, which were called chicken 65 for some reason. He said that they made up some strange names here. All the food was delicious. Syd's wasn't too spicy, but it had a good kick. It wasn't too expensive either, at $35 for the two of us (about 20 quid), I can't complain. Looking at the receipt, it does say "mgr" under the cashier section, which probably means manager, I guess I was right.

I looked on the map to see what was nearby. I saw another mall called City Square Mall. We weren't too close to the city centre, but nonetheless, the mall was an actual mall this time. With arcade games, kids' shops, cafés, restaurants, a cinema etc.

On the way there Syd asked what mutton was. I knew it was an older sheep but didn't know the exact definitions. So, I Googled it. It turns out that mutton is usually just a sheep that's over 3 years old. With a lamb being a sheep under a year old. I wonder what the sheep between the age of 1 and 3 years called? Donna, Shaun, who knows?

The mall was interesting, the first half was only four stories high, with a large glass and metal ceiling. Then when it went round the corner, it went up two more floors, filled with shops. But above that, all the way up to floor nine was filled with a school and offices.

On this odd-corner part of the mall, there was also a massive, netted play-zone, that was suspended in the air above the mezzanine below. I'd have liked to try it, and it did hold adults, in-fact it was designed for offices for team-building exercises. But I didn't want to do it solo, as that's no fun.

From here, we walked up to the cinema. We noticed that the new Marvel movie, Doctor Strange in the Multiverse of Madness, was showing in just five minutes. I booked two tickets, and we made our way to the screen. We were the only people there originally, a few more walked in during the adverts. Not many though, maybe only six in total.

During the movie, we had some of the crisps that had come with the room, as I had bought them along with us today too. They were truffle and black pepper. I liked them, I'm not sure Syd was the biggest fan, but she had them anyways. She didn't have much for lunch as she had felt full early on, for some reason. Needless to say - I then finished the rest of her dish for her.

Once the movie finished, we walked around the mall for a bit more, sitting for a while opposite the Toys R Us store. Syd got the "when I grow up, I want to be a Toys R Us kids" song stuck in her head. Which she continued to repeat for what seemed like the rest of the day...

On the way back to the hotel, we stopped off at Koi The again to have some more bubble tea. This time Syd went for a fruity one, it was very sweet and had chunks of orange peel in it. I quite liked it, but Syd didn't like the texture. I had a milky honey one, with 120% honey and 2 times the golden balls. This time I got my balls!

It wasn't as sweet as Syd's, but I liked having all the golden balls! We then walked back to our hotel, passing two very nice-looking cars (one Ferrari and one Lamborghini). Even after all of today's walks, Syd was still feeling okay. Which was good news. She was a little gassy, but that's probably more down to the mutton earlier, as she gets that way with lamb.

Back in the room I was replying to a few messages and talking to a few people about Kieron. We rested up for a bit before getting ready and heading out for our evening meal. We walked over to Suntec City and made our way across to Tempura Makino. I asked if we could sit right up at the counter to watch the chefs, there were two seats available, but they did let us, even without a reservation.

Syd ordered their Makino Tendon & Soba Set. It consisted of a bowl of soba noodles on ice, a miso soup, Japanese pickles, a bowl of rice, a mix of tempura vegetables, a tempura poached egg (which I'd never seen before), tempura prawn, and tempura squid. I had Executive Tempura Bento. Mine had a miso soup and pickles too, a smaller bowl of rice, some sashimi (scallops, salmon, and I think tuna), some sort of fresh crispy bean sprouts, tempura vegetables, tempura prawn, tempura squid, and a tempura chicken filet.

Both of us had a ginger ale to drink. We enjoyed the meal, but there were a few things we picked up on. One was when the chef washed his hands, it was in the same sink he prepped food. Also, he wouldn't wash his hands from going between the raw prawn, chicken, and squid while he was breading them. I'd have expected a kitchen working with raw served ingredients (sashimi), that their hygiene would have been higher than usual not sub-par. But other than that. It was good. 7/10 is what we would rate it, as it was fairly expensive for what it was.

We then returned to the hotel to watch more of the Depp vs Heard trial. We watched it in bed for a few hours before falling asleep.

BUS, BOAT, DUCK?!

SINGAPORE | DAY 5

19th May 2022

https://twobritsinasia.com/bus-boat-duck/

Syd woke me up this morning around 5. She needed to go to the toilet but couldn't find the light switch. We managed to drift back off to sleep for another few hours. Once we were awake for good, I made up our cereal bowls again. I used up the rest of the cornflakes, so we had larger bowls than before. There wasn't much milk left, so we only had a dribble each. It made for a very sweet milk slurp at the end!

I had a shower while Syd packed what she could. Then I finished packing up for us both. We dropped our bags off at reception and made our way over to the Duck Tours. The midday tour that was leaving in five minutes was fully booked. So, I paid for the 1 pm one, just an hour later.

While we waited, we went into the Suntec Center and sat on the charging station table again. This time they were empty. Actually, the whole mall was a lot less busy today. Syd had brought over the rest of her sweet fruity drink that she didn't finish yesterday from Koi The. She didn't want to finish it today either, so she let me have it.

After having a sit-down and finishing the drink, we walked around the mall again. I wanted to try the duck poop tea. However, by the time we got there, we were already past the 12:50 meet-up time for the bus. So, without ordering, we briskly walked back to the meet-up point. Getting there at 12:57 with everyone else already on the bus, ooops.

We got on and then about a minute later, the tour began! It first made its way to the water's edge. It was a bit of a bumpy ride; this was because the boat bus was an old, converted war tank bus. Which was left over from the Vietnam war. We were going quick down the ramp towards the water. It made a big splash! Thankfully no one got wet!

On the water, we walked around the marina, seeing many famous buildings. First passing the Singapore Flyer, which is their large Ferris wheel. Then along past the gardens. Next, we went under the Helix bridge, which as its name suggests, looks like a DNA Helix spiral. Passing the floating stadium which can seat up to 30,000 people! It's usually used for concerts and New Year's celebrations. But it has also been used to host a football match every now and then.

Next, we sailed past the Marina Bay Sands hotel where we would be staying for a few days, soon. Seeing the gardens from the water was very special. The lion statue was interesting to see from this angle too. The driver then did a 180-degree turn, and we headed back to dry land, passing the F1 Grand Prix course on the way, which I had missed the first time.

The guide was asking quiz questions, and the winner would get a pencil with a duck on top as a souvenir. One of the questions was how many F1 teams were there racing in the Singapore Grand Prix. Syd Guessed 12, which was correct, so we won the pen! Syd claims it wasn't a guess, but I'm not too certain...

While on the water we spotted a Chinook and a few other war-like aircraft. Some older styles, and even a jet fighter. Back on the land, we saw a military base, set up on the side of the water, it had a few tanks too. I wondered if they were getting prepared if anything gets worse with Putin's invasion of Ukraine...

Back on dry land, the tour continued around the city centre, passing the city hall, the Supreme Court, and the parliamentary buildings. The Supreme Court and the Parliament buildings both have new and old versions – which seemed funny to me. The older parliament building is now being used as an art gallery, and the older Supreme Court is used as Singapore's national gallery.

We went past a skyscraper which was Hotel Swissôtel. This is where they run the largest Asian "upward" marathon, where around 2,000 participants run up 70+ stories in the fastest time. The quickest time is sub 7 minutes! After seeing this, the tour made its way back to Suntec City, doing a lap of the Fountain of Wealth. Before dropping us back off where we had Started.

Syd had packed my sunglasses in the bag today. No prices for guessing... Of course, they broke... That's the fourth pair now that she's either broken or lost and this time they were mine! Not ideal, especially as in Singapore the sunglasses are expensive I didn't buy a replacement, I'd only had these from Mallorca, and have plenty more at home.

Making our way up to LiHo (the shop that did the poo tea), and I ordered the infamous drink. At first, it just tasted like normal green tea. But then I realised I needed to mix in the milky substance at the top. Once I had done this the whole drink changed to a white, dare I say, duck poo colour. It was sweet and still had that under-tone of green tea. It was nice.

I noticed that Jo (Kieron's wife) had invited me to connect to my Linked in. I messaged her sending my condolences, along with my number in case she or Alexander (their son) wanted somewhere to vent. She replied that she appreciated the message, and that Alexander was still going ahead with his GCSEs, the brave soul

Syd was getting hungry and fancied a chicken wrap. She was so hungry in fact, that she originally said "chicken wap" which made me laugh for some reason! After looking around we found a place called "Donergy". On the way here we saw a very nice matte black Lamborghini.

Syd had her chicken wrap. I had a calzone-type thing, it was stuffed with mixed meats and cheese on top. It was like a stuffed boat actually. We also shared a bowl of French fries which were nice and thin! After eating we walked back towards the hotel, on the way I saw a gold bar shop.

They were selling gold at £46,000 a kg. I thought about getting 10kg and selling it back home (it was about 47k back in England at the time). But I was worried that it would get confiscated or heavily taxed at customs, so I decided against it. Shame as it could have been a quick 10k profit just to bring it across the border.

Back at our hotel, we picked up our bags and then I ordered us a Grab. It was a fully red car, with tons of supreme stickers in and around it. It was a smooth ride. We enjoyed going over the bridge to Sentosa island. Then onto our hotel, Amara Sanctuary Resort, to check-in.

It was a fancy lobby, but the check-in process took a while, and they also wanted a $100 deposit for the room. Even though they had my card on file. This is the first place to ask that, but whatever. Our room was nice though, top floor with views of the Singapore Strait. There were lots of shipping container boats out on the water. These could also be seen from the rooftop pool, which was just down our corridor.

It had been raining, but it had settled down a bit, so we decided to go for a walk to look around the resort. The gym and spa centre had been closed, there were workers actively making a new outside one, it seemed, down below. There were offices on-site with people inside, not many desks, maybe 10 tops.

This resort had clearly been hit hard by Covid. The two bottom pools were dirty, and the wood surrounding them had rotted. Although the pool's slide pump was still on and so were the water features. Very strange.

There was also a mansion on site that had clearly been abandoned, with the roof breaking and vines starting to grow down it. Also, the decking was rotting away. A real shame as it was a beautiful-looking property. We also saw five peacocks on site. Syd was worried that they would attack us, but of course, we were fine.

I decided I wanted to go to the sky pool for a bit. Weirdly we must book it, as still only 10 people are allowed in it at any one time. You need to book it using their online reservation tool. I did, but honestly, I don't think it really matters now, so if I decide to go in again, I don't think I'll bother reserving it, as the pool was empty the whole time we were there.

It was cool to see the boats lights out to sea. Syd didn't come in, but she sat on a lounger watching me. We also saw a fire, light and water show from down below up here. It started to rain a little bit, so I got out. While I was getting out, I noticed a circular cut-out in the decking. I could see a hot tub below, there was also a button by the side of it. I pressed the button thinking it would open the decking, but it only just started the bubbles below. I tried to lift the decking up by hand, but it was very heavy, so I think it's closed for a reason.

Back in our room, I ran Syd a bath, as we took her bandages off. While she was in the bath, I had a shower. The small showerhead didn't want to stay up, so I just switched to just using the rain head above. Syd was able to have more movement in her hand which was great!

I tried to order some food on Grab, it was about 8:30. There wasn't much selection, but I found this Chinese place doing noodles and dumplings, perfect. I ordered; however, an hour later the restaurant hadn't even started cooking yet. I tried to order from elsewhere, but basically everywhere was closed or over an hour wait. Which would be almost 11 by the time it arrived.

We weren't too fussed as we had eaten a late, big lunch, but still annoying as I had paid for the meal and now, I have no idea what was going to happen with it. I guess we will find out in the morning... We had the snacks (crisps and nuts) we took from our last hotel, along with some chocolate we got from this hotel. Not a great dinner, but better than nothing. I had looked at room service, but it was $30+ for a basic pasta dish. No thank you.

We watched some more of the Johnny Depp and Amber Heard trial before heading off to bed.

UNIVERSALLY UNIVERSAL

SINGAPORE | DAY 6

20th May 2022

https://twobritsinasia.com/universally-universal/

We woke up later this morning. I did some LISA and ETF trading and documenting then ae walked over to Universal Studios at about 12ish, the park's opening time. Since it was only across the road it took us about 5 minutes to get there. On the walk over we shared the last Kit Kat bar from our room, we also had a can of Coke each.

It was a hot day, but there weren't many people compared to what would be normal for a park like this. We made our way to the park entrance, after taking a few pictures of the classic Universal Spinning Globe. These are "Universally Universal" for every park entrance.

The first ride we went on was the Sesame Street Spaghetti Space Race. It had the same walking conveyor belt as some Disneyland Paris rides. You stand on the conveyor belt, and it moves at the same speed as the ride so it's easier for you to get on and off. Without the riding stopping. This ride was held on top rails, in fact, basically, all the rides here were held that way. I wonder if this is the new standard for rollercoasters, since it gives that extra sense of suspension in mid-air, with our legs dangling below.

We then tried to get on the Transformers ride, however, there was a massive queue, stated to be 50 minutes. The other attractions had queue times of about 5 minutes! So, we decided to come back to this later once it had quietened down. This meant we could go on to the other attractions now their queues were much lower and back to this later once everyone else was in other queues.

To start with we went on the ride next door: the Battlestar Galactica Ceylon ride. We had to put my bag and everything in my pockets in a locker. We were given 45 minutes free before getting charged. Thankfully we didn't take any more than 20. It was quite a cool system; you just entered your birth date and your favourite colour, and it would tell you a locker to use. It would then unlock that locker for you when you returned.

The ride itself was great fun. It was also hanging from rails above. It had 5 upside-down loops in it. It was very fast, and after not eating properly for almost 20 hours now, we both almost fainted on the first loop. Defiantly light-headed after that ride. We decided to go try and get some food.

There weren't many options open. We saw a fried chicken place called Goldilocks, so we made our way there. It was quite expensive, $43 for some fried chicken and chips. Syd and I both had a Pappa Bear Box, which was three bits of chicken and some fries. It also came with sweetcorn in a milky sauce, and a drink, we both opted for Sprite. We also got a side of chicken strips. The chicken bits were very big, and we couldn't finish everything, we certainly didn't realise how big they would be. I reckon it must have been an ostrich!

After lunch, as we were both full we didn't fancy going on any harsh rides, so we decided on Puss in Boots Giant Journey. There were a lot of jolts, but it was a fun ride. It had a cool spiral mechanism which pushed the cart up the outward-spiral rails.

We weren't in the queue very long for that ride and we opted for another softer ride. We had looked at watching the Shrek 4D experience, but the next show wasn't for another 30 minutes yet. So, we went next door to Enchanted Airways instead. The first drop surprised Syd, I was glad to be sitting on the right-hand side, as I was thrown on the side of the cart. This would have hurt Syd's arm.

By the time we had queued and ridden the Enchanted Airways, it was time for the next viewing of Shrek 4D. We made our way into the waiting hall, and then into the theatre when the doors opened. We sat far back as these types of attractions sometimes can make Syd feel sick. Thankfully this one didn't. It was cool to have the chairs move around too. They did a great job on the lights around the side of the theatre interlinking what was being shown on screen. At one point the lights made it look like a fairy was flying around above us.

We then decided to head over to Jurassic Park, our first ride bring the Canopy Flyer. The queue was the longest we had been in, so far today, at about half an hour. There were bugs in the amber which was dotted around the wall for decoration. The ride was fun too. We sat backwards, Syd was worried about that at first, but she really enjoyed it when it got going. I could hear her giggling, which she does instead of screaming on rollercoasters.

Next, we tried the Jurassic Park Rapid Adventure, they wanted to charge for the lockers! It was $4 for an hour. I thought this was a bit cheeky as it also said you would get wet (soaked actually) on this ride. So, you don't have much choice. We thought maybe we would come back just before we left in case we get wet we needn't be wet all day.

We made our way round into Ancient Egypt to ride Revenge of The Mummy. This queue time was only about 5 minutes. It was a great ride. There was pyrotechnics, which was very hot on our faces. It also had an amazing statue design within the ride. Syd said it scared her a little bit, we had a sit down outside for a few minutes so she could have a drink and compose herself.

It was only about halfway through the park's open time; however, the sky had started to get a little grey. So, we had to think about what rides we really wanted to do in case it started to rain and restrict the rides that were open. We decided to try out the Transformers ride which previously had a big queue this morning.

On the way there we saw Megatron, Syd originally wanted a photo with him, but then decided she was a bit scared of him. We walked a bit further towards the Transformers 4D simulator ride. It was amazingly done. I sent some photos to Syd's Dad as he likes Transformers. We both felt a little queasy after it though, especially Syd as we sat close to the screens.

We only had two rides left, the Rapids and the Human. This was the other Battlestar Galactica ride and only opened from 4 pm onwards, once this one was open Ceylon was closed. However, when walking past, the queue was too big, so went to see the Puss in Boots live show.

The show was funny but didn't last long, maybe 5 minutes. It then turned into a meet-and-greet for photos etc. This was more for the kiddos, so we went to head back to the Human. On the way there we saw another section of the park, Water World, but unfortunately, that was closed off.

So back we went to Human. We still had over an hour of queuing time, but we didn't have anything else to do, so we waited. We were about 10 people behind the front, but unfortunately, the ride broke down. Thankfully no one was stuck mid-ride! They said it was a technical issue, and we could wait in the queue, but they didn't know how long it would take to fix it, if at all.

We decided to go on the wet raft ride instead. I used a locker that was in the Ancient Egypt area as this was free for 45 minutes. We got very wet on the raft ride, but we both really enjoyed it. Syd was worried at one part when we were about to drop, grabbing onto me. But she explained she enjoyed it when it was over, and it became one of her favourites of the day!

On the way out of the park, we noticed they had literally just opened Human up again, so we got in the queue. It instantly said 25 minutes which must have been the people that had stayed in there. It ended up being 30 but whatever, we both really liked this ride. And so glad we did it as it was one, if not the, best ride of the day, for me.

We started heading back to the hotel but then we spotted some food options. Not wanting a repeat of last night, we made our way into a building that had lots of little street-stall-style shacks on the walls. We went with two pork noodle dishes. Syd had red pork, and I had a roast pork topping. They both came with some prawn wantons which were nice. Syd's red pork wasn't very red though, nonetheless, it did taste good.

Back at the hotel, I jumped and played about in the pool for a bit. Syd just sat on the side and watched; she wasn't feeling up to it just yet. We could see the light, water, fire, and fireworks display down below again. I might see if we can see that close-up tomorrow.

After I was finished playing in the pool, we walked back to our room and had showers. Our chocolate supplies had been restocked. We will have this tomorrow for a bit of breakfast. I still had a packet of nuts from the Naumi, so I ate those while we watched The Beach. We managed to finish it before falling asleep, which is a first...

LUNCH NEXT TO A SHARK

SINGAPORE | DAY 7

21st May 2022

https://twobritsinasia.com/lunch-next-to-a-shark/

We had a later start this morning, having the free chocolates and orange juice in bed for breakfast. We then got ready and made our way across to the S.E.A. Aquarium. The walk was the same as Universal yesterday, as they're all part of the same larger Resort World Sentosa complex.

On the walk over we saw a bunch of large red ants swarming on the walkway handle-rail. Thankfully we didn't need to use it! At the complex, we made our way around to the aquarium. I bought Syd one of those squeezed pennies with a pattern on. She chose one with a dolphin on.

There wasn't any queue, so we got right in. Next to the entrance, on the waterfront, there was a pirate-looking ship. We joked that it was my ship (I had my pirate necklace on from Thailand). I joked to say the necklace was the key to the ship. We could also see the cable carts in the distance.

When we went in, we were greeted by the first large glass panel. It had a type of shark that we had not seen before. It was half shark half manta-ray. Next, we saw a smaller tank which had loads of smaller fish, at least 250, all hovering in the same position. Great formation.

In some of the viewing spots, the glass had built-in magnifying lenses. This really helped to see the smaller fish and to see the details of the coral and other intricate things to see. As usual, there were a lot of noisy children. It was a Saturday, so I had expected it.

It was either Universal today and the aquarium yesterday, or this way around we did it. I decided to do Universal yesterday as we would be spending more of the day there. Also, Universal would be the busier attraction on a weekend, causing the queues to be longer. Within the aquarium, there are no queues, just busier sections.

Using one of the magnifying lenses, I was looking at a thin greenish starfish. Its legs had lots of spikes on. I wouldn't want to step on it! It was in the same tank as some bright, red-coloured shrimps. Some of them were fully red, ruby red, and some had yellow strips down the side. Next to this was a glass walkway with sharks below! It was cool to walk over it.

Further down the building was a large cylinder, about three stories high. It had a massive rock with tons (literally) of coral on it. I wonder how they lowered it in there. I wonder if they put it there and then build the tank around it. Although that may have killed the coral for being out of water for so long. A mystery!

The tank room itself was cool too. There were LEDs around the tank at the top which made an awesome effect, like the Tardis from Dr Who. In the tank were all sorts of different fishes, there were even a few large eels! We carried on around to the next section, where there was a tank with smaller sharks. These had long noses and they could also open their mouth up huge, just like a basking shark.

We also saw some sea snakes. There were about 20 of them in their tank. I have no idea how long they were, as a section of their bodies was buried under the sand. They looked funny all lent over the same way moving with the water. Next, we saw an enclosure with dolphins in it! They were swimming around doing different movements. They seemed to like to swim upside down.

The next section was all about jellyfish. We even saw one of the workers feeding them with what looked like a mix between a large injection needle and a turkey baster. It was full of tiny little shrimp. They were aiming the nozzle directly into the jellyfish's mouth. We had seen another penny impression machine; this one had a hammerhead imprint. I had used my last $2 note up on the last machine though, and that's what they need, these machines had the pennies built in.

Now onto the main attraction! The ocean hall. It had a massive glass wall, like the one in Phuket. This one was bigger though! The glass was 36 meters across, 12 meters high, and 0.7 meters thick! There were so many fishes, sharks, and rays in there. It had 18 million litres of water in it! Syd spotted the hammerhead straight away! Not surprising, as these are her favourite sharks.

We could see two smaller manta rays playing about with each other. There was also a side dome room, which has glass on all walls (other than the door in), it even had glass viewing on the ceiling. We had started to get a little hungry, so we made our way out to look for food, as we were able to get back in later.

On the walk out we stopped at another large tank. This had a walk-through tube, and the water around us was filled with loads of different sharks! Multiple hammerheads! There was one shark that was much bigger than the others, it had a mean-looking bite too! Lots of teeth on show, like a snarling wolf.

Further nearer the exit, there was a section of tiny rainforest frogs. They were about the size of my thumb, but very poisonous. They were all black with bright coloured stripes. The staff had separated them into yellow, green, and red. There was a massive boat structure in the foyer too, it was really something to look at.

I had seen publicity for a restaurant called Ocean, where we could sit and eat next to some viewing sections of the tank. However, it was difficult to find the entrance. It turned out we were on the wrong floor. But either way, it was also expensive, over $80 each for three set courses, which at that price, the menu didn't actually sound too exciting.

Instead, we decided to go find something else cheaper and maybe use the money saved on a shark experience Syd had seen. So, we walked down to the food area. I had fancied either a cook-it-yourself place or some dim sum or dumplings. We found a freshly made dumpling spot, but they had 6 tables already ahead of us waiting to be seated. The takeaway was a 40-minute wait too!

We decided to keep looking. During our search we saw the casino, we tried to go in, but we needed our passports, which I didn't have on us. So, the search continued. We found ourselves in one of the car parks. It was massive, all underground. There were bus routes here too, which I suspect people from the city centre had used to get here.

We eventually found a place we liked the look of. It was some noodle bar which did dumplings. We had a bowl of their chilli pork wanton with noodles. We also shared a slow braised pork rib side dish. I asked if we could have it as a takeaway so we could take it back to the ocean room at the aquarium. They said that was fine, so we sat and waited for our food.

It didn't take long to come out, he had said ten minutes, but it was out in about three. Perfect. We made our way back to the aquarium. Syd was worried that we might not be allowed in with the food. She asked if we could go into the Lego shop and get a bag, so it looks like we had purchased toys, rather than food. I laughed and said I'm sure we will be okay.

The guy at the entrance recognised us, he had complimented Syd on her tattoos the first time. So didn't even bother asking for our tickets again. However, on the bit where the turn-gate was, the lady asked if we had a stamp as we had left. We didn't see anywhere to get stamped on our way out, we explained this to her, and she let us in any way.

We made our way back to the ocean room with our food. None of the staff said anything, so Syd started to get excited to be able to eat the food with such an amazing view of all the fish! Unfortunately, on the way, a kid bumped into Syd which caused her arm to start hurting again. She had a painkiller once we had sat down.

After finding the perfect spot, we sat down and started eating our food. It was a little spicy but really nice. It also came with an interesting-looking toothpick. One end was the normal style, however, the other end looked almost like a feather. We used it as a tiny brush.

We sat watching the fish for a few hours, we had also seen divers come and go from the tank. The first time they had a long blue hose. It looked as if they were hovering over the bottom part. The viewing platform was three tiers high, there were a few seats too. However, it was difficult to get a seat as soon as one became available, someone else jumped onto it. Luckily with Syd's sharp eyes and my ninja skills, we got one after we finished our lunch.

We sat here for a bit, then we saw a girl next to us with candy floss. I haven't had one of those for years! Neither had Syd! So, we decided to get one. It came on a flashing wand! There was quite a big queue for the snacks at the aquarium. People were trying to push in, but the woman at the counter was doing a good job telling them to get to the back of the queue!

I got to the front of the line and paid for my candy floss. I had to then go to the candy floss stand to show them my receipt. As this lady was making them. As she was making mine, a kid came along with two women. The little girl had also bought one and given the lady the receipt. When the woman went to hand me mine, I let the little girl have hers first. It's a lot easier for me to stand around waiting than it is for two adults with an eager child waiting for a sugar hit!

They both said thank you, and I also think the lady making them made my next one bigger. Good karma ey. We enjoyed eating it! Very very sweet! After it had gone, we cleaned our hands up with some alcohol gel in Syd's bag. We then made our way out of the aquarium. On the way out we saw another diver in a smaller tank. He was cleaning the rocks with a toothbrush; he also had a hoover type thing.

We walked around the rest of the complex for a bit, seeing an interesting elephant statue. It had very very long skinny legs. Next, we walked down to the beach, to see where the show would be later. We were able to find it, and it was only about a 5-minute walk from the hotel. Perfect.

While we were down on the beachfront, Syd wanted a drink. The first shop we went into was $2.80 for a can! I had thought we'd just hold on till back to our hotel room. But in another shop, we saw a purple Fanta can, we'd never seen this before. It was grape flavour and was $2. So, I bought us each a can, it was very sweet. We drank them on the beach. The beach itself wasn't very big, well there are a lot of small beaches, with crab claw-like islands off them all.

We made our way back to the hotel, having a cool down in our room before both getting in the pool. We didn't stay in long as the temperatures had dropped. But Syd's arm was doing better which was great news. After the swim, we got ready for our evening show and headed back out.

The walk down didn't take long, Syd had looked at the shuttle service, but I reckon it would have taken longer to use that! We were going to sit on the steps to watch the show, which would have been free. However, I saw a worker and asked if it was worth it to buy the tickets. He said since it was just the two of us then it is.

In the queue, a guy behind us kept getting really close. Even one of the staff told him to back up. He still didn't, so I looked him dead in the eye and said, it's time to give us space now, which did the job. The tickets weren't too bad, ($18, just over a tenner each). The show was about 20 minutes, but well worth it!

They used the water as a projector, and it really made the whole thing feel life-like. I'd 100% recommend it. The staff were friendly. Also stopping people pushing in, telling them to wait their turn. It was interesting that people were so pushy, all of whom were Indian men, not just now but all the pushy people today. This surprised me.

After the show, we started looking for some food. Most of the places directly outside the venue were cocktail bars, with very expensive small plates of food. So, I looked on Google and found an

Italian place about half a mile down the road. We made the walk down, which didn't take too long. We saw cool graffiti on the way there too, of a man and a bird.

It was funny seeing how quickly the businesses disappeared when we left the main part of the prom. We also saw a bungee jump tower; I think I'd be a bit too scared to do that by myself. I reckon if I was here with Lawrence, we would convince ourselves to do it. That's probably not a good thing to admit...

Once at the Italian, Trapizza, there wasn't anyone at the front of the house to show us where to go. So, we walked around the side where a waiter showed us to our table. It was another place where we had to order with a QR code. It's quite smart I think, as it stops people doing runners since they would have their phone details from visiting the website to order the food. Well, maybe the people who do runners might not realise that. Either way, I liked the idea as it also saved paper when the menu changed. Allowing for the menu to change in real-time if needed, for example, if something became out of stock.

The service wasn't great, they were clearly understaffed at the front of the house, with no apparent front-of-house manager. We could see the chefs getting visibly annoyed when they dinged the bell for service, and no one would come to collect it. The food was nice though, although the fries came our way before our pizzas did.

We both had pizza Sicilian, which had peppers, onions, salami, pork sausage, and spinach (as well as the usual tomato and cheese). The fries came with a little pot of ketchup, which is about good for 2 dips... When I finally managed to get one of the server's attention, I asked for some more.

But he took ages getting it, that our pizzas turned up. So, I asked the server who was delivering our pizzas instead. They both came back basically at the same time with more... Oh well, at least we had our food and sauces now. We were both stuffed after this, we had shared a large jug of ice water too. I paid up, which was very expensive for two pizzas (around $80) and made our way back to the hotel.

I really needed the loo on the way back. Thankfully I made it without any issues. We were both fairly tired so just lay down, using our phones. Syd was watching reels on Instagram while I was replying to messages, before heading to sleep.

HOME HUNTING

SINGAPORE | DAY 8

22nd May 2022

https://twobritsinasia.com/home-hunting/

We started the day late today. Both of us felt tired from the last two busy tourist days at Universal and the Aquarium. For breakfast we had, what seems to be the standard breakfast at this hotel, our Kit Kats and Oreo chocolates... Once we finished these, we got ready for the day.

While brushing our teeth this morning, I sat on the balcony watching the ships. There was a massive one today called CMA CGM, which was taking up a fair portion of the horizon. With nothing really planned other than going to look at the expensive houses on the island, we made our way downstairs.

The walk was about 30 minutes, so I asked reception if we could have some umbrellas for shade. They only had white ones, they didn't seem to be doing a great job, however, they did cause a shadow so better than nothing. By the time we had left, it was already 13:30!

On the way to Sentosa Cove, there are two routes to the harbour. The top route, which is the quicker route, or the bottom route, which is longer, but more scenic next to the waterfront. I asked Syd which way she wanted to go first; she said the top way as it was the hottest part of the day. Fair enough.

Both paths surround the golf course, it was funny seeing all the buggies in the houses, along with their normal cars. During the walk, we also saw a massive satellite dish. It must have been at least 50 meters in diameter, if not more! Syd is convinced it was a UFO!

There were so many fancy cars going past, Porsches, Ferraris, Lamborghinis, Bentleys, Rollers, the lot! Once we got to the houses, they were all behind gate houses, with manned security!

Even the pedestrian entrance had a heavy-duty electromagnetically locked gate!

I walked over to one of the security guards, pretending I was interested in buying one and wanted to look around the area. He let us in. Which surprised me. The number of cameras in the street was almost overwhelming, to be honest!! I bet nothing bad ever happens here.

After looking around the streets, my previous prediction was confirmed. Basically, everyone just left their bike unlocked by the side of their house, in plain view of the street! Some of the houses looked like they were being renovated. But the houses that were lived in looked amazing! So beautiful. These contemporary designs are exactly what I like.

All the houses that were lived in had expensive cars out the front. One, number 39 no less (same as our house number at the time), had three Ferraris out front! As well as a modded G waggon! Some serious serious money here.

Also, all these houses backed onto water, each having its own private pier, with many having luxury yachts, with jet skis attached to them! Interestingly a lot of the houses had a lot of Chinese lanterns out the front. Syd and I wondered if this were like their version of Sandbanks, where a lot of it is owned by the Russian Mafia (Bratva). Maybe this lot is owned by the Chinese Mafia (Triad).

We found an ally which went close to the shoreline. We could see the Marina Bay Sands from here, along with loads of containers waiting to be loaded onto the ships in the harbour. It was an impressive industrial view. We also saw a man on his bike come down here, we later saw him when we were having lunch too.

There were a few people running up and down the street for exercise. It felt very much like Beverly Hills. I bet there are a few famous people here too!

After about an hour or so of snooping around, and taking photos, we both started to get a bit hungry. We made our way back out of the gated community, the gate automatically opened as we approached it. Syd didn't see the sensor so was confused about how it knew when to open. I clocked the sensor but didn't say anything as she was enjoying the mystery of it.

On the way to the marina, we saw an estate agent, but for super luxury yachts. A lot of the adverts were POA (price on application), which is no good for us wanting to be nosy! A few did have prices though, not as bad as I thought. Some really nice ones were "only" around $1.8 million, with the most expensive one with a price we saw at just under $3 million USD. Honestly not as crazy as I would have thought. Although I suppose we are used to the crazy Sunseeker prices in Poole.

There were quite a few restaurant options on the front. Most of them with stupid prices, three digits for a simple plate. We found ourselves some Thai food right at the front, which seemed silly after being able to get a whole meal for about £4 back there. But still, this was one of the cheaper options, and we fancied eating it.

We ordered some chicken wings and prawn spring rolls to share. The spring roll design was something I had never seen before. They were like a thin isosceles triangle. Tasty. I ordered a Pad see ew with beef, and Syd had a pad Thai with prawns.

Unfortunately, her first plate had hair in it. Which we had only spotted after getting our hands messy with separating the prawns from their shells. Not to worry, they brought out a new dish promptly, with new prawns... which meant I had to de-shell these ones too.

Oh well, it was very tasty, but not as good as the real deal, or anywhere near the price point... It was about $60 odd, but they gave us a 10% discount to apologise for Syd's hair debacle. Originally the guy at the till didn't, but I think the manager shouted something from where she was sitting down, and then he changed it.

We were both very sweaty, even before sitting down, my top was soaked from carrying the bag. I had hoped it would dry off while we ate, but it didn't. We continued walking around the marina. It's a shame we couldn't find any fish and chips really, but we still enjoyed our lunch.

I wanted to walk along the man-made shoreline, however, it was for residents only. I tried moving the gate but no luck. Thankfully though one of the residents saw me, and he used his card to open it up for us . We then walked along the winding path along the walkway.

We found a bench a little way down, it wasn't like a normal English park bench, but more like a Japanese-style table. We sat here for a while watching the boats go in and out of the harbour. After a little rest, we continued to walk along, first noticing interestingly designed sky risers. Some looked like the front of boats, with others with massive balconies. The communal pools looked nice too. We couldn't decide if we'd prefer the bottom floor to have direct access to the pool, or the top floor to have the views.

These buildings also looked like the backside of a boat, which I'd assume was the design they were going for being this close to the sea. We walked a little further, crossing a loch bridge. I took some photos of Syd with her umbrella crossing it. On the other side, we saw some really amazing houses. All of them had their own pools, some of which were only a few meters wide but the full length of the house. The houses didn't seem to have much garden space, as most of the lot was taken up by the house itself.

One house looked like it was fully covered in a mosquito net, as part of the design. I'm not sure I like that idea, as it restricts their view. Further down we saw some more apartment complexes, they had an infinity pool, which I'd assume would look like it was going into the sea if you were to swim in it.

We found the gate to exit back onto the main road, but it didn't automatically open to let us out. Oh no, and to make things worse, no one was about. Thankfully there was a button to press for the intercom, I pressed it and a man said something to me in a different language. Not sure what he said but the gate started to open so we scampered on through.

Syd was starting to get a bit hot and bothered with all the walking. We were at the beach now so weren't too far from the hotel, I don't think she realised how much further this bottom route was. Well saying that: it wasn't much further, only an extra 10 mins or so, but in this heat, that feels a lot longer!

We cooled off at the hotel and went into the pool together. While in the pool looking out, I did get a little sad realising that we didn't have much longer left of our trip. Also, just sad about Kieron, which brought up feelings of missing my own Dad. I wish I could have taken Dad on an adventure like this with us, after all the holidays he had taken me on, I wished I could have re-paid the favour.

Back in the room, we had a bath together and I ordered us an Indian for dinner. It took a while to arrive, I was worried it was going to get cancelled again like the first night's noodles. Thankfully it didn't, but it was slightly delayed, so I get a $5 voucher for my next order!

I had asked for cutlery, which it didn't come with. Luckily at reception, I asked for two plates and accompanying cutlery set for both. Reception said they would have catering bring it up to us. It had been about 5 minutes and it had not turned up to the room. I called reception and they said they had let catering know.

I didn't want the food to go cold so I laid out a pool towel on the bed and took out our bowls and spoons. I served us both up a bowl, and we put Jackass 4.5 on my laptop, as it had just come out on Netflix. About 2 mouthfuls in the door rings... Brilliant.

I took the plates and cutlery, but they were tiny side plates. So wouldn't have been much use anyways. We continued eating out of our bowls. I had ordered a mutton dum biryani, mutton rogan gosh (which is what it was spelt like on their menu, I think was a typo for josh as it tasted similar), chilli chicken, butter chicken, and paneer paratha. Quite the feast!

About halfway through our first bowl, Syd asked if we could put something else on while eating. Which was fair enough as the new recruits on Jackass were putting chilli sauce in their anus, not great for dinner-time watching... I chucked on The Night Shift on YouTube. We had another bowl each, finishing the order.

Syd couldn't finish all of hers, so I finished hers too. I was very stuffed!

We finished watching Jackass and then went to sleep. Looking forward to seeing our room at Marina Bay Sands tomorrow!

AIRFORCE CIRCLING US

SINGAPORE | DAY 9

23rd May 2022

https://twobritsinasia.com/airforce-circling-us/

We both had a bit of a lie-in this morning. Syd had woken up in the night, for some reason she was not At ease in this room. She says the high ceilings create very dark shadows that she doesn't like. Either way, she was able to fall back to sleep.

Once we had both woken up, we heard what sounded like the universal rides. This was strange for two reasons. Firstly, it was 9:50 am and the park doesn't open till 12. And for the second, it was a Monday, and the park doesn't open on a Monday. So, I opened our balcony doors to try to get a better sense of where the noise was coming from.

As I stood on the balcony, I saw a plane circling the boats below. It was a big plane, and it wasn't far off the water either, around 200 meters tops. It also had its wheels down the whole time which I thought was strange. I went on Flight Radar 24 to see what it was.

Turns out it is part of the Singapore Airforce; it was an Airbus A330-243MRTT. It had been airborne for about an hour, continuously circling the area. I took some photos of it with my camera, before packing up and getting ready to go to our next hotel, the Marina Bay Sands!

Down at reception, my $100 hold was released, and I had fully checked out. I'm not sure why they kept that hold on the room, as they didn't do a final check before we handed our keys back. Oh well, I ordered us a Grab, this time the executive one, it was more than double the price, but I wanted a luxury arrival to MBS.

A Mercedes Benz C-class! Syd liked the ride, and it made me miss my two-seater AMG Merc. He dropped us off at Tower 1, there were so many porters waiting for us. They opened our doors and took all our bags, including hand luggage. Giving us a slip to hand to reception when checking in for our bags to make their way to our room for us.

The check-in process was easy too! There was a guy who met us by the line with an iPad, he took our basic details like name etc. He then showed us to one of the 16 desks within this tower. Behind the row of desks was another desk, which is where the manager was standing. I suspect it's so he keeps an eye on what everyone is doing from here.

Our receptionist was very friendly. We were very early, it was about 11:30 at this time, and check-in wasn't really meant till 15:00! As expected, our room wasn't ready, but the lady gave us a temporary card so we were still able to use the facilities. She also gave us lots of advice on what was good to eat, and what light shows to see.

We made our way up to the top of tower 1. There was a permanent pair of binoculars up there which we looked through. We could point them at the ships below, I put my phone camera up to the lens, and it made for a cool photo. Next to this, we saw one of the three main restaurants on site, Lavo. They had some expensive-looking steaks, we may be back later to try them out on our last evening.

Next, we walked along the decking, next to the infinity pool. It was beautiful seeing the city this high up. The pool looked as if it was going off into the sky! There was also a mini kids' pool next to the main one, I found this funny. I could see JP's office directly opposite.

From here we made our way across the whole top of the platform. All the way to the sky deck, which is open to the public but was basically empty. I think they said it's the largest overhanging platform in the world. At 68 meters, it is quite something. It's 2/3rds the height of the Eiffel Tower, you get a great sense of height up there.

Syd was a little worried to go right to the end peninsula point. I made my wobbly legs joke again (like I had back in Paris a few months earlier at the top of the Eiffel Tower), which made her laugh. We then made our way back to the pool, I already had my trunks on, and thankfully had my spare shorts in my backpack which I had kept on me.

However, I didn't have any spare boxers. Thankfully there were loads of towel pickup points all around the pool. I went to get me and Syd one, they were massive! About two to three times the size of a normal towel! I wrapped it around me to take my trunks and boxers off, and then to put my trunks back on. This way I had dry boxers after I had been for a swim.

While I was swimming, I had an email come through to say our room was ready, it was only just past 13:00 at this point. Great news! I got dried up and changed into my shorts, and we got the lift back down tower 1. These lifts are so fast, from the top floor (57) where the pool was, to reception at the bottom in about 20-30 seconds. They reminded me of the lifts at JPs Canary Wharf office, and the ones in New Jersey too.

Back down at reception, another lady tended to our needs, she started checking us in again. But I said we had already done that and just needed the key. She then got our keys for us. We were on the highest floor which has rooms (54), the penthouse suite! Over in tower 3. Floor 55 is used for the spa, gym, and Club 55 (which is another restaurant on site). 56 is used for staff offices and 57 is the pool deck.

Our room was the biggest, and certainly the fanciest room I have ever stayed in. And rightly so! Just these two nights cost me more than Syd used to bring home in a month! With huge floor-to-ceiling windows, spanning one whole wall of our room looking over the marina, Merlion park, and the business centre. A truly breath-taking room. Even the free shampoo and other gels were from the luxury Paris brand, Hermès!

Our suite had its own lounge area, with a sofa and two chairs, an office space, a walk-in wardrobe, and a massive toilet and shower room. There was a massive TV in the room too, around 65 inches, maybe bigger, it's hard to tell in such a big room. Anyways, it was on a swivel stand, with a mirror behind it!

The room next to us (5427) also had a window on the back wall, so they could also view the gardens. I phoned reception to see if it was available, but unfortunately, someone else was going to be staying there throughout our stay.

We had both started to get a little hungry, we didn't even unpack. Our bags had made their way to our room before we had even got there, which was impressive! We decided to go to the mall downstairs, which is owned by the hotel too. It looks as if they lease out shop space to high-end luxury brands, such as Louis Vuitton, Gucci, Chanel, and Montclair, just to name a few.

There was a casino here, it's one of the two casinos in Singapore (the other being next to universal studios we saw the other day). But even with just two, it ranked 4th in the world for the most money played. We aren't too interested in this, but it would be cool to go in and try a game or two while we are here.

I had fancied a Japanese BBQ for lunch, but we couldn't find any. So, we made our way to the food court instead. We both had some noodles with a fried chicken cutlet, I also had a portion of pork dumplings. We do like this food hall/court idea, it would be good to see these where we live.

We then explored the mall, or what it's referred to as "The Shoppes". I saw some bubble tea, so I had one of those. I went with caramel milk with golden pearls. They also offered this as a crème brûlée option too, but I was already fairly full of lunch.

There was a cool indoor water fountain, which came down from a central upside-down dome in the ceiling. It flowed into a river, which was inside the mall. There were gondolas on this man-made river, giving people boat rides up the river, around the waterfall, and back down to the start again. These were all man-powered by a worker at the back of the boat. It reminded me of The Venetian Las Vegas, which Lawrence and I stayed in, one Christmas, a few years prior.

After a while, the waterfall stopped. I'm not sure why, it did start up again later. It seemed to be a bit sporadic when it started and stopped. We also went for a walk along the front of the mall. It was warm outside, but we were the only people about, which was nice after being in the busy building.

Syd obviously noticed the Louis Vuitton shop, and wanted to go in... So, we did. It was interesting how it was on the water, with links under the water back into The Shoppes. We didn't buy any-thing, just had a look around. Once we were finished, we made our way back out to the front of the mall. There was, what looks to be, a blow-up crocodile. It looked like people could take photos standing in its mouth.

Next, we walked around the second half of the mall. Looking for a Japanese BBQ place for dinner, as we couldn't find one for lunch. We didn't find any on this side either! However, we did see Gordon Ramsey's "Bread Street Kitchen", where Syd stood crossed-armed next to the picture of Chef Ramsey who was also crossing his arms.

We decided to see how we would get to the gardens later to watch the light show. The reason for going now was so that we would be able to find it easier later. Thankfully we did as we walked a long way around, instead of using the cut-through bridge we found later.

The mega trees were truly something special. Big red/purple metal "wire" frames, interconnecting acting as branches. I say wire, but they were beams really, just so high up off the ground they look smaller than they are. There was one big tree, surrounded by many smaller trees. These smaller trees weren't small though, not by any stretch of the imagination.

All the trees had many different plants going up the side of them. The main tree looked as if we were able to go to the top, and the smaller trees had a bridge between a few of them to get a view from above. We decided not to do any of that today as we would be coming back here on our last day, before our night flight.

On the way back to our room, the cleaner had the door to the room next to us open (5427). I asked if we could go in to look at the views it had. They were amazing, seeing the gardens as well as the city skyline. This room was bigger too, somehow! It had a bath, lounge area, and dining room.

Since the cleaner was still cleaning that room at 16:30, and check-in is at 15:00 I wondered how it could be booked up. I called reception again to ask, and they said this time that I could have it, but it would be an extra $470 odd a night. I didn't think it was worth that, so we didn't. Our room is immense anyways.

We then got changed into our swimming kits and made our way up to the infinity pool right at the top. It was amazing views of the city below. Something completely different from anything else, and hard to imagine if never done before. The pictures do not do it justice. We spent quite a bit of time up there.

Back in our room, we got ready for our evening plans. While we were getting ready, we took a funny photo of me "flashing" the business park. It made Syd laugh. Once we were ready, we went to see the garden's light show, going over the bridge this time. On the walk over lighting started. I managed to get a cool shot of it forking over the skyline.

A lot of people were already there, but we managed to find somewhere to sit. Most of the people were also laying back on their seats, as they were large benches surrounding the bottom of the trees. Syd and I did the same. Even though it was now dark, the concrete was still hot from the sun during the day. The light show was quite spectacular, it had music too which made the lights seem to be dancing to it. There was a little French boy who was dancing in front of his parents next to us.

We left before the show finished as we wanted to avoid the crowd, and we could make it to the first showing of the laser, light, and water show at the front of the mall. It was quite a close call to make it in time, as the escalator up to the bridge had stopped working. I was sweating as I had chosen to wear jeans for some reason tonight, for the first time on this whole Asia tour no less!

There was a great spot we found, right on the roof of the mall. I'm not sure if we were really meant to be here as we were the only people up here. Either way, we watched the show from up here, heading down about halfway through to get a closer look at the ground level.

We also saw the waterfall from the top view, watching the water drain down the dome to the river below. I wouldn't want to fall into the dome, it looked quite slippy, and would be hard to get out again. I think I read it was 48 meters in diameter!

It was a good show, not as good as the one on the island I paid for the other day. But this one was free, so can't complain. I had seen a Japanese BBQ place, on the opposite side of the marina. So, I ordered us a Grab, trying the hitch option, which is a reduced fare but takes between 15-30 minutes for the car to arrive.

There could also be other passengers and the driver makes other stops on the way. It's about half the price so I thought I'd give it a go and try a different experience. Annoyingly when it got to 20:30, no drivers were found so the app cancelled the ride. I had to order a standard Grab instead. It would have been quicker for us to just walk the 20 minutes over the marina at this point...

When the driver dropped us off, the mall looked dead. There were two entrances to the mall, and the driver had asked where we wanted to be dropped off. I had just said the first one as thought that would be the main one. We were worried that all the shops in the mall would be closed since all the shops at this entrance were closed. Google had said it was open, but that has been wrong a few other times during this trip.

Thankfully after walking towards the other entrance, other people started to appear, and shops were still open. We found the Japanese BBQ place, but unfortunately, we were too late for their buffet option. The kitchen would close in about 40 minutes, and usually, you get 90 to finish. If we had just walked originally, we probably would have made that. Not to worry.

I had asked if they'd do it at a reduced rate, but they weren't having it. Oh well, we ordered quite a bit off the menu anyways, basically what we would have wanted from the buffet. Since it was off the menu it was better quality anyways and ended up being cheaper. So, a win-win really.

We ordered all sorts of different cuts of wagyu, some black pig bacon too. Two different types of chicken, and a plate of pork crispy dumplings. It was interesting cooking the food ourselves on the BBQ, since they were thin slices it cooked so quickly. The bacon made some quite big flames from the fat dripping!

It's interesting how we had these BBQs indoors. They had these smart venting mechanisms on the side which took away the smoke. Also, there was an oxygen supply at the bottom of the BBQ. This flowed onto the coals either quicker or slower depending on how hot we wanted the grill to be. The BBQ was very hot, the technique is to use the outermost part of the cooking area to cook these thin slices of meat.

Once I had paid up, we decided we were just going to walk back, instead of faffing with a Grab again. When we left the mall, we saw Suntec City only over the road but we didn't bother going in again as it was quite late, and we were getting tired.

We did, however, walk past the Youth Olympic Park. They had the famous five rings on show, not as good as the ones at Portland though! We also made our way over the Helix Bridge which was nice. It was lit up with blue and purple LEDs. We also stopped to take some pictures of the floating stadium, while we stood on one of the four viewing platforms which were built into the design of the bridge. From this angle, it was great to see our hotel and exactly which room we were in.

Back in our room, we got ready for bed. We decided to sleep with the curtains open as it was such a beautiful view of the city below. Syd had originally chosen the side by the window, but one building had a flashing light that was keeping her up. So, we swapped sides.

Usually, I like sleeping closest to the door, just in case any-thing happens. But with the room this big, it didn't matter what side of the bed you were on. As it would take an intruder about 20 seconds to get to us anyways! As I had checked earlier by running around like a bit of a loon. And I had also dead-locked the door closed anyways. We went to sleep quickly after we swapped sides.

FOODIES

SINGAPORE | DAY 10

24th May 2022

https://twobritsinasia.com/foodies/

We both slept well last night. We were up and ready by about 10:30. It was a bit of a faff getting out of bed and making the long walk to the toilet. Ha! There are worse problems to have though, ey! While Syd was still going through her phone on Instagram, I took a panorama of the room, my foot looked massive in it!

Once Syd had finished her scrolling, we made our way up to the pool. This time having to register as the staff on duty wasn't as blasé as the people yesterday. Oh well, it didn't take long to register, I'm not sure the point of it, it would just be easier to use our room key to badge in and out.

We saw two fighter jets cross the sky, the same place where the other Air Force plane had been circling yesterday. I wonder if they like to keep an eye on the ships below to make sure nothing "under the cuff" is going on.

While walking to find a lounger by the pool, we were given some complimentary fruit drinks. They were very nice, they had mango, orange, and pineapple in them. It was a warm day, but thankfully we were able to get some loungers right at the pool's edge, under a palm tree.

We had asked about a photo shoot yesterday, but we didn't end up getting enough time to go back. So, I went to see him this morning, he was just dealing with his last customer but said he would come over to find us when he was done. It didn't take him long, maybe 5 minutes before he was by our loungers.

All of us got in the pool. He had us doing all sorts of poses, it was great fun! Other guests even complimented us on our poses. We bought the highest package, which gave us a white leather booklet, with 8 large-scale photos. Along with all the photos taken as a digital download online.

We stayed up by the pool for the rest of the afternoon, re-applying sun-cream every now and then. Although when it got the hottest part of the day, we decided to try and find some more shade. The palm tree wasn't doing a great job. There weren't actually many shaded spots across the whole of the deck, which is interesting.

However, we were able to find a little corner above tower 1. There were a bunch of larger trees here, their canopy made for a good cover. There was also another couple sitting here, they were from down south (of England) too. Us soft southerners ey... We sat and chatted with them for about an hour, before heading down to the mall for some lunch.

I had seen a hot-pot place, near Gordon Ramsey's yesterday, and wanted to have it for lunch today. On the way down we saw a Fendi baby pram stroller, God knows how much it would cost. I didn't ask! The plan wasn't to have much as we had an expensive dinner booked later tonight at CUT. But as per, I ordered basically everything.

The soup pot was separated into four segments. We had one hot, and one that was sweeter, these were diagonal from each other. The other two segments just had water in them, with some sort of small red Chinese fruit to make the water sweeter. The idea was to cook the noodles in the water, and the meat in the flavoured soups.

Talking of the meat, we ordered wagyu and Kobe beef. We also had some pork, I'm not sure what type, to be honest, it was nice though! We had a portion of dried instant noodles each (which is funny as this wasn't a cheap meal). A portion of rice to share, some chicken dumplings (Syd's favourite of the dishes), chilli chicken, garlic chicken, some sort of cheese tofu dumpling (Syd wasn't a fan of these) and some fried tofu with fish flavouring.

As well as this, we were able to use the selection of dipping sauces, there must have been about 50 to choose from! My favourite was their satay sauce. On this help-your-self bar, they also had some sort of noodle, I'm not sure what it was made of, maybe tofu, maybe soy. I'm not sure, it was almost rubbery to bite, it was spicy (from the topping) but was very nice.

Originally the spicy soup came with lots of chillies in it, which was getting too hot for us, so our server removed them. Usually, we are good with spice, especially after climatising in Thailand. In the segments, there were metal baskets, in which we could put our noodles or meats. This way if we lost them, we only had to pick the basket up and they would be there.

The service was great. Our guy helped us choose dishes that he recommended. The main part of the meal was delivered to us by a robot. It made funny "robot" noises as it was gliding across the floor to our table. It made Syd laugh out loud. The robot had a funny face on it too, it was interesting to see the human and robot servers working together.

Syd had seen this technique online, where she would grab a little slice of the meat with her chopsticks, then swing it around making a twirly motion. This would make the meat wrap around the chopsticks and could then easily be lowered into the soup. Not having to worry about losing the meat in the liquid. It worked well, other than if you wrapped it too tight, the layers closest to the chopsticks didn't cook properly. I tried too, but I wasn't as good at this as Syd was.

You could make up so many different combinations of flavours with all the dipping sauces available. I can't even begin to compute how many different mouthfuls we had, no two were the same! It would be good to see England have the quality and quantity of food selection like this, however, I'm not sure they're quite ready for the rawness of the ingredients coming out. It's certainly a gap in the market though.

After lunch, we spent some time in the room, just recovering from such a feast! Once we had regained some energy, we made our way back up to the pool. It had gotten cloudy, but it was still warm and sunny enough. So, we found some more loungers on the poolside and lay down on them (with some more of those massive towels). The couple we were speaking to earlier were just leaving as I went to pick up the towels. We wished them a safe flight.

The clouds started to look a little worse, although there was a hole in them, and it looked like a circular rainbow around the entrance. I tried to take a photo of it, but it was too bright to see in the pictures. Not to worry, it was cool to see anyways.

Syd didn't fancy getting in the pool again just yet, so she lounged on the loungers and read her book. I went back in though! While I was in the pool a worker came up to our loungers, asking Syd if she wanted some more complimentary juice. She took one of the same from this morning for me and an apple juice for herself.

We had brought up some drinks from the room, so I mixed mine together to make a soft punch. My phone was also getting quite hot, so I asked a server for a cup of ice, it took maybe 30 seconds to arrive, yet he apologised for the delay. I laughed and said it's all right, I didn't even think there was a delay! Impeccable service.

It started to get a bit warmer again, so we went back to where the shade was earlier. Although once we got there, Syd said why don't we just go back to the room and rest before tonight's meal. It was probably best to get some time fully out of the sun anyways, so we went down to our room. I caught up on some messages I needed to reply to and then just chilled for a bit.

We watched the 20:00 o'clock laser and light show up from our room. We both got ready for our evening plans, getting dressed up smart. Well Syd did, I didn't really have anything too smart with me, so I just wore some chino-type trousers and my usual white top. I only had my trainers for actual shoes, so I wore those too.

Once we were ready, we made our way down to CUT, thankfully they let us in. The receptionist didn't say anything, but I did notice the porter looking down at my shoes, she didn't say anything either though. We were shown to our seats, it was dark in the restaurant, but it had a good atmosphere.

Since we had that big lunch, we weren't too hungry. So, we decided to order the expensive A5 Japanese Wagyu Ribeye to share. It was $295 for 230g (8 ounces)! I also ordered us a side of onion rings, fries, and mac n cheese.

We also had a cocktail each. Syd had something called along the lines of "Heading to London", which I thought was fitting as we were flying there tomorrow (well setting off tomorrow, landing the day after). Syd found it quite strong though, so I had to help her finish it. I had a cocktail too, it was one with Hendricks in, I can't remember the name, but it was nice too! It came with some liquor cherries.

The server also managed to persuade me into ordering a $42 crab cake! Blooming heck! It was nice though to be fair, but very expensive. Everything here was expensive; the fries and onion rings were $18 each too! And the mac n cheese was over $20 too! Although it was probably the best mac n cheese we'd ever had!

Our cocktails took a while to come out, but we had some fancy breadsticks to keep us going. They also brought out a selection of freshly baked bread. These were very tasty! When the crab cake arrived, it was small but tasted amazing.

They had cut our steak in two for us, as we had told the server we were sharing, as he thought when I was ordering it was all for me! Usually, I could have probably finished it all, but not after all that food at lunch! I wasn't the biggest fan of the onion rings, I think they had too much oil on them or at least had been cooked in oil that wasn't hot enough, as they came out greasy.

The chips were nice, and like I'd already said, the mac n cheese was great. The main event, the meat, was beautifully cooked. Melt in your mouth, literally, as A5 should do. Even though it was a small portion, it was more than enough. It's so rich that if one was to have a lot of it, it can become un-enjoyable, due to it being so rich

Syd couldn't finish all of hers, so I cleaned it up! It was also served with 5 different dips. Mostly mustards, and one in the centre, which was rock salt. It was all very flavourful. We even had some mini macarons and some type of jelly square for dessert, on the house. The bill was less than ideal, more than $540 :(! I'd spent more today on food than we usually do on food shops for the month back at home... Ooops.

After dinner, we made our way to the casino. They needed our passports, I had them on us as I knew we would need them based on the experience we had at the Sentosa casino just under a week prior. Once we were in, we walked around the floor watching others play.

There were some tables going up to $800,000 bets. This was just on the ground floor! There were loads of private rooms which would have gone into the 10s of millions! We found a Monopoly slot machine, for which I put $2 just for fun. Each pull was $1. I won the first pull (making 30 cents) but lost it all on the next go.

We then found the blackjack tables; it was the only card game I knew that was on offer. I exchanged $30 for chips. The min bet was $25, so I kept the other $5 chip as a souvenir. I won the first game ($50 to play with now). Lost the second (back to $25). Won the third (back up to 50). Then lost the fourth and fifth, so down to nothing.

Annoyingly the games I lost were because I went over 21. But so did the dealer! So, if I had just stuck with the lower numbers I might have won. But you never know as the dealer wouldn't have had the cards they had if I didn't ask for mine. The house is always the winner, I know this, and it was only a small amount and purely just for some fun. So happy faces all around really. Syd didn't fancy having a go, she doesn't really know how to play properly.

We made it back to our room, after having our passports checked again on the way out of the casino. We were so tired that we both went to sleep immediately! It was already tomorrow morning really though, by the time we got up to our room. Syd was excited to be starting the journey home to see Buttons, our cat, tomorrow.

THE GARDENS

SINGAPORE | DAY 11

25th May 2022

https://twobritsinasia.com/the-gardens/

I had woken up early this morning before my alarms had gone off. I could see out the window that it was going to be a bit of a wet day as visibility was low. I think the top of the hotel may have even been in a cloud. I managed to drift back off to sleep, waking again a few hours later.

We had a chilled morning, taking it slow and getting up. I ordered two more sets of shower pots, as I wanted to take them home with us. I also got a pair of slippers for us both. We packed our bags, and I had a shower, Syd didn't have one as she was worried about time.

After I'd had my shower, we did our teeth, and I called the reception to let them know we were ready to check out. Someone came up to our room shortly after to pick up our suitcases. We then made our way down to reception to check out.

Unfortunately, the receptionist said that once we had checked out, we weren't able to use the pool. Not to worry, we had planned on going to the gardens anyways today. The pool was only a time-filler if needed.

We made our way down into the mall, heading towards Toast Box, which was opposite Gordon Ramsey's. Every time we walked past it always had a queue, so we thought we give it a go for our final breakfast of the Asia part of our tour.

I ordered French toast. It was two slices of bread, which had some sort of lava ooze coming out the side. It was very sweet, I think it was a mix between sugar, butter, sugar, egg yolk, and more sugar. I enjoyed it, it wasn't very big and was fairly expensive for what it was, but I enjoyed it. I also ordered a cold hot chocolate; I didn't really understand the difference between that and chocolate milk. But basically, the cold hot chocolate wasn't as sweet.

Syd ordered a thick slice of toast, with peanut butter on top. She had a honey and lemon drink. She enjoyed them both but also commenting on that there wasn't much to eat. Once we had both finished, we made our way across to the gardens.

On the way, we popped into the Apple store, which was the shape of an apple (funny that) on the water. Syd had tried a trick to keep her mask off by carrying her leftover drink. But one of the staff members in Apple said she had to keep her mask up and quickly take it down for a sip and then put her mask back up again. He seemed a bit of a jobsworth, no one else seemed to care, even the mall's security.

We also stopped back off at the bag storage to hand in Syd's bag, as she didn't want to keep carrying it around the gardens. We were given another tag for these items, as she had a bag of snacks that she dropped off too. Annoyingly the cut-through door to the bridge was having work done on it today, so we had to walk out of the front of tower 1, and around the side.

On the walk, we saw a beautiful Ferrari, with its owner getting in and revving it about. Wonderful. We also walked past a couple of signs about cyclists. One of them had a rider wearing pink, so I just had to get out one of the Elmer (the cycling club I am part of) stickers and put it on him. It looked genuine too, I wonder how long it would stay there.

We walked across the bridge, thankfully the escalator was working today! We made our way down and towards the large trees. Annoyingly the skywalk was closed for maintenance today, so we were unable to go on the high bridges between the big trees. Oh well, we were still able to go into the two domes.

I bought us a special package, which gave us access to both domes, and the flower park. It also came with a shuttle service, as the flower park wasn't directly next to the domes. It also came with a $4 souvenir voucher, and a $12 food voucher. It was $100 total for the two of us.

We first started in the flower dome, there were lots of different sections within the dome. From different cactuses to Italian villa-themed, Californian gardens, African, Australian, basically, you name it, it was probably there! They had lots of cool wooden sculptures dotted around the displays. These ranged from goats to monkeys, snakes, sloths, horses, and even a dragon! Just to name a few!

There was also a sculpture of a family with their tummies missing. It was a clever bit of artwork. There was also a display of old paintings, such as the famous The Last Supper by Leonardo Da Vinci. My favourite part of this dome was seeing how they wove the wooden sculptures into the scene. Syd's favourite part was seeing the sloths, as it reminded her of Sabbie, her travelling teddy.

It was interesting that in the dome, even though it was basically like being outside because it was so big we still had to wear masks. Even when taking photos, which usually is deemed acceptable here in Singapore. It's strange as the air quality here would be amazing with all the trees and plants producing all that oxygen.

The exit of both domes went into the souvenir shop. I tried looking all over for a shot glass for my Nan, as in every country I go to I buy her one as a gift. In the end, I had to ask the lady at the till if they sold any. Funnily enough, they were directly opposite the tills, in a tiny gap. It was $8, but it looked cool, with the Singapore skyline, and the gardens surrounding the glass in 3D.

At the till, after I handed her the $4 voucher, she asked for $6. I thought, hang on a moment, that doesn't seem right. So, I asked, isn't this $8, to which she said yes. I did the maths for her, 8 minus 4 equals 4. She realised her mistake and apologised. A genuine mistake.

While we were in the flower dome, the rain really started to hammer down. Thunder and lightning too! I'm glad we did this today and the pool yesterday when it was hotter and clear skies (for the most part).

Next, we made our way to the cloud dome. This had a huge rock face, with a waterfall coming down it. I had expected the domes to be quite hot inside, but quite the opposite, they were chilly. I wonder if this makes it easier to maintain them as they don't dry up so quick.

At the entrance of the cloud dome, we saw a couple taking wedding photos. They had three photographers with them and a stylist. Her wedding dress looked nice, and I bet the photos with the waterfall behind them came out amazing. They weren't wearing their masks for the photos, which I think is a good thing. Seems a shame to ruin such a nice photo with a mask.

This second dome was colder than the first, I felt okay, but Syd started to get some goosebumps. It was amazing seeing all these flowers. On the rock face, they had air outlets, where they were pumping the dome with cool air. It made the leaves around this part look like they were shivering. I made a joke, saying they must be cold too. There was a beautiful purple flower walkway. I think this was probably Syd's favourite part of this dome. Outside of this walkway was a bright electric aqua statue, the exact colour I love. This wasn't my favourite part though, that came later...

We then made our way up the cliff. Getting in the lift right to the top. There were walk-way bridges in this dome which we were able to go on. Syd was a little worried looking over the edge. I did the usual leg wobble to try and make her laugh, she didn't find it too funny this time though. I think she was getting hungry.

I was teasing her a bit by jumping up and down, a bit naughty but she was making it too easy to wind her up. These walkways were my favourite part of this dome. It was great to be able to look at the plants and trees below. There was also a section in which we could stand next to the falling water of the waterfall, which was neat!

The rain was quite hard outside now. So much so that we could barely see our hotel, which was only just across the road!! We had made it down to the bottom of the cliff by this point. There was a secret garden at the bottom, with magnifying glasses as part of the display, showing us where to look.

In the dome, they had misters to keep the humidity up, and these had been on while we were in the secret garden. It made for a cool effect while walking through the grounds. It was like being in the middle of a rainforest. There was also a learning centre, where we spent some time. Trying to jump as far as a kangaroo (nowhere near, they can jump 12 meters, but I only managed 2...) Syd didn't want to try in case she hurt her arm again.

We learnt that if a flee was the same size as a human, their jumps would make it over 30 stories high! Also, the smallest street in the world was in Germany, and it's only 1 foot wide! Along with some other facts such as some dogs are allergic to cats. And lots more! We also watched two short (very short) movies about climate change.

After we had left the cloud dome, Syd started to get really hungry now. I saw a cafe in the wall, which we stood next to. The server had gone for a quick toilet break. Once they were back, they explained that the voucher couldn't be used there, only certain establishments on the site.

Next door was one of these said establishments. It was a Chinese-looking place, which offered a buffet. Unfortunately, though we only had half an hour before this sitting ended, and the next wasn't for another four hours. So, it wouldn't be worth our money to go in now.

We decided instead to just get the shuttle to the flower garden and see what was there. We looked around the flower garden, seeing the couple taking a few more wedding pictures. This time the lady was in some sort of oriental blue dress, it looked very pretty.

This flower garden wasn't very big and only took us about 10 minutes to walk around it. Probably hurried up the fact we were both hungry now, especially as breakfast hadn't been very big. This exhibit also had cool statues, one looked like an old tree man. Another was a cross between a man and a lion throwing a spear. We also saw some more poisoned dart frogs. These were black and aqua.

After looking around the flower garden, we found the cafe which was accepting the vouchers. We ordered a chicken burger meal (basically just a chicken burger with fries), and a hot dog. We shared this between the two of us. Finishing off with a vanilla ice cream cone.

The woman at the till was a delinquent, she couldn't understand how the voucher worked. First, she gave us a 20% staff discount, I mean, do we look like staff, with my backpack and camera out? Anyways, she had to get the chef to come to help her. In total the meals only cost me about $1.90 so can't complain.

When we finished eating this, the same lady came to get our plates. She then walked over to the bins, where there were other plates and just stood and looked at them for about a minute, before picking them up and taking them back to the kitchen. Very strange. Syd and I exchanged glances, as if to say, what on earth is going on? We left shortly after, as there was a break in the weather.

We made it back to the hotel, but it was a bit too early to go to the airport yet. I wanted to go up to the top deck to see the bad weather from up here. They let us look, the pool was closed though as the lighting flashing light was on. Which would warn the staff if the lighting was likely so to clear the pool. It was very windy up here today, interesting to experience being that high up in a storm.

After, we made our way down into the mall food court again. We sat here for a couple of hours while I was messaging Mum about her new house purchase. She had just had an offer on her house and was asking for some advice. She ended up accepting the offer and making a great offer on the house she wanted. All in all, coming out of it with a lot more than she was expecting, thanks to my persuasions. It will be sad to see my childhood home sold to someone else. But I think it's good that Mum is moving on now.

Syd was still a little cold from earlier, so she wanted to get a hot drink. I gave her my card, and she got herself a hot chocolate. She also brought me back another one of those milk drinks. This time with the crème brûlée on top. It was much sweeter today with that on top.

Once we had finished our drinks, we made our way back to the hotel to collect our bags. The guy at the desk was scrolling on his phone. He didn't hear us turn up. We both stayed quiet to see how long it would take him to realise, but one of the porters came over to tell him we were there.

The porter apologised on his behalf. He even made a comment to another porter who came out to us. They both went into the storage room with the desk guy, I think they probably had a stern word with him to focus, as when he came out, he looked forlorn and apologised to us.

I ordered us a Grab exec again. It was another Mercedes, but this time it was a V220 (or something like that). It had lots of room, with 6 seats at the back, two rows facing each other. Even with all this room, Syd decided to sit right next to me anyways. It was a smooth ride, we got to the airport quickly.

There wasn't any queue at the BA check-in, unfortunately, there weren't any upgrades available as it was a full flight. The passport check was quick too. I was able to go through the automated ones, however, Syd's passport wasn't working on that for some reason. She went to a manned one instead. That didn't take too long anyways.

We explored the airport for a bit. Making our way up to the BA lounge. Unfortunately, since it's been so long since I've had to fly with them, I lost my level of membership which gave me access to the lounges, even on an economy flight. Not to worry, SIN airport is well known for being plush anyways.

We found ourselves some comfy seats and sat watching the planes while we waited. There was even an area where you could snooze on loungers. We didn't go here as we wouldn't be here for that long. Also, what was nice was every seating area had plugs, which is just a great quality-of-life addition to an airport.

The actual bag security check was at the gate itself. Each gate had its own security team. It made going through very quick. It would be good to see this elsewhere. However, it does take up a lot of room. I like it though. Meaning we could have if we had known, brought our own food and drink from outside the airport. Which would have been a lot cheaper than the airport offerings.

We were only waiting at the gate for about 10 minutes before being called onto the plane. This was Syd's first time flying with BA, she was excited with her own TV, blankets, and complimentary snacks and drinks.

HOME!

SINGAPORE | DAY 12

26th May 2022

https://twobritsinasia.com/home/

Praise the lord! We don't need to wear masks on this flight! We were all so relieved by this news. We made our way through business class and into our seats. Unfortunately, not stopping in business class, I had asked about an upgrade, but it was a full flight.

I was trying to sort my bags out to see what I needed for the flight. Unfortunately, the guy who was going to be sitting next to us was behind me. So, I had to rush. I managed to get my joggers out and went to the toilet to change into them. Once I sat back down, I still had my backpack which I wanted going into the overheads. But he had already sat back down. I passed him my bag to put up for me. He seemed okay, but what can you do, that's the life of an aisle seat.

There were a few babies and younger kids on the flight. When we sat on the tarmac one mother was doing some seriously annoying baby voice talking to it. Hopefully, that won't go on for long! I plan on trying to go to sleep at 1 or 2 am (Singapore time) which means by the time we land in England, I should have had a full night's sleep, with a bit of time to wake up before we land too.

Thankfully during take-off, the kid (and mother) had quietened down. The take-off was smooth, however, the oxygen cabin above our air hostess swung open! She didn't notice originally but when she did, she just closed and locked it back in place. She made a remark about it to her college when the seatbelt signs were turned off.

Syd made herself comfy, wrapping herself up in her blanket, and pillow provided for us. She asked me to get her teddy bear out too! She was so excited to see all these freebies on this flight. She put Clifford The Big Red Dog on her inflight TV.

The first beverage trolly made its rounds. Syd thought we had to pay for it. I chuckled, explaining that it was all part of the ticket price. I ordered a Brewdog Jet Stream beer, as I thought it was appropriate. I also ordered a red wine ready for dinner time. Syd went with cranberry juice, the hostess asked if she wanted vodka in it. Syd turned her nose to that, and they both laughed. Syd also ordered a white wine to go with her dinner. We were both given sour cream and onion pretzels, to keep us going before our main meal arrived.

I was getting a little sleepy, after having my beer and not really any food. Plus, it was past midnight Singapore time! Thankfully our main food wasn't much longer. We both went with the chicken curry; it was very nice. It also came with a quinoa and sweetcorn salad, the classic bread roll and butter, some crackers and cheese, a pudding of some sort (not entirely sure what, it was similar to a bread-and-butter pudding, it was nice), and a bottle of water.

I asked the hostess what the pudding was. She wasn't sure either, she guessed banana cake or a walnut cake. Syd originally thought it was meat?! She ended up thinking it was a mix of different puddings. Our hostess brought me over another one as I said I liked it. I was stuffed after eating it all! We didn't end up drinking the wine with dinner. So, we saved it for later.

As we were eating Syd goes, "that baby is behaving itself". Within 30 seconds it then started crying... I looked at Syd to say, "you jinxed that". Thankfully it didn't cry for long. Syd had finished her first film and had now put on Godzilla. It wasn't long till she had fallen asleep.

We both had a sleep; however, the baby was crying for the rest of the flight. Really quite annoying, the parents didn't do anything to try and stop it either. On a plane is not the time to do that "leave them crying" therapy! Everyone in our section was awake most of the flight because of it! Everyone gave the sleeping parents' death stares. They must just be able to drown out their children crying from being used to it at home.

Oh well, we managed to get somewhat little interrupted rest. I decided to put on Clifford The Big Red Dog myself. Syd restarted Godzilla. About an hour later our breakfast came along. Not sure if it's breakfast or lunch, but it was a cheese and ham mini sub, it had tomatoes in too. It came with yoghurt and some Oreos. There was also another bottle of water with it, along with an orange juice. Syd had apple juice.

The sun was red out of the window. It was quite a sight. It was interesting seeing it then light up the plane as it got higher. The sky looked clear above England from the plane. I put my UK SIM card back into my phone while we were descending, ready to use it when we land.

Anddddd TOUCHDOWN!! The security check and baggage re-claim took about an hour. It's funny, in Asia we were out of the airport, with our bags within 10 minutes of hitting the ground. Annoyingly my big bag had been damaged in transit.

I didn't faff about finding someone at the airport to report it, as I didn't want Toby spending a million pounds on parking as he had driven this morning to pick us up. Also, the world duty-free was closed so I couldn't get even get him the promised Toblerone. Oh well, on to the car and the ride home!

Toby stopped a few times for coffee and loo breaks, but me and Syd really just wanted to get home as fast as possible after such a long time away. Once we did get back, Syd ran straight upstairs to find Buttons. Syd may have had a few tears of happiness seeing her again. It was interesting to see how much the plans in our garden had grown. While Syd was sorting out the dirty clothes for the wash, I pulled up the weeds.

My Mum and Nan then arrived, and we all went out for another Toby Carvery. It felt fitting to do this as it was how we started the tour almost two months earlier. It was great to catch up with them and go over our adventures! Albeit short, as within a day or so, we were off to Barcelona. I had booked this as a post-tour holiday to let us relax by the pool and down the beach for a week... That wasn't quite the case, but that is a story for another day...

Ingram Content Group UK Ltd.
Milton Keynes UK
UKHW020858040423
419625UK00014B/788